TIME STOP HERO

2

STORY & ART BY
**YASUNORI
MITSUNAGA**

CONTENTS

▶START
PAUSE

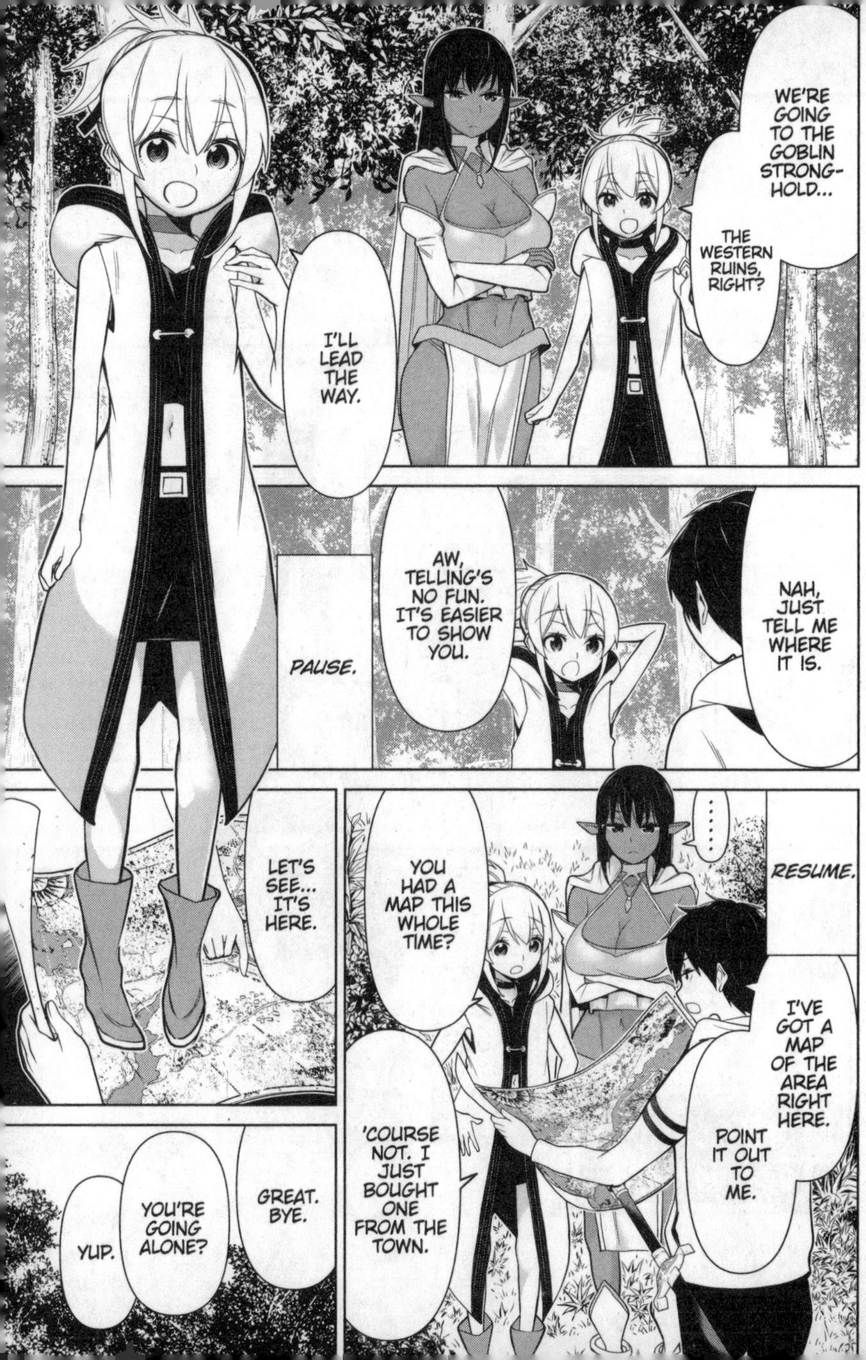
WE'RE GOING TO THE GOBLIN STRONGHOLD...
THE WESTERN RUINS, RIGHT?
I'LL LEAD THE WAY.
NAH, JUST TELL ME WHERE IT IS.
AW, TELLING'S NO FUN. IT'S EASIER TO SHOW YOU.
PAUSE.
RESUME.
......
I'VE GOT A MAP OF THE AREA RIGHT HERE.
POINT IT OUT TO ME.
YOU HAD A MAP THIS WHOLE TIME?
'COURSE NOT. I JUST BOUGHT ONE FROM THE TOWN.
LET'S SEE... IT'S HERE.
GREAT. BYE.
YOU'RE GOING ALONE?
YUP.

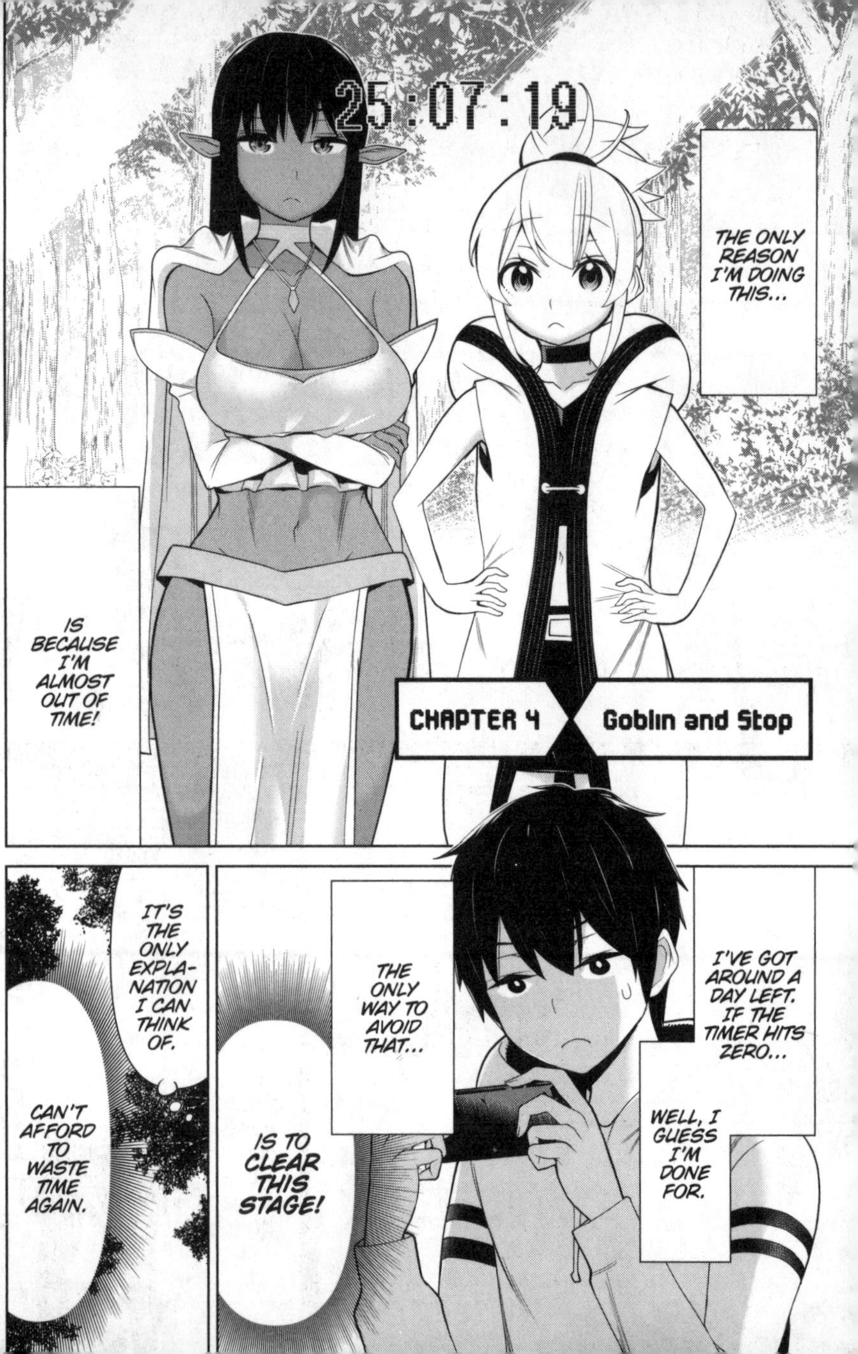

25:07:19
THE ONLY REASON I'M DOING THIS...
IS BECAUSE I'M ALMOST OUT OF TIME!
CHAPTER 4
Goblin and Stop
I'VE GOT AROUND A DAY LEFT. IF THE TIMER HITS ZERO...
WELL, I GUESS I'M DONE FOR.
THE ONLY WAY TO AVOID THAT...
IS TO CLEAR THIS STAGE!
IT'S THE ONLY EXPLANATION I CAN THINK OF.
CAN'T AFFORD TO WASTE TIME AGAIN.

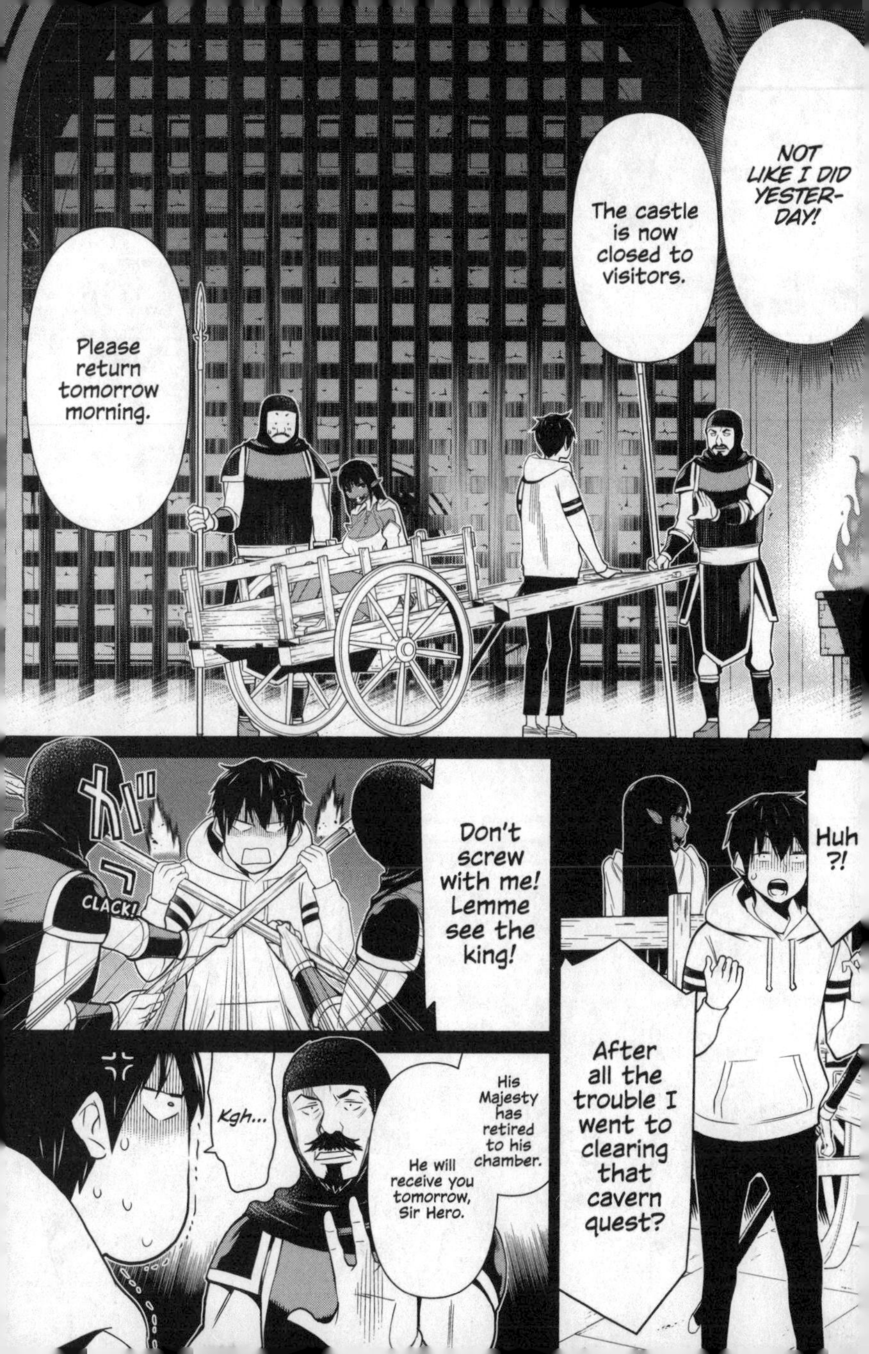

NOT LIKE I DID YESTER-DAY!
The castle is now closed to visitors.
Please return tomorrow morning.
Huh ?!
After all the trouble I went to clearing that cavern quest?
Don't screw with me! Lemme see the king!
CLACK!
His Majesty has retired to his chamber.
He will receive you tomorrow, Sir Hero.
Kgh...

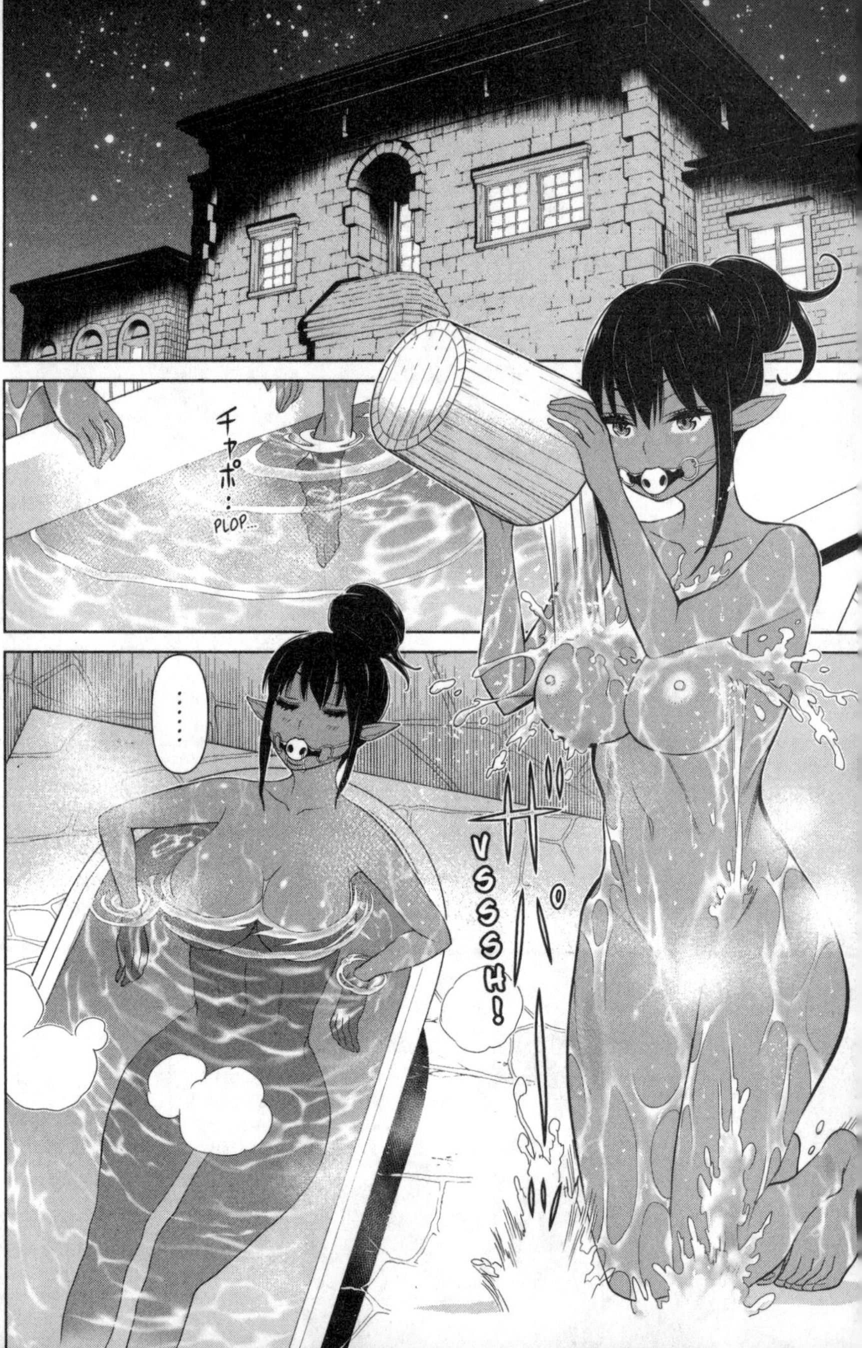
チャポ…
PLOP...
……
VSSSH!

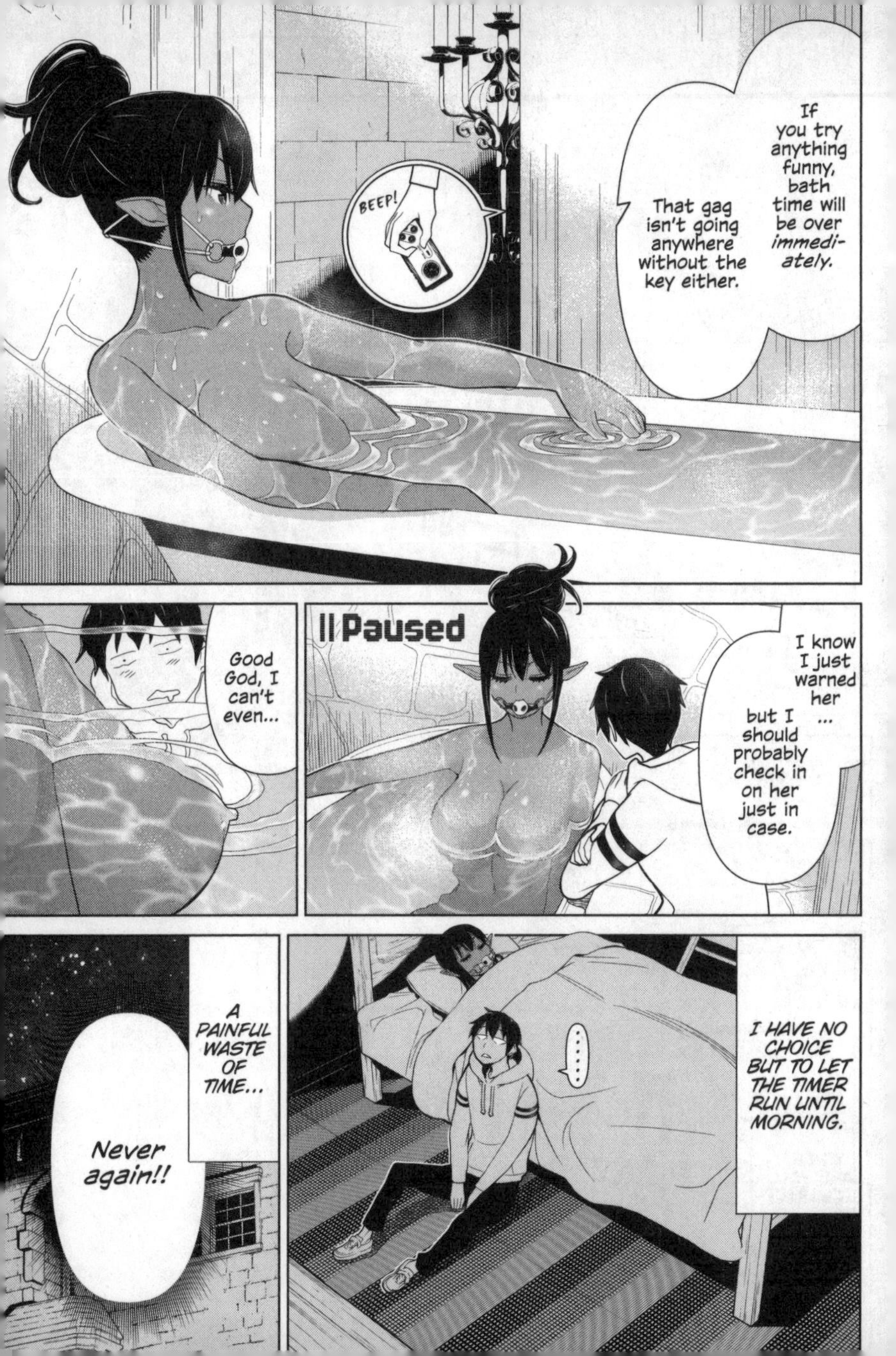
If you try anything funny, bath time will be over *immediately.*
That gag isn't going anywhere without the key either.
BEEP!
I know I just warned her ...
but I should probably check in on her just in case.
Paused
Good God, I can't even...
I HAVE NO CHOICE BUT TO LET THE TIMER RUN UNTIL MORNING.
......
A PAINFUL WASTE OF TIME...
Never again!!

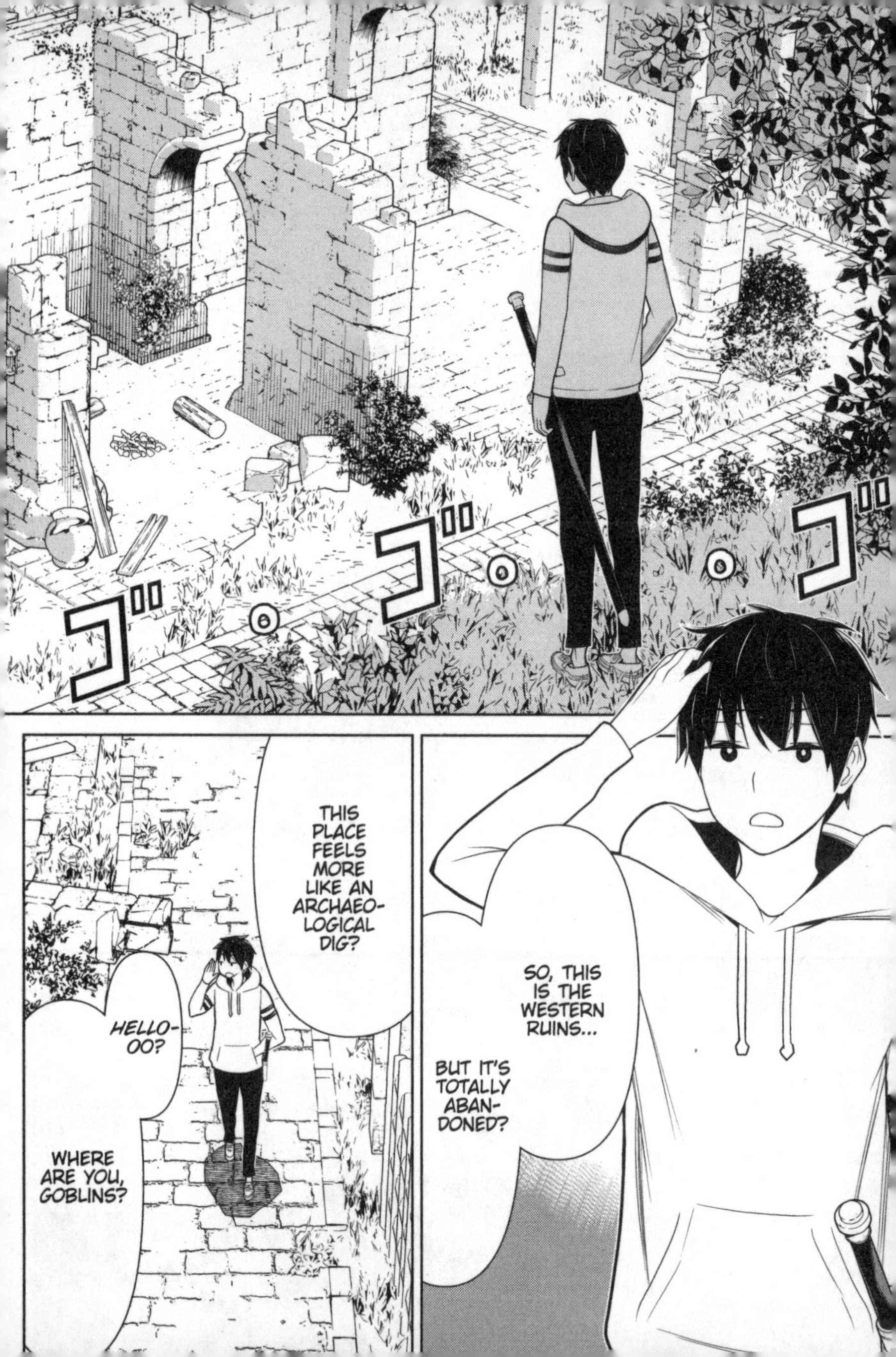
ゴ ゴ ゴ
SO, THIS IS THE WESTERN RUINS...
BUT IT'S TOTALLY ABAN-DONED?
THIS PLACE FEELS MORE LIKE AN ARCHAEO-LOGICAL DIG?
HELLO-OO?
WHERE ARE YOU, GOBLINS?

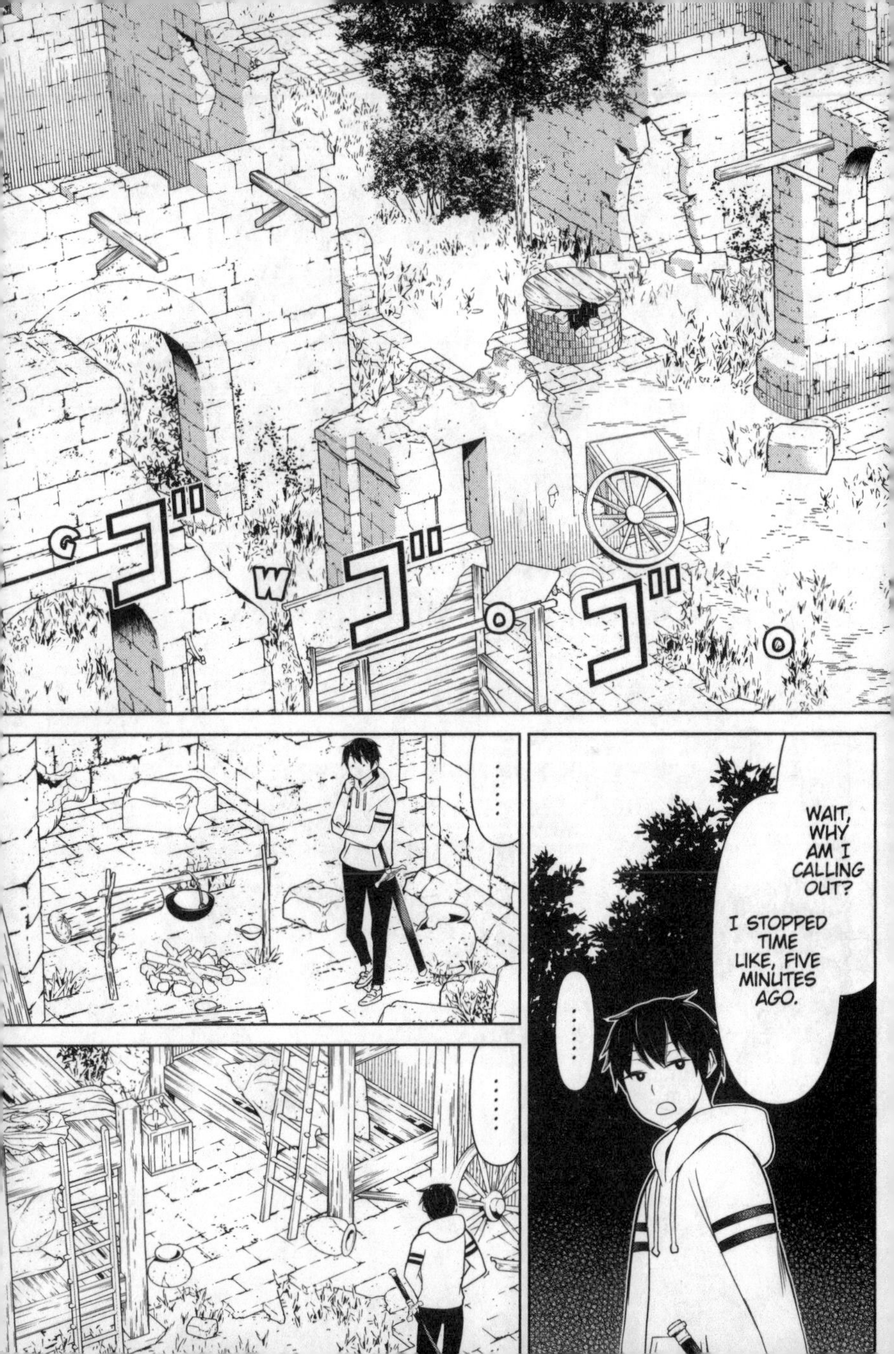

Gゴ Wゴ Oゴ O
WAIT, WHY AM I CALLING OUT?
I STOPPED TIME LIKE, FIVE MINUTES AGO.
......
......
......

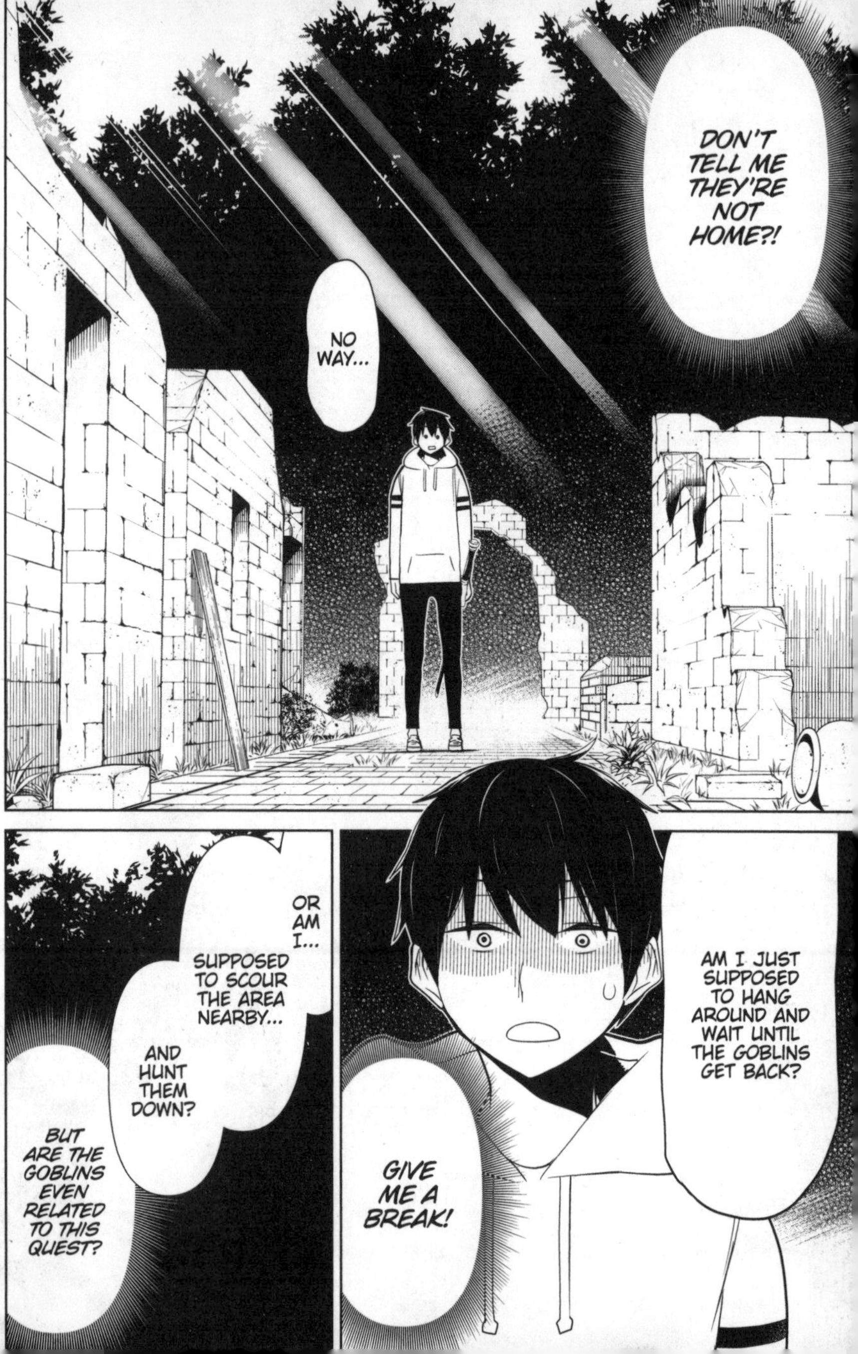
DON'T TELL ME THEY'RE NOT HOME?!
NO WAY...
AM I JUST SUPPOSED TO HANG AROUND AND WAIT UNTIL THE GOBLINS GET BACK?
GIVE ME A BREAK!
OR AM I...
SUPPOSED TO SCOUR THE AREA NEARBY...
AND HUNT THEM DOWN?
BUT ARE THE GOBLINS EVEN RELATED TO THIS QUEST?

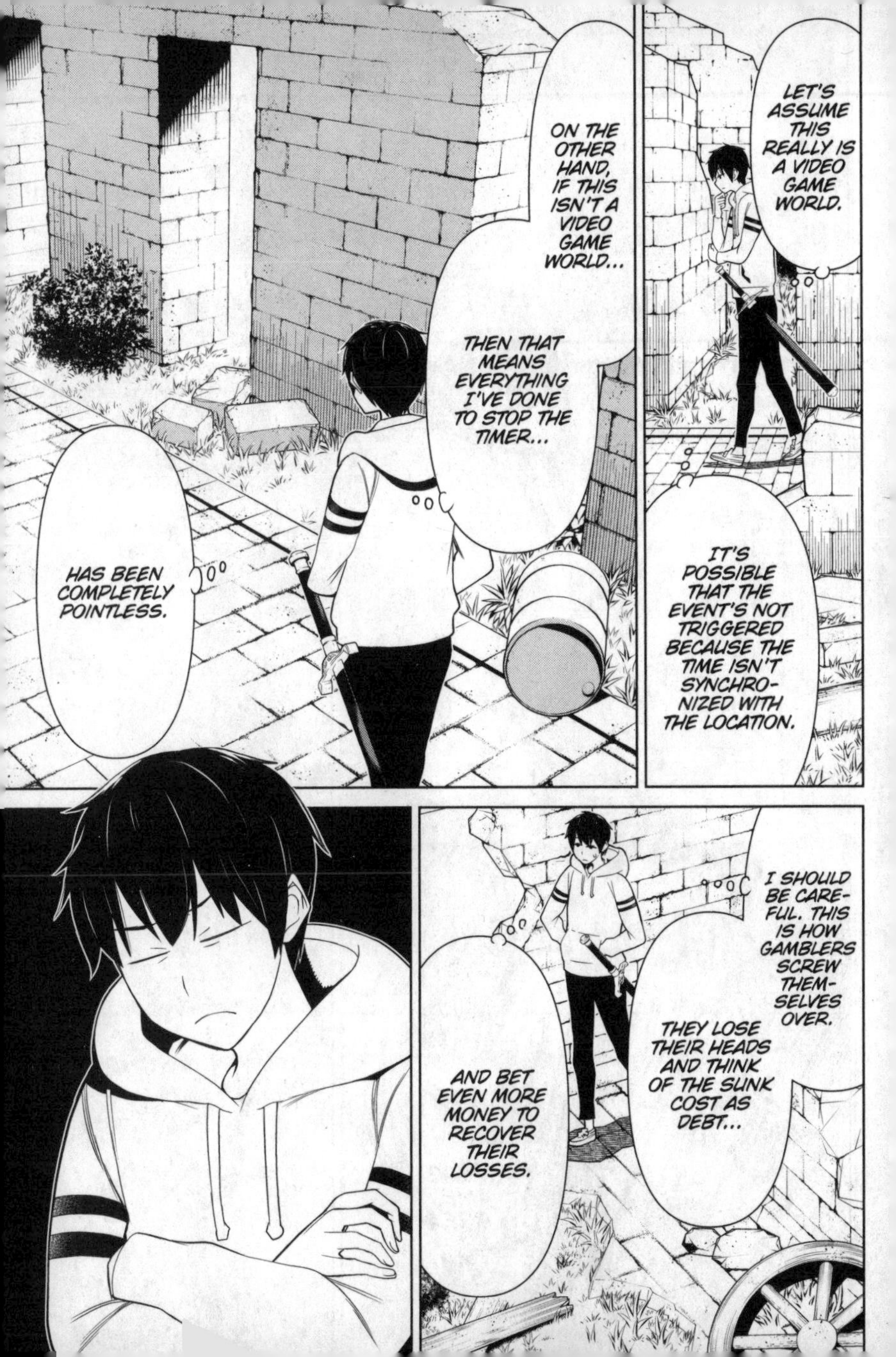
LET'S ASSUME THIS REALLY IS A VIDEO GAME WORLD.
IT'S POSSIBLE THAT THE EVENT'S NOT TRIGGERED BECAUSE THE TIME ISN'T SYNCHRONIZED WITH THE LOCATION.
ON THE OTHER HAND, IF THIS ISN'T A VIDEO GAME WORLD...
THEN THAT MEANS EVERYTHING I'VE DONE TO STOP THE TIMER...
HAS BEEN COMPLETELY POINTLESS.
I SHOULD BE CAREFUL. THIS IS HOW GAMBLERS SCREW THEMSELVES OVER.
THEY LOSE THEIR HEADS AND THINK OF THE SUNK COST AS DEBT...
AND BET EVEN MORE MONEY TO RECOVER THEIR LOSSES.

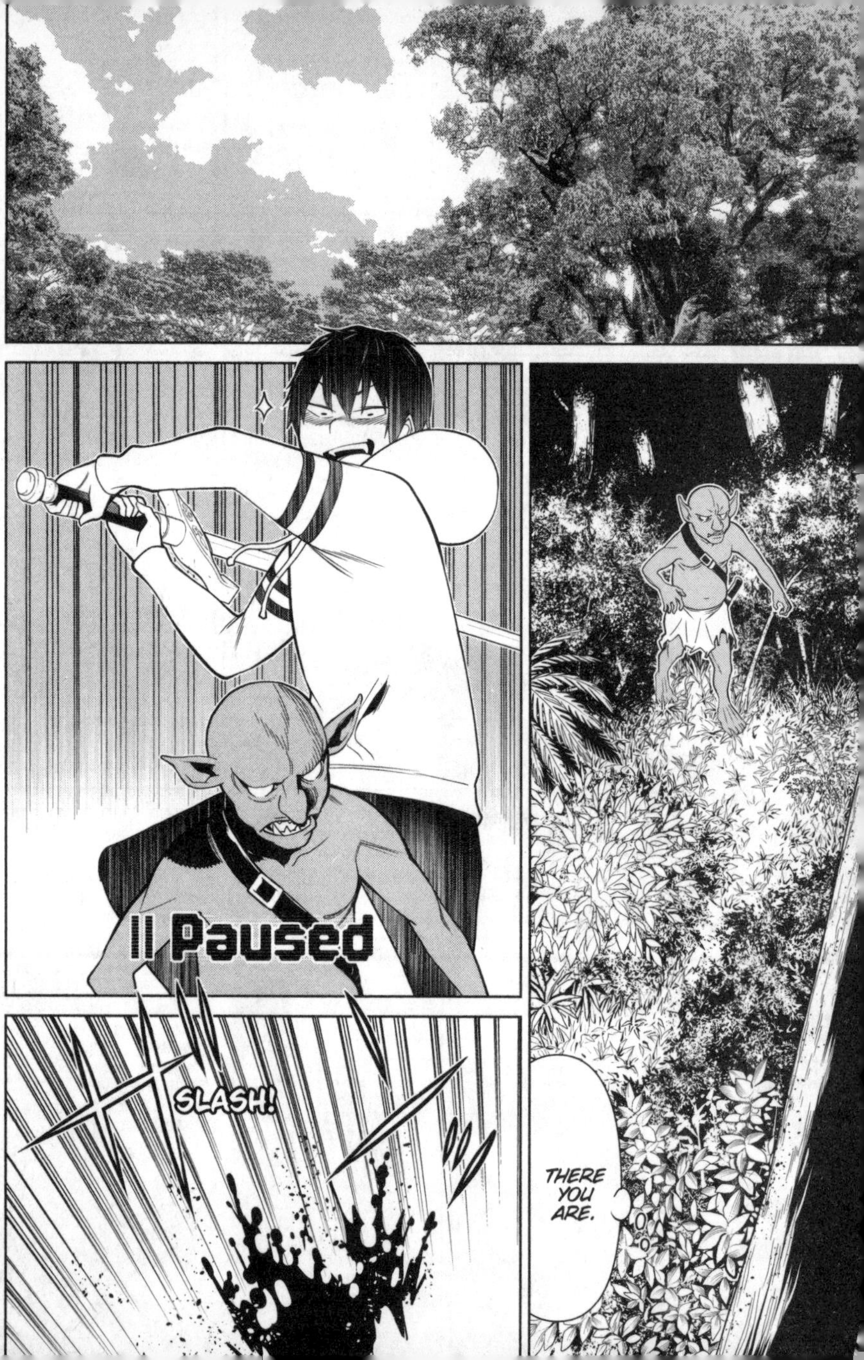
THERE YOU ARE.
Paused
SLASH!

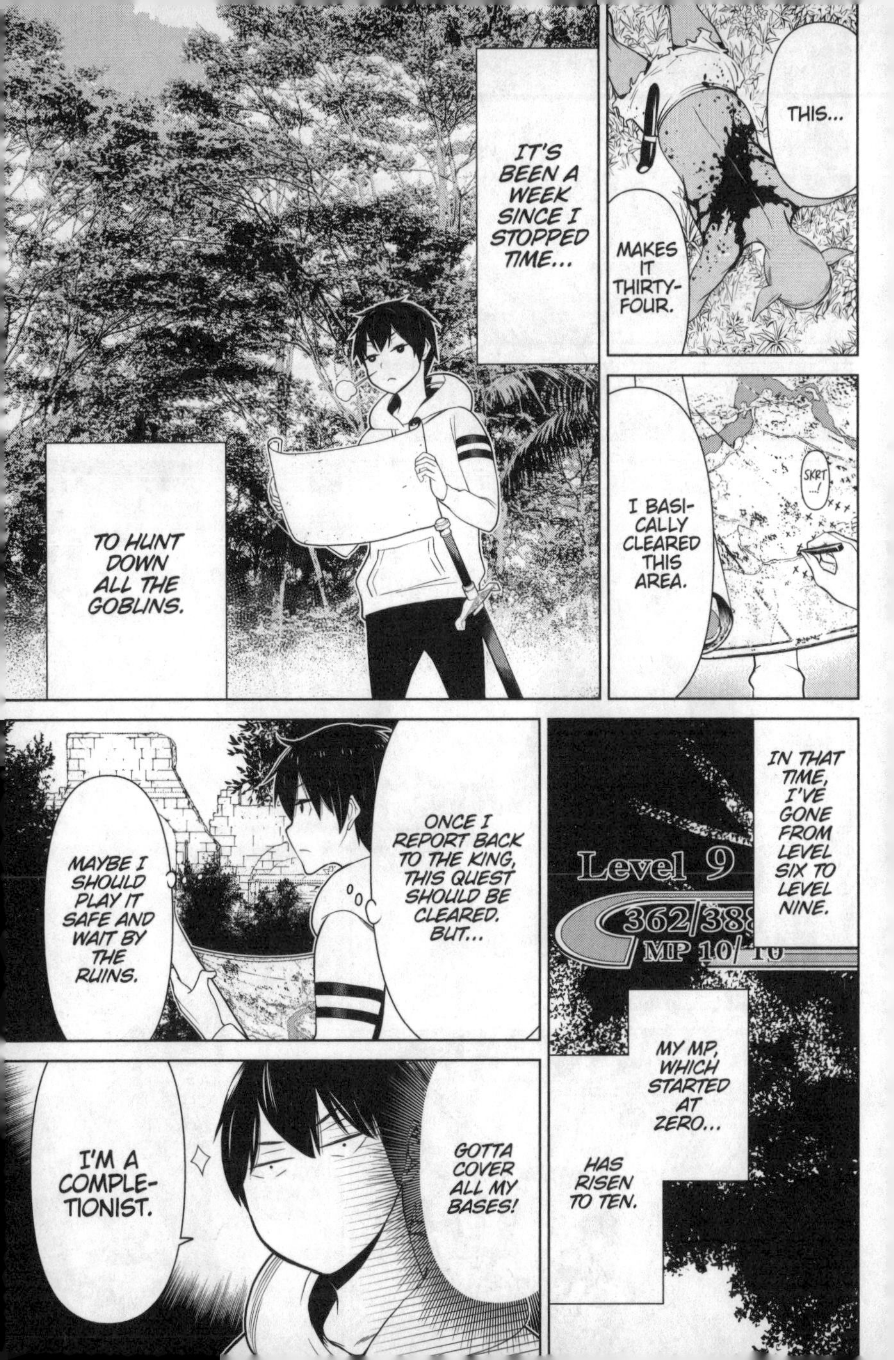
THIS...
MAKES IT THIRTY-FOUR.
SKRT...!
I BASICALLY CLEARED THIS AREA.
IT'S BEEN A WEEK SINCE I STOPPED TIME...
TO HUNT DOWN ALL THE GOBLINS.
IN THAT TIME, I'VE GONE FROM LEVEL SIX TO LEVEL NINE.
Level 9
362/388
MP 10/10
MY MP, WHICH STARTED AT ZERO...
HAS RISEN TO TEN.
ONCE I REPORT BACK TO THE KING, THIS QUEST SHOULD BE CLEARED. BUT...
MAYBE I SHOULD PLAY IT SAFE AND WAIT BY THE RUINS.
GOTTA COVER ALL MY BASES!
I'M A COMPLETIONIST.

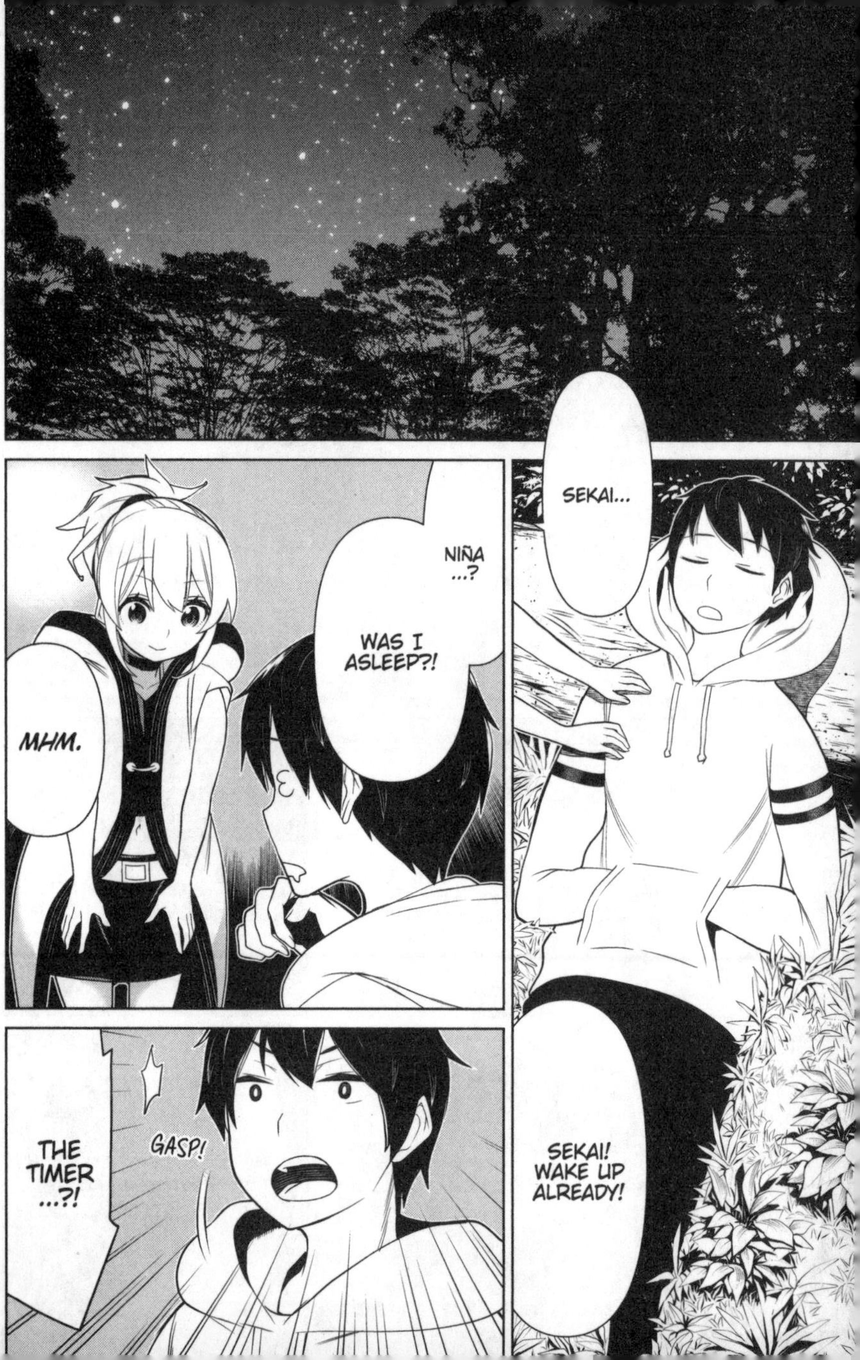
SEKAI...
SEKAI! WAKE UP ALREADY!
NIÑA ...?
WAS I ASLEEP?!
MHM.
GASP!
THE TIMER ...?!

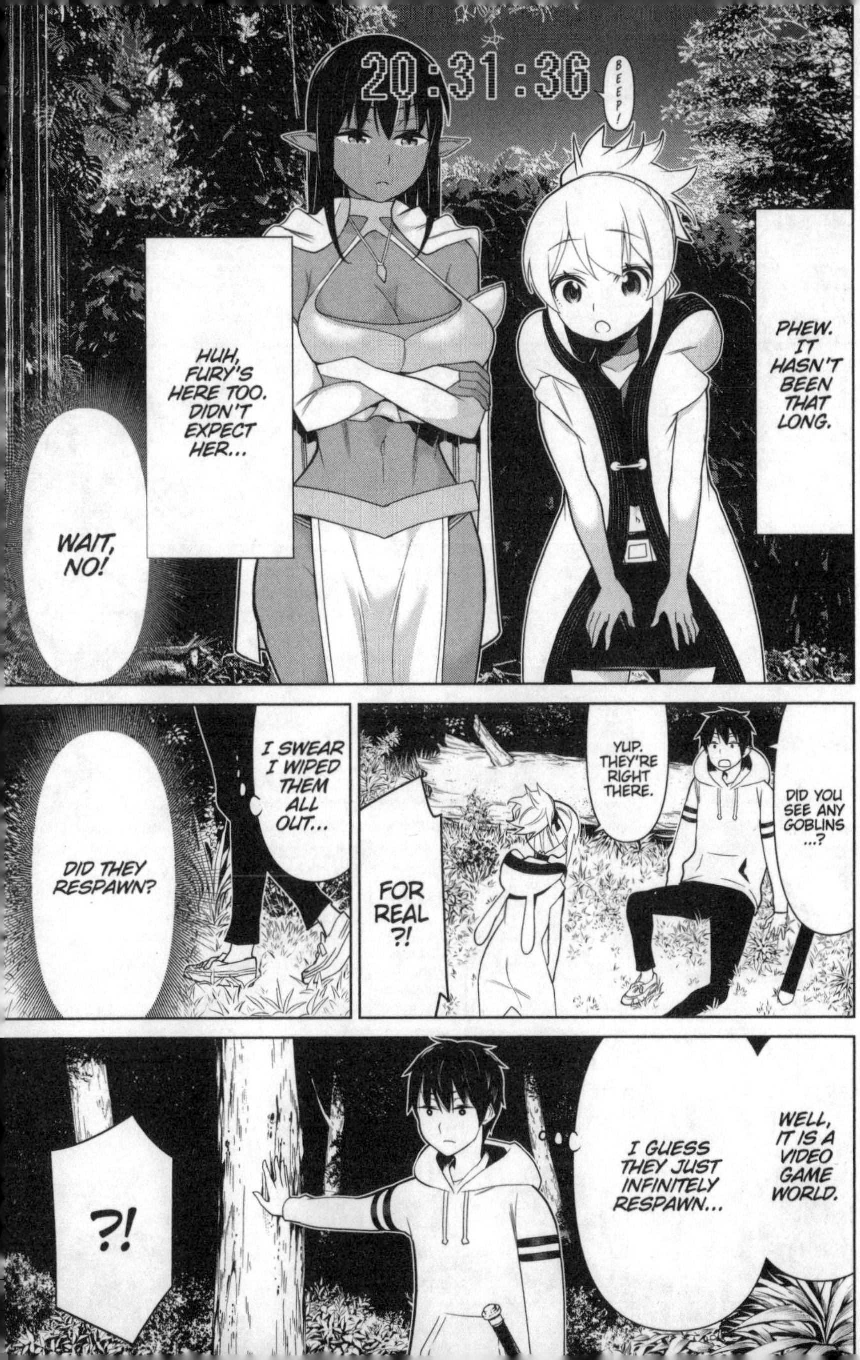
20:31:36
BEEP!
PHEW. IT HASN'T BEEN THAT LONG.
HUH, FURY'S HERE TOO. DIDN'T EXPECT HER...
WAIT, NO!
DID YOU SEE ANY GOBLINS ...?
YUP. THEY'RE RIGHT THERE.
FOR REAL ?!
I SWEAR I WIPED THEM ALL OUT...
DID THEY RESPAWN?
WELL, IT IS A VIDEO GAME WORLD.
I GUESS THEY JUST INFINITELY RESPAWN...
?!

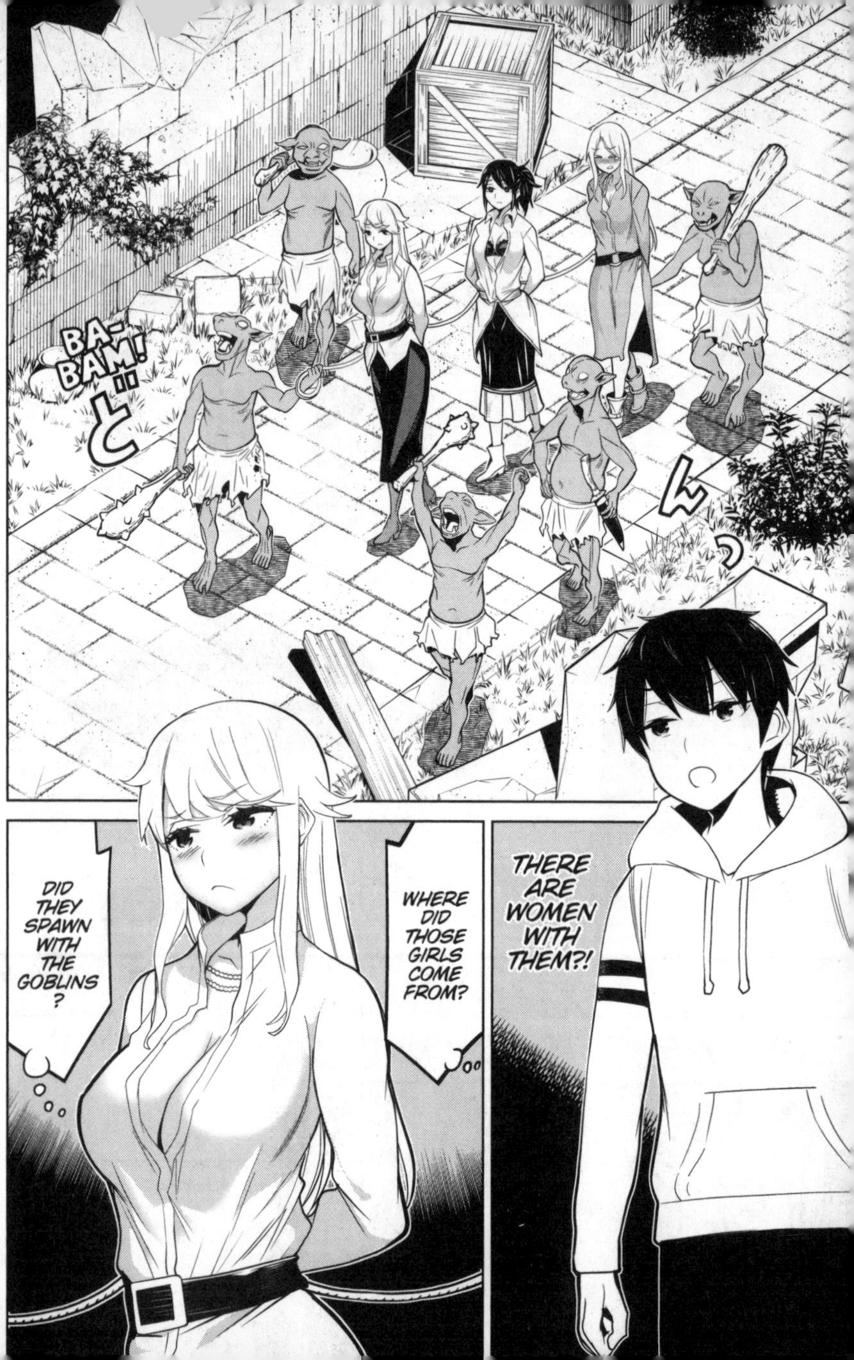
BA-BAM!
と
んっ
THERE ARE WOMEN WITH THEM?!
WHERE DID THOSE GIRLS COME FROM?
DID THEY SPAWN WITH THE GOBLINS?

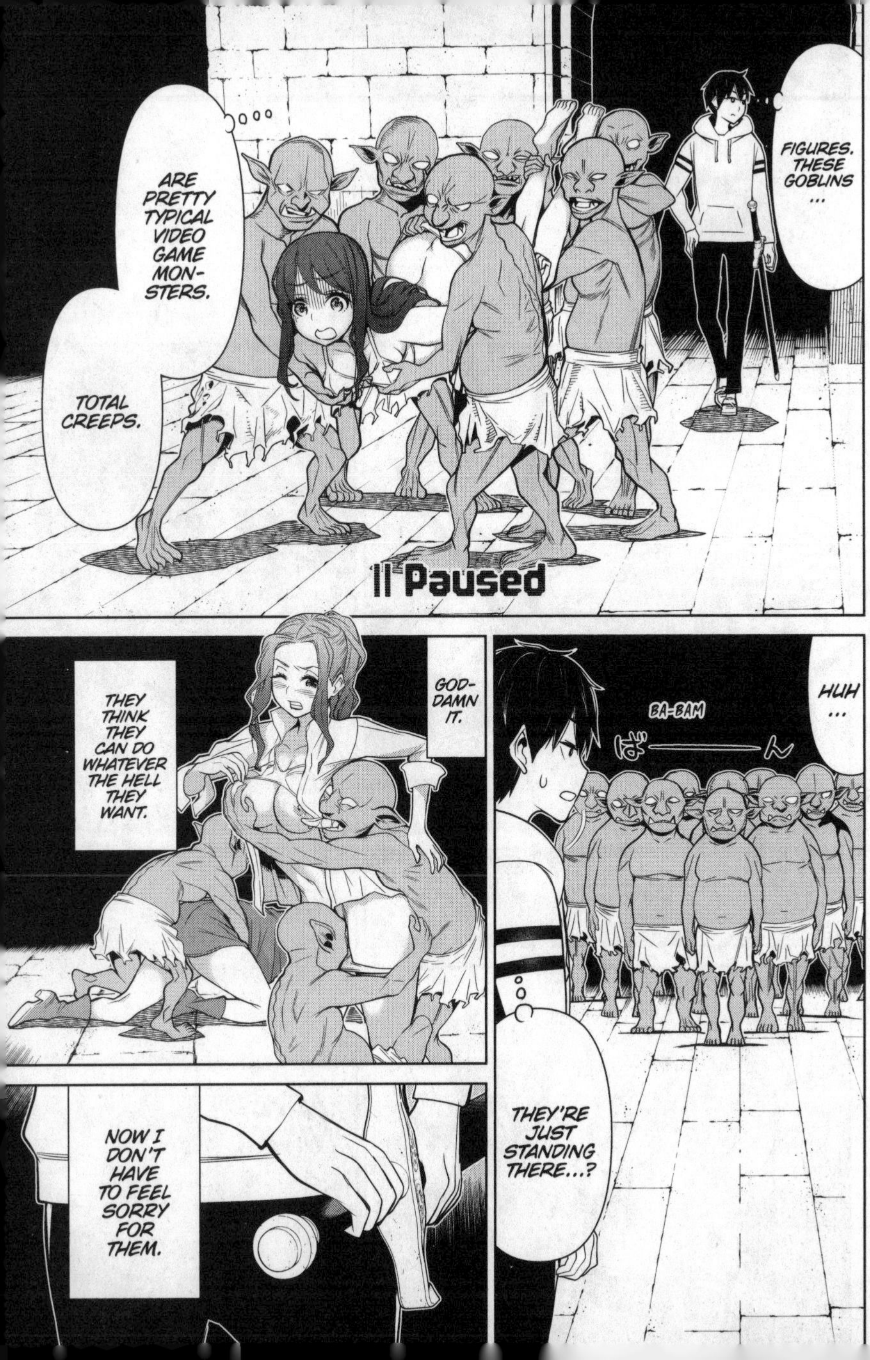
FIGURES. THESE GOBLINS ...
ARE PRETTY TYPICAL VIDEO GAME MONSTERS.
TOTAL CREEPS.
II Paused
HUH ...
BA-BAM
ばーーーん
THEY'RE JUST STANDING THERE...?
GOD-DAMN IT.
THEY THINK THEY CAN DO WHATEVER THE HELL THEY WANT.
NOW I DON'T HAVE TO FEEL SORRY FOR THEM.

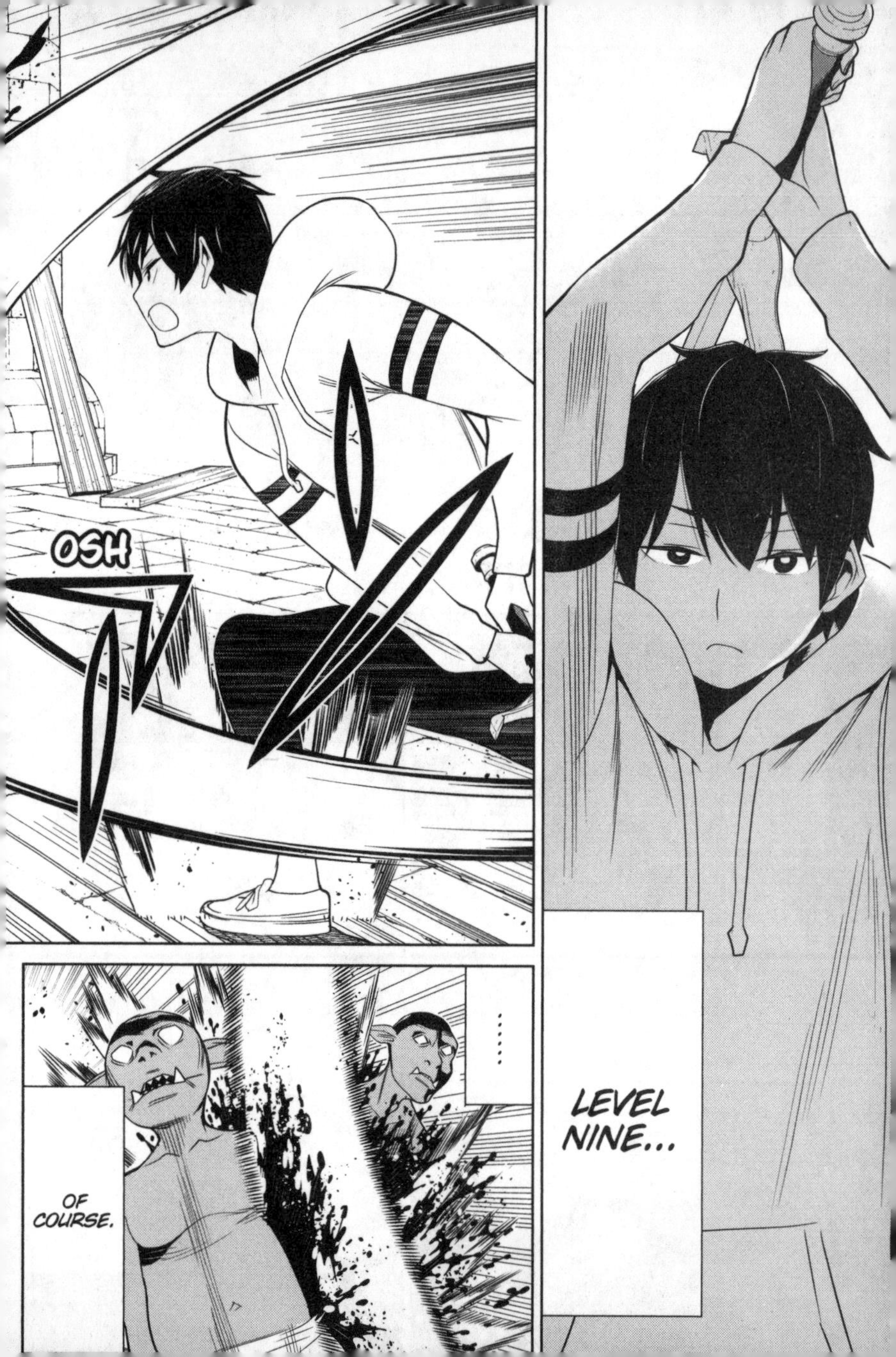
LEVEL NINE...
OSH
......
OF COURSE.

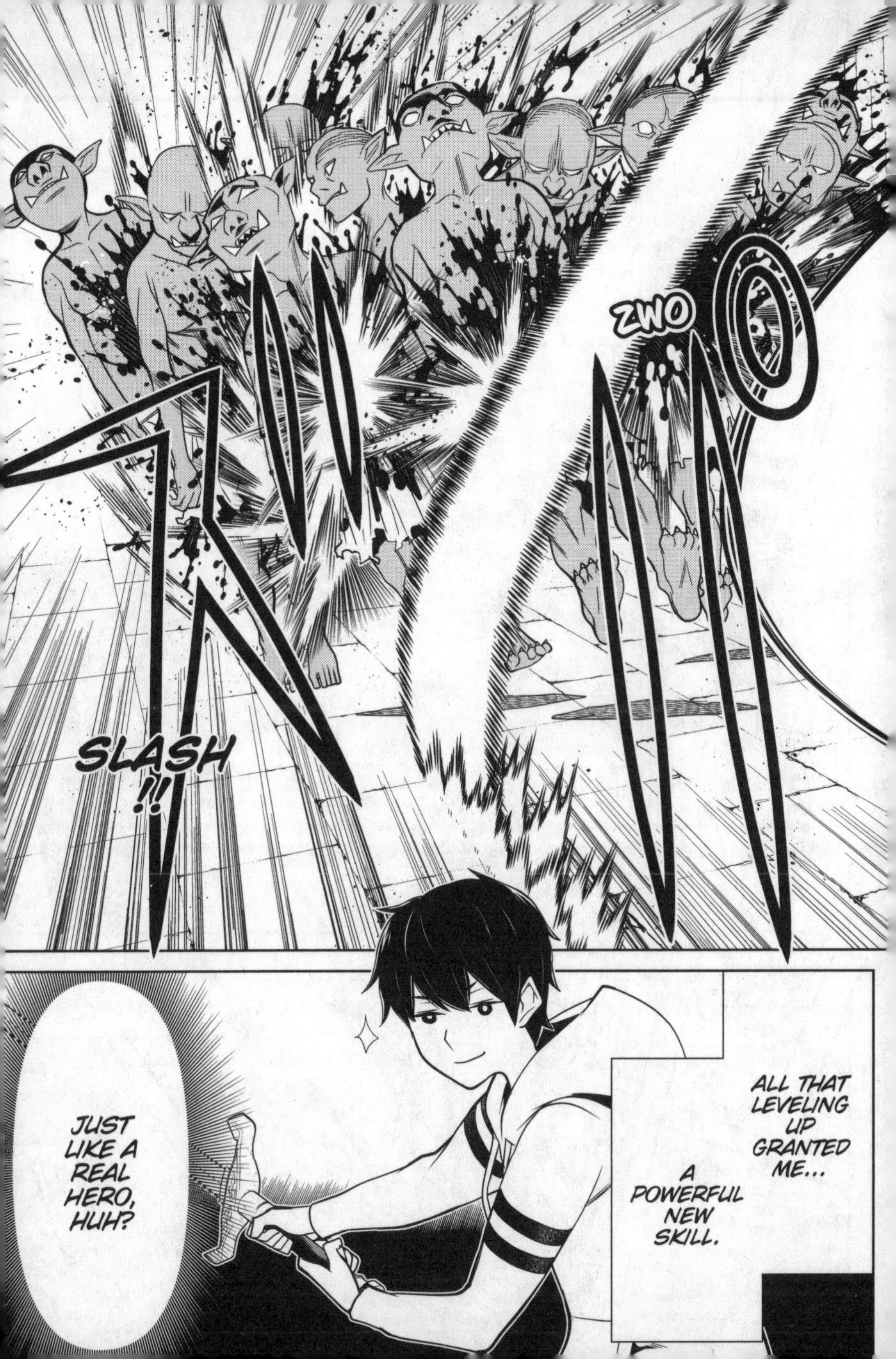
ZWO
SLASH!!
ALL THAT LEVELING UP GRANTED ME...
A POWERFUL NEW SKILL.
JUST LIKE A REAL HERO, HUH?

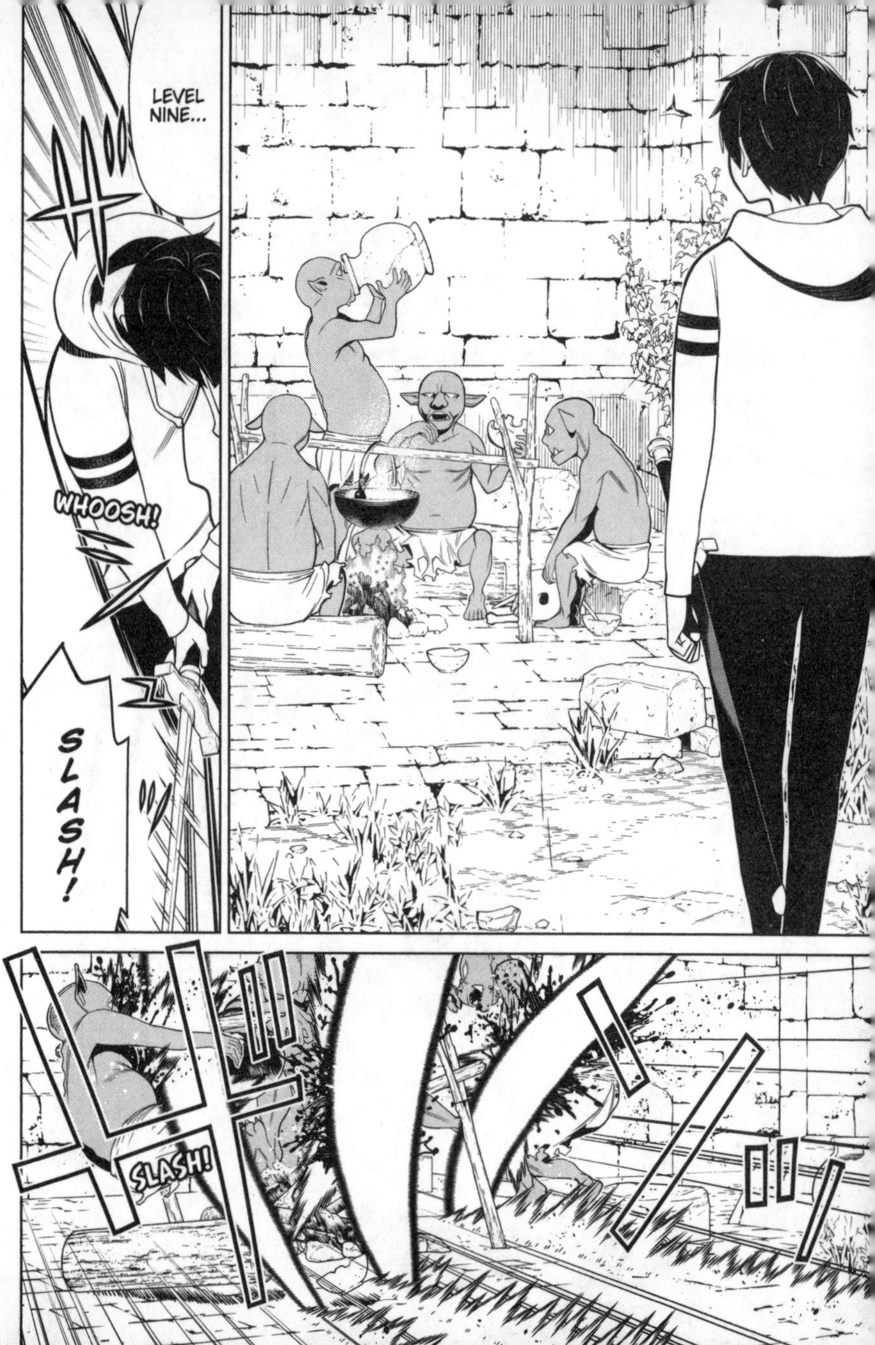
LEVEL NINE...
WHOOSH!
SLASH!
SLASH!

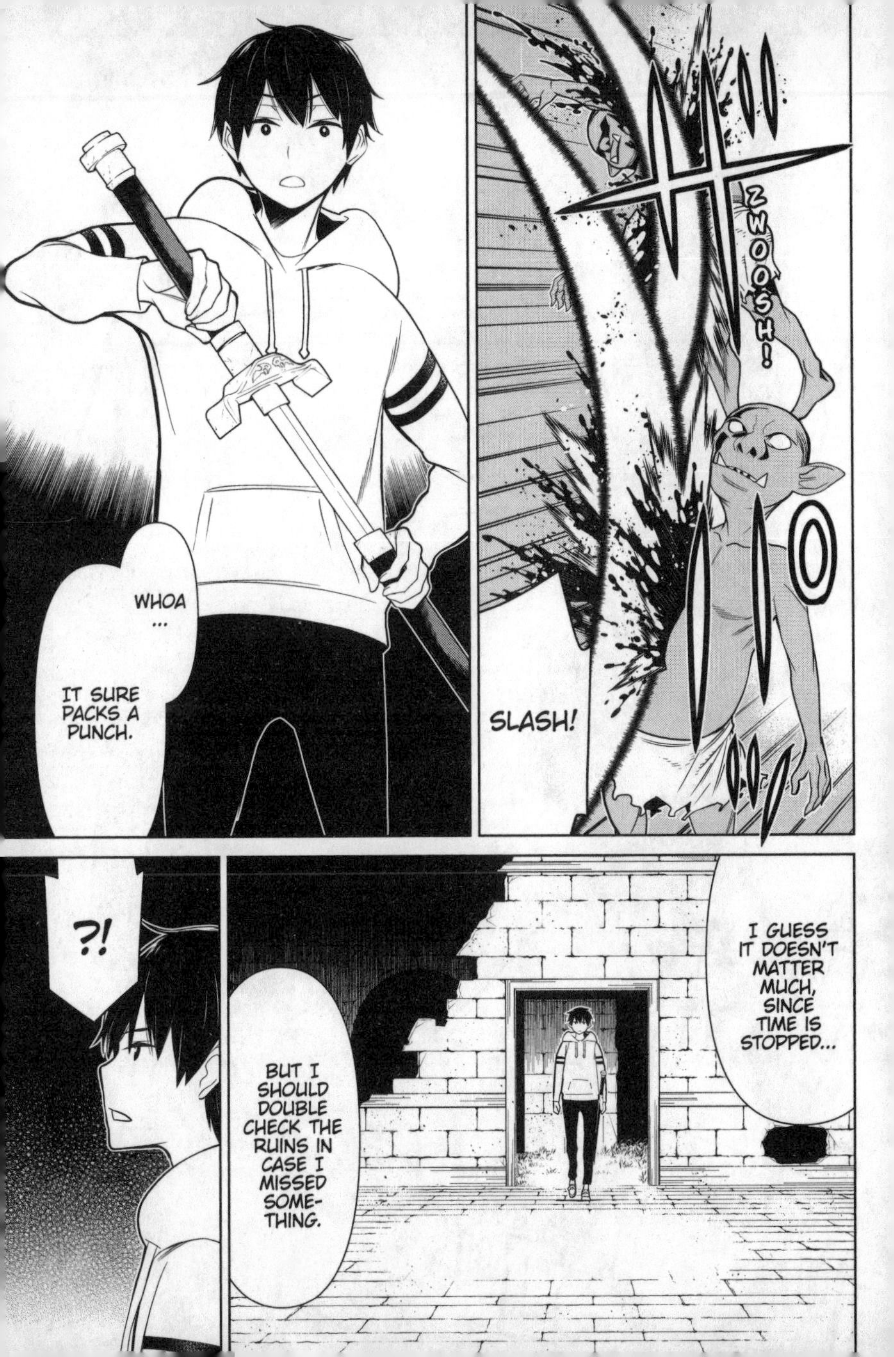
ZWOOSH!
SLASH!
WHOA ...
IT SURE PACKS A PUNCH.
I GUESS IT DOESN'T MATTER MUCH, SINCE TIME IS STOPPED...
BUT I SHOULD DOUBLE CHECK THE RUINS IN CASE I MISSED SOME-THING.
?!

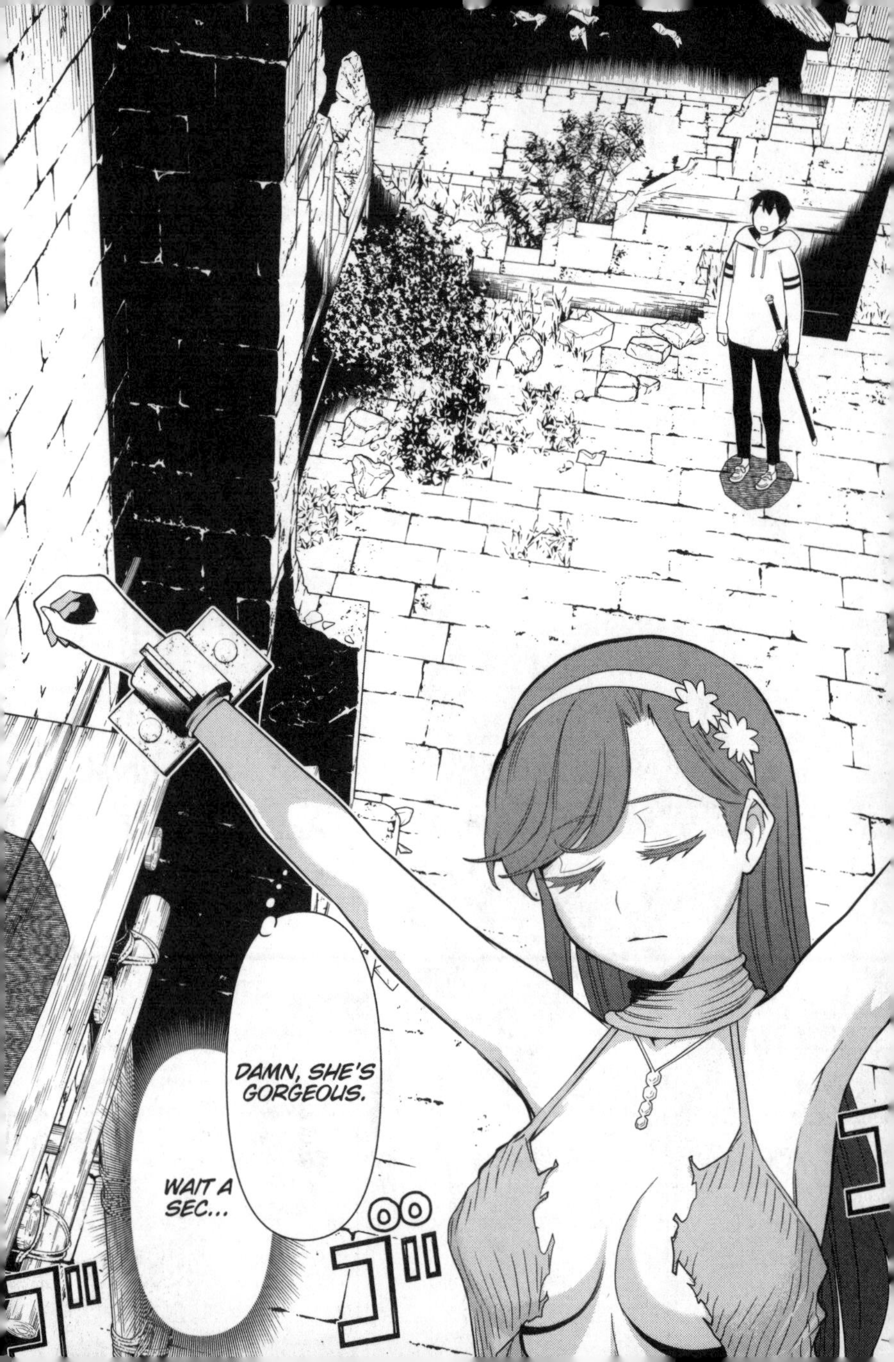
DAMN, SHE'S GORGEOUS.
WAIT A SEC...

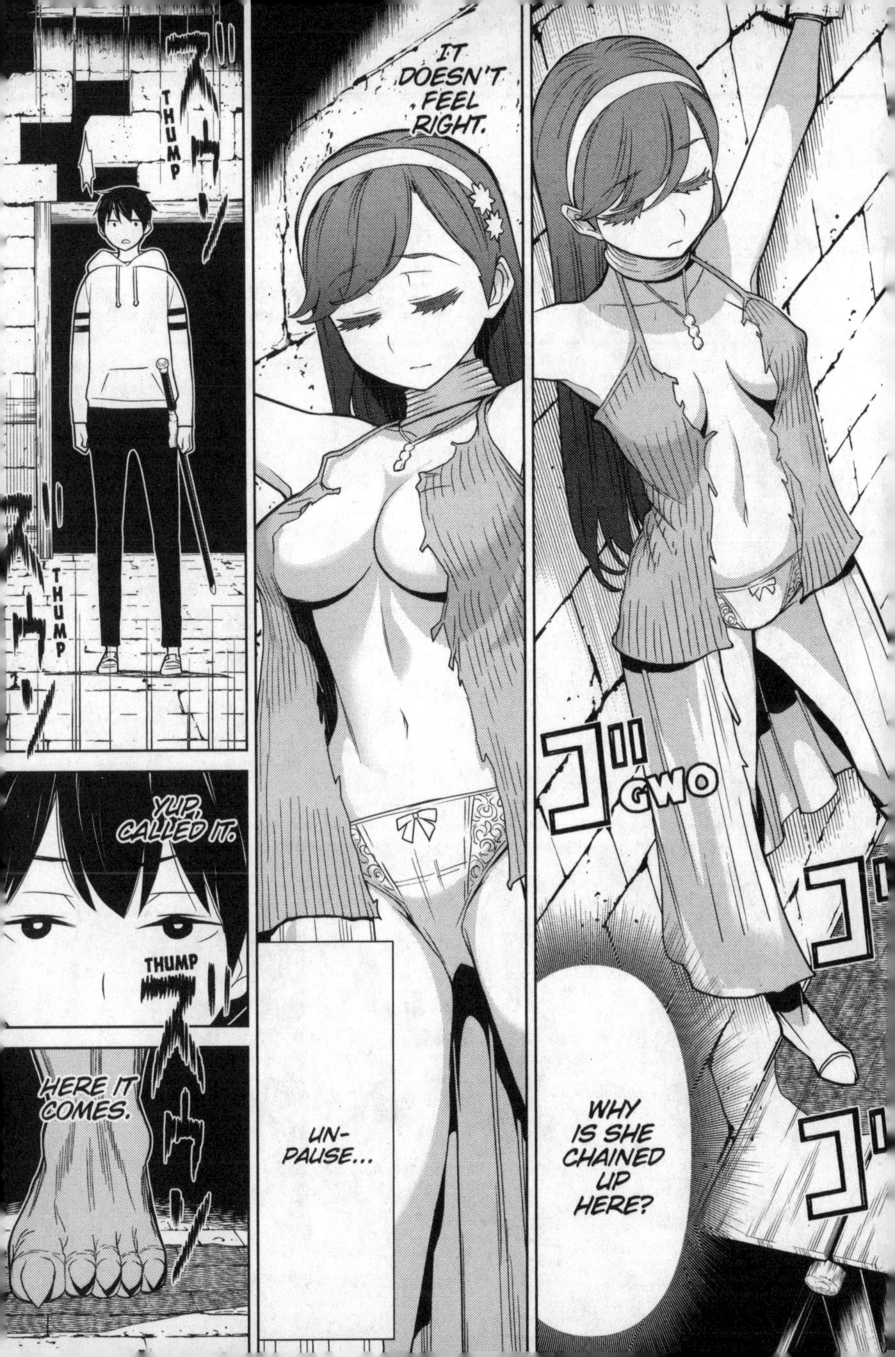
GWO
WHY IS SHE CHAINED UP HERE?
IT DOESN'T FEEL RIGHT.
UN-PAUSE...
THUMP
THUMP
YUP, CALLED IT.
THUMP
HERE IT COMES.

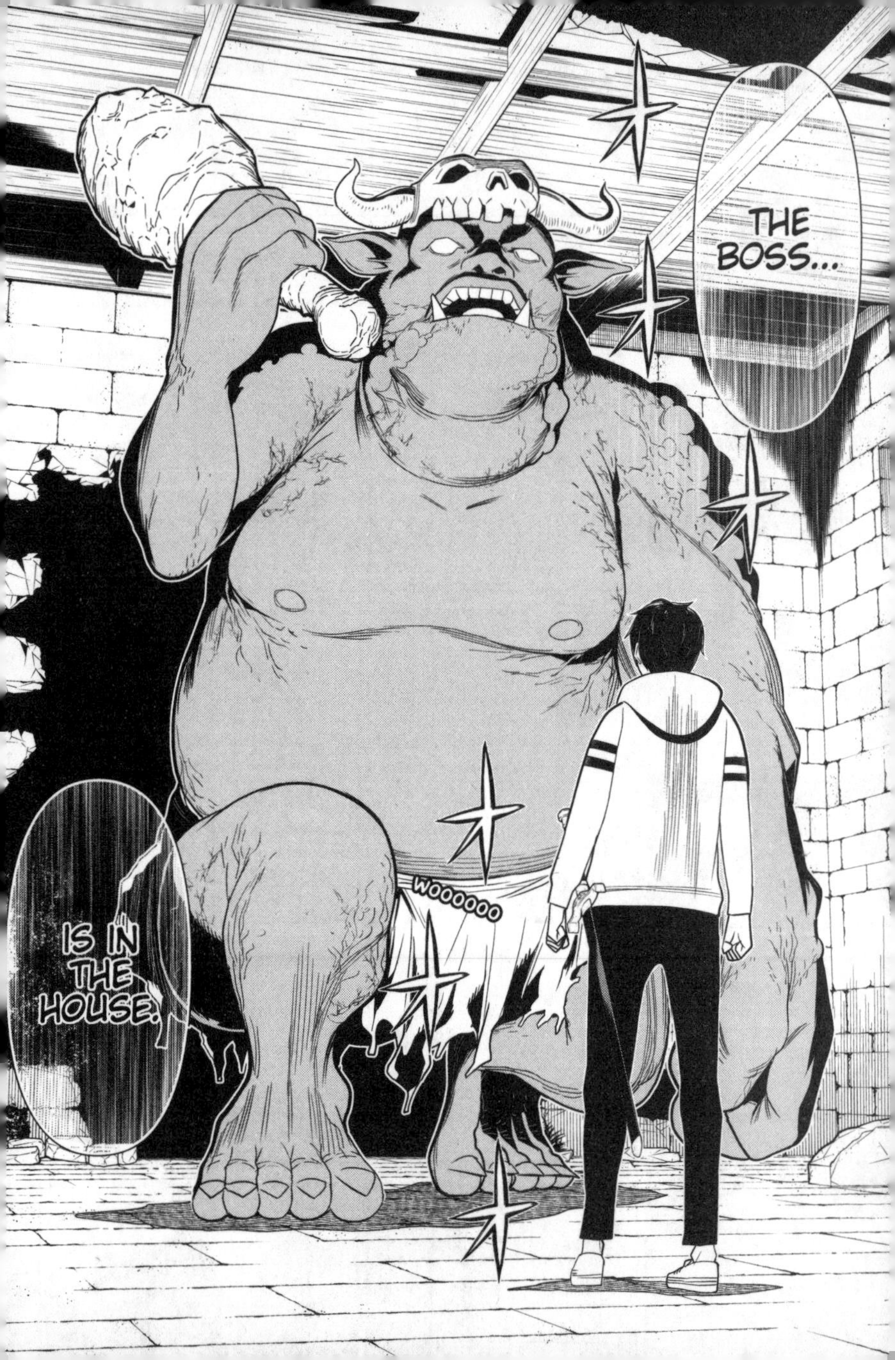
THE BOSS...
WOOOOOO
IS IN THE HOUSE.

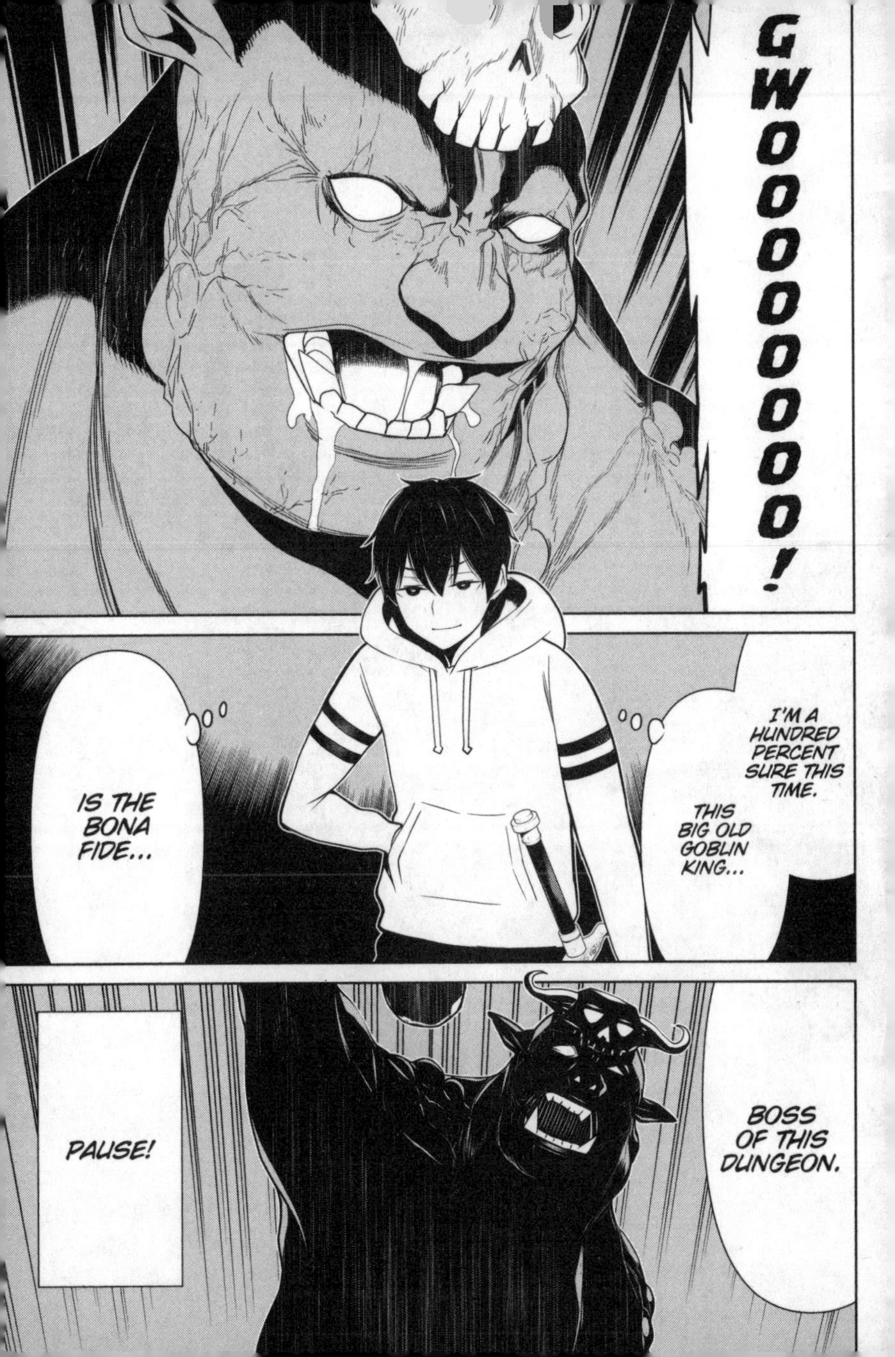
GWOOOOOOOO!
I'M A HUNDRED PERCENT SURE THIS TIME.
THIS BIG OLD GOBLIN KING...
IS THE BONA FIDE...
BOSS OF THIS DUNGEON.
PAUSE!

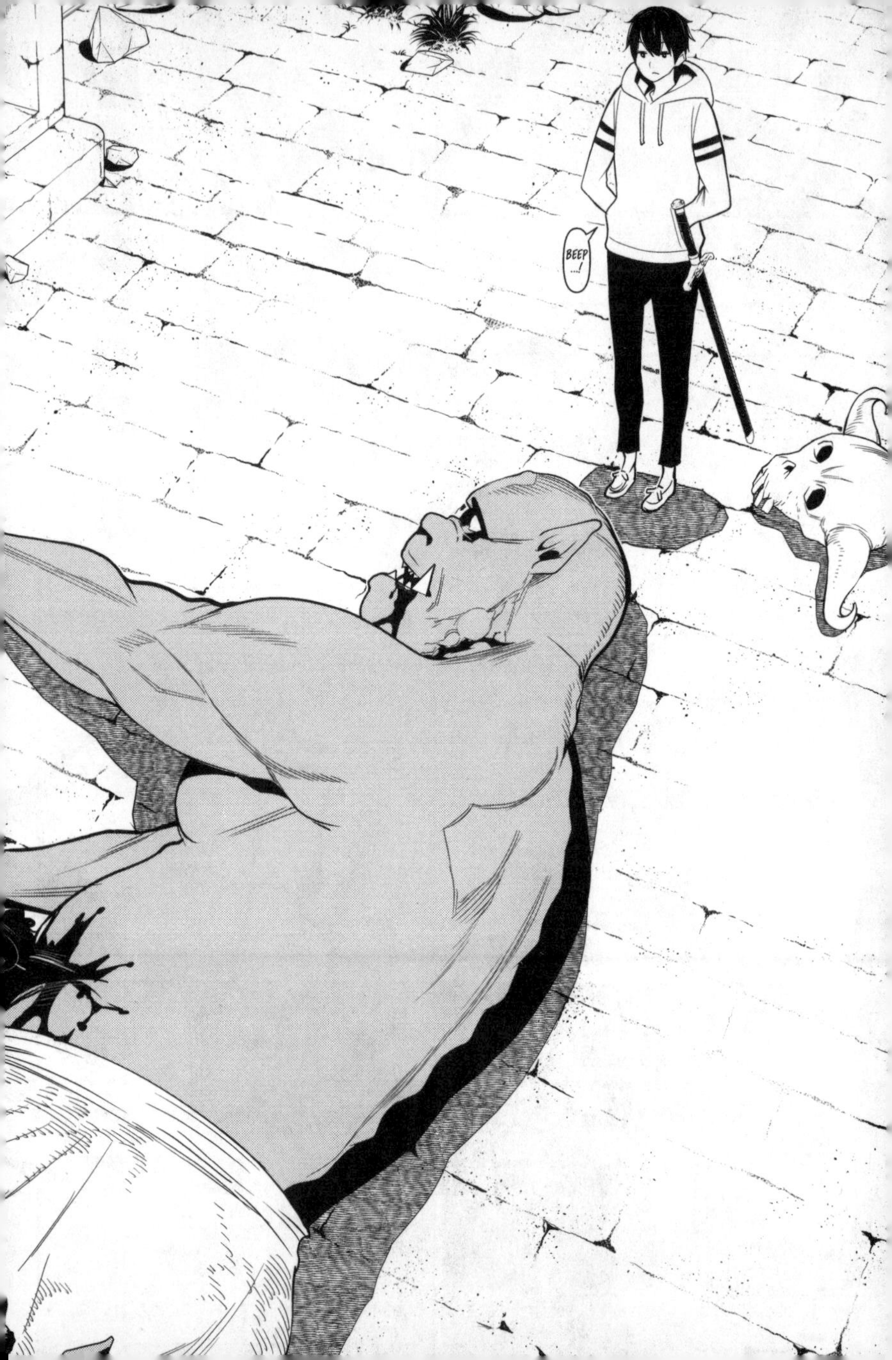
BEEP ...!

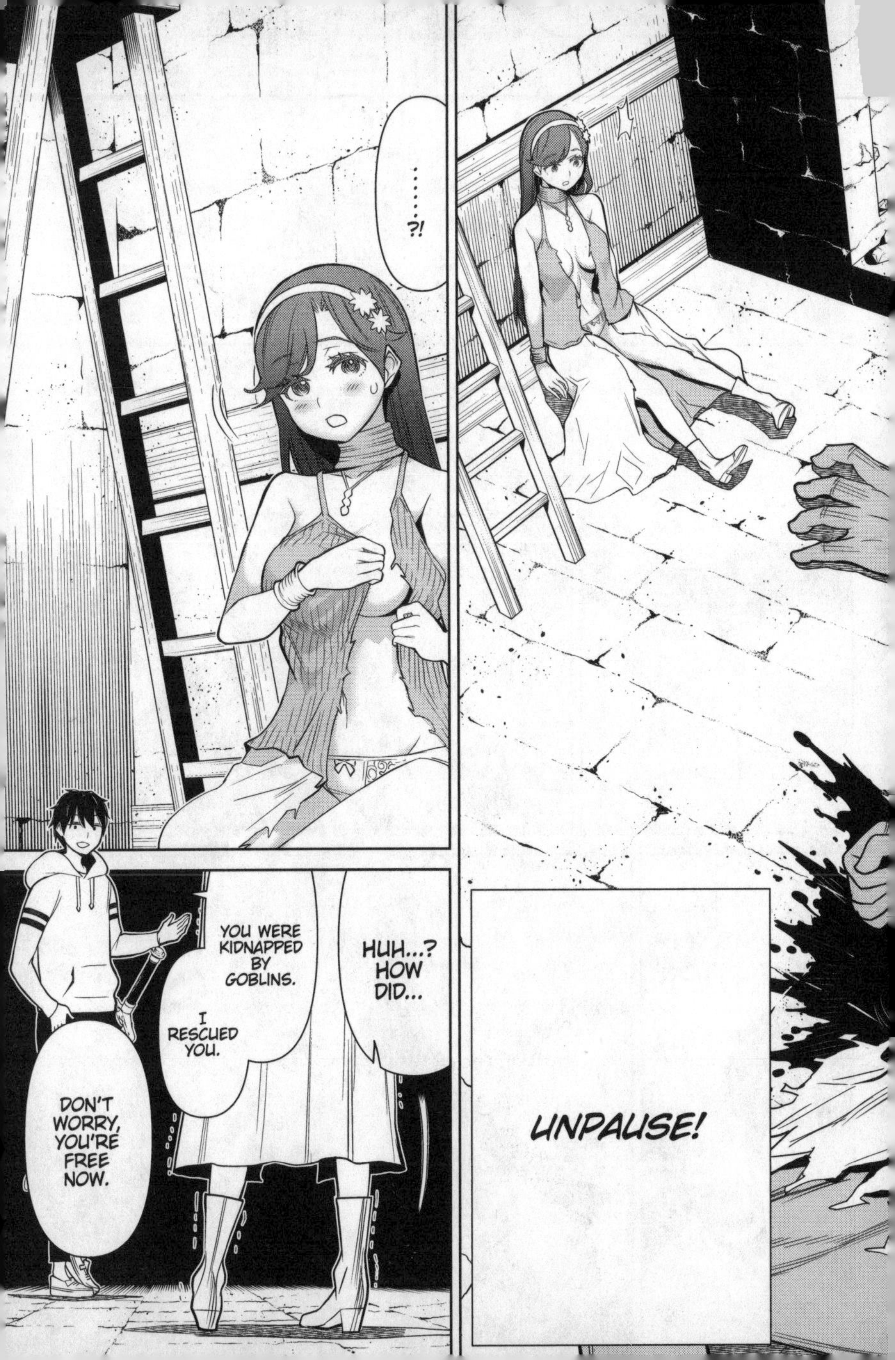

......
?!
UNPAUSE!
HUH...? HOW DID...
YOU WERE KIDNAPPED BY GOBLINS.
I RESCUED YOU.
DON'T WORRY, YOU'RE FREE NOW.

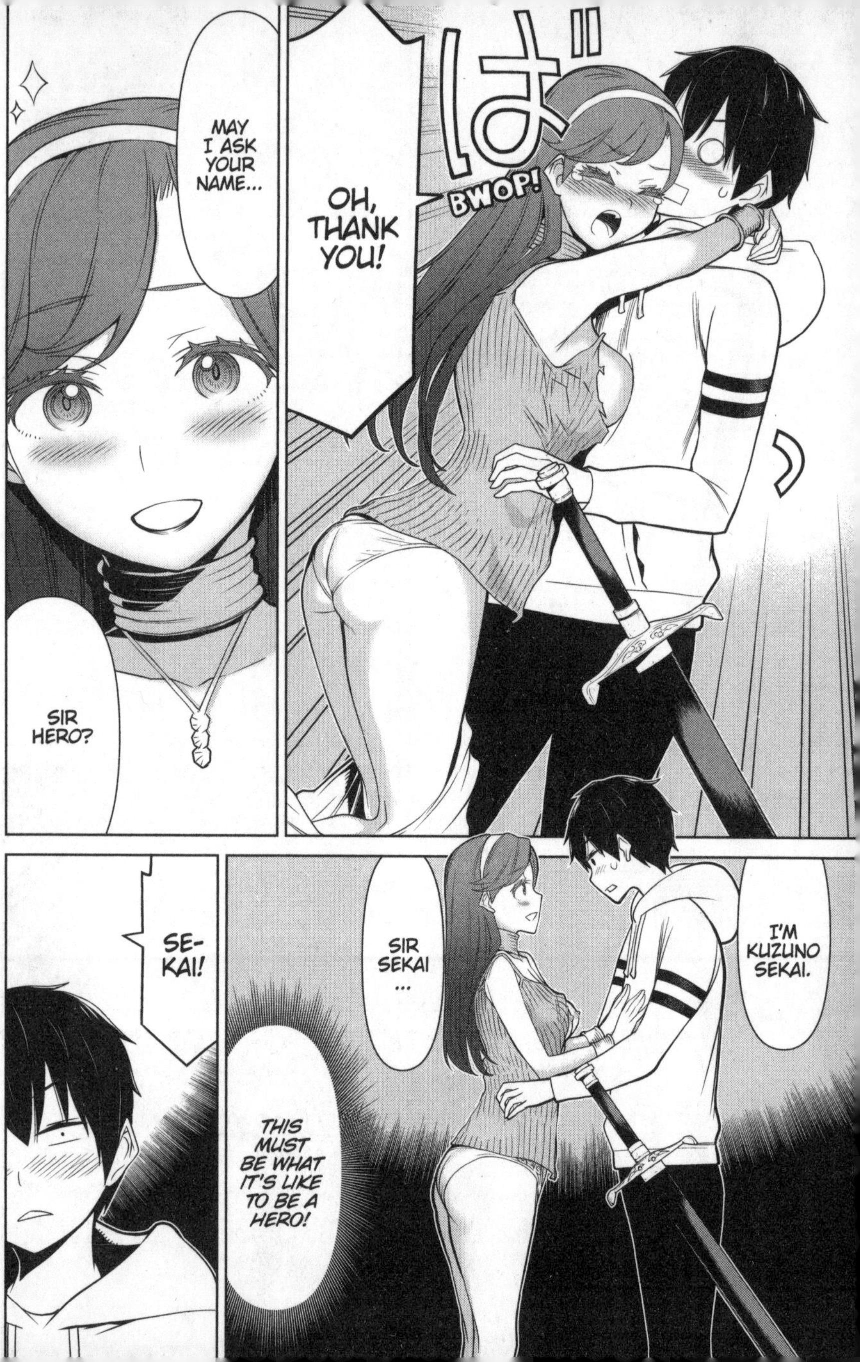
ば
BWOP!
OH, THANK YOU!
MAY I ASK YOUR NAME...
SIR HERO?
I'M KUZUNO SEKAI.
SIR SEKAI ...
THIS MUST BE WHAT IT'S LIKE TO BE A HERO!
SE-KAI!

NO WAY!

YOU CLEARED OUT THE GOBLINS ALREADY...?

PRETTY MUCH.

IN LESS THAN A MINUTE?!

YOU'RE TOTALLY AWESOME!

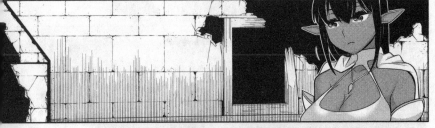

APPEARS TO BE ABLE TO STOP TIME.

KUZUNO SEKAI...

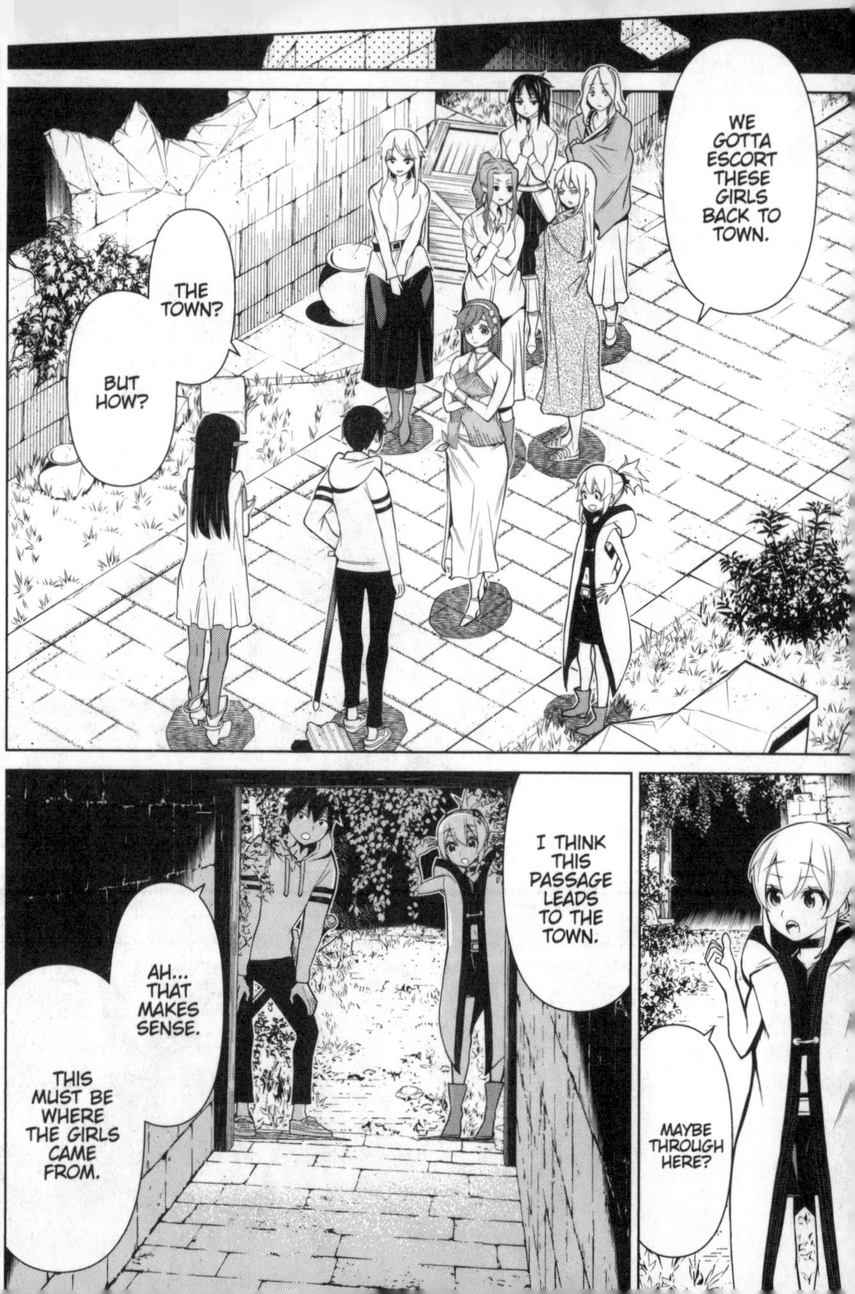
WE GOTTA ESCORT THESE GIRLS BACK TO TOWN.
THE TOWN?
BUT HOW?
MAYBE THROUGH HERE?
I THINK THIS PASSAGE LEADS TO THE TOWN.
AH... THAT MAKES SENSE.
THIS MUST BE WHERE THE GIRLS CAME FROM.

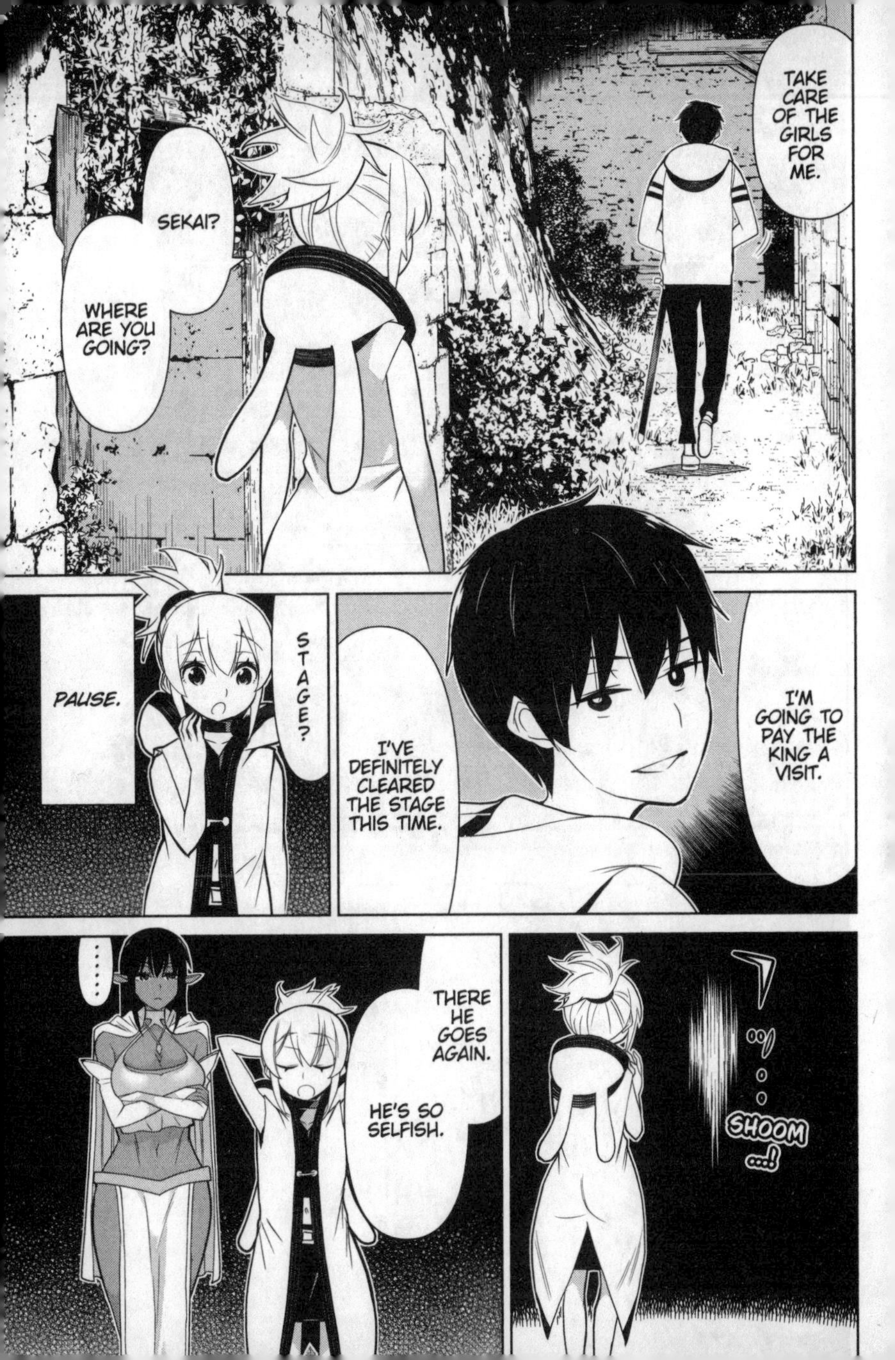

TAKE CARE OF THE GIRLS FOR ME.
SEKAI?
WHERE ARE YOU GOING?
I'M GOING TO PAY THE KING A VISIT.
I'VE DEFINITELY CLEARED THE STAGE THIS TIME.
STAGE?
PAUSE.
SHOOM...!
THERE HE GOES AGAIN.
HE'S SO SELFISH.
......

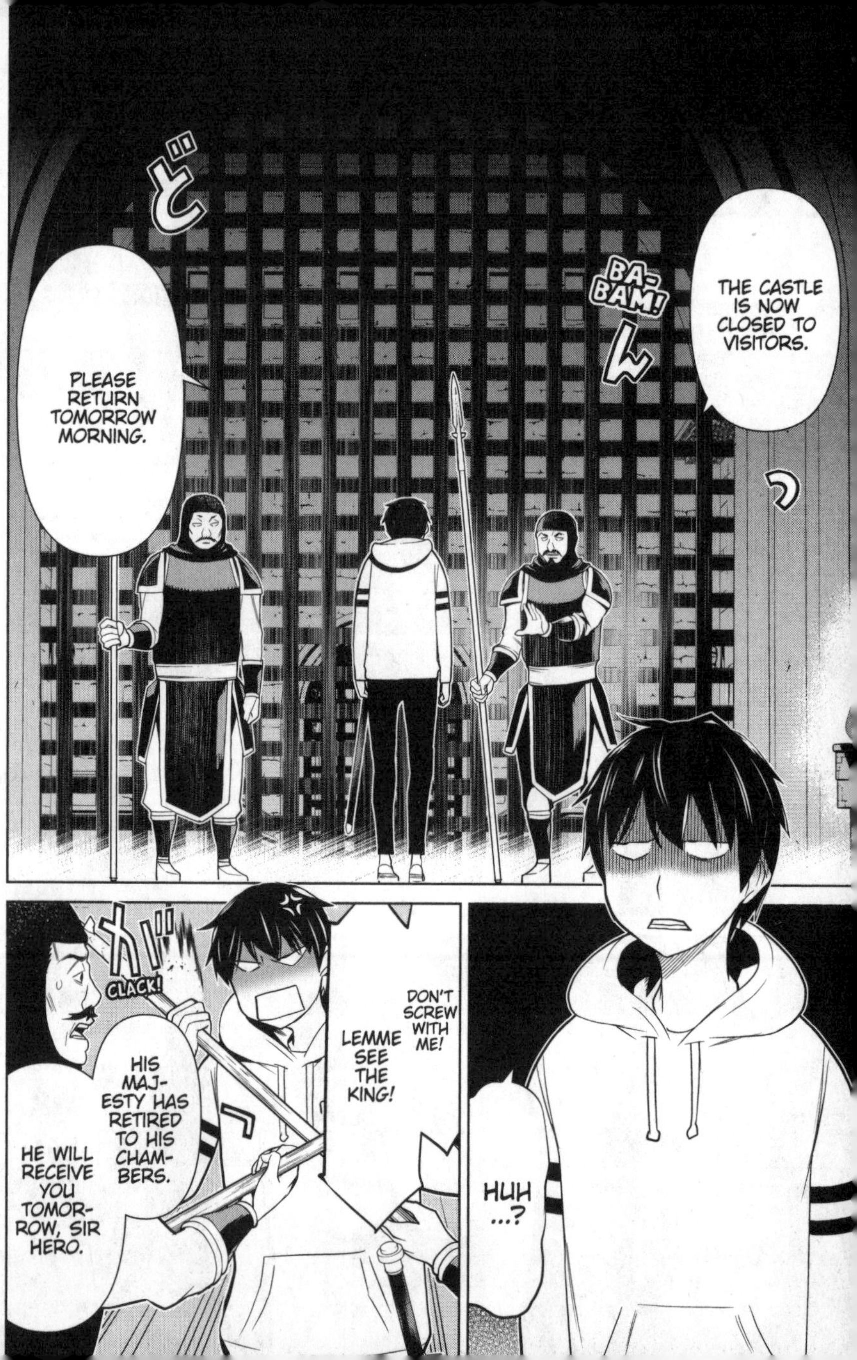

THE CASTLE IS NOW CLOSED TO VISITORS.
BA-BAM!
PLEASE RETURN TOMORROW MORNING.
HUH ...?
DON'T SCREW WITH ME!
LEMME SEE THE KING!
CLACK!
HIS MAJESTY HAS RETIRED TO HIS CHAMBERS.
HE WILL RECEIVE YOU TOMORROW, SIR HERO.

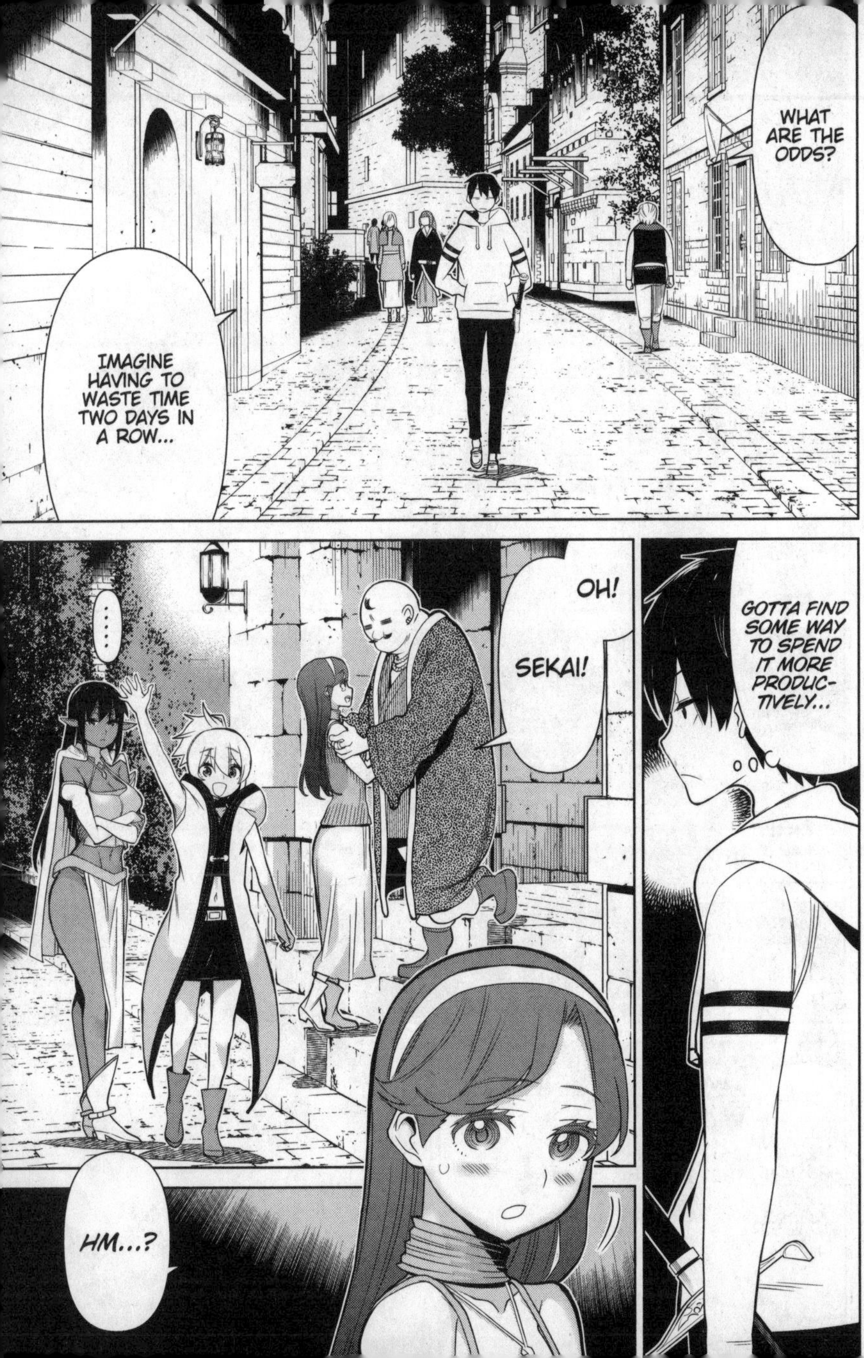
WHAT ARE THE ODDS?
IMAGINE HAVING TO WASTE TIME TWO DAYS IN A ROW...
GOTTA FIND SOME WAY TO SPEND IT MORE PRODUC-TIVELY...
OH!
SEKAI!
......
HM...?

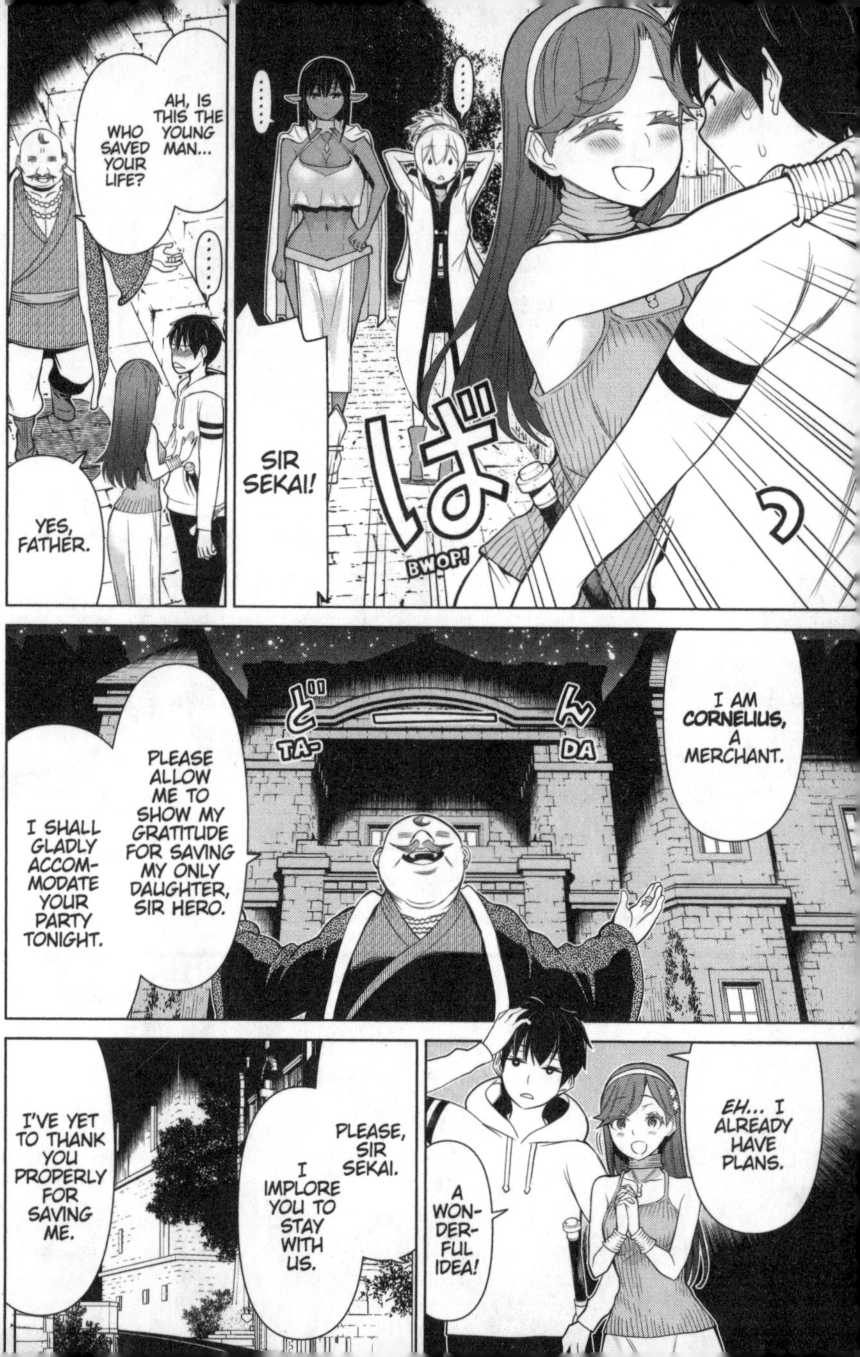

ぽっ
BWOP!
……
……
SIR SEKAI!
AH, IS THIS THE YOUNG MAN... WHO SAVED YOUR LIFE?
……
YES, FATHER.
I AM CORNELIUS, A MERCHANT.
どん
TA- DA
PLEASE ALLOW ME TO SHOW MY GRATITUDE FOR SAVING MY ONLY DAUGHTER, SIR HERO.
I SHALL GLADLY ACCOMMODATE YOUR PARTY TONIGHT.
EH... I ALREADY HAVE PLANS.
A WONDERFUL IDEA!
PLEASE, SIR SEKAI.
I IMPLORE YOU TO STAY WITH US.
I'VE YET TO THANK YOU PROPERLY FOR SAVING ME.

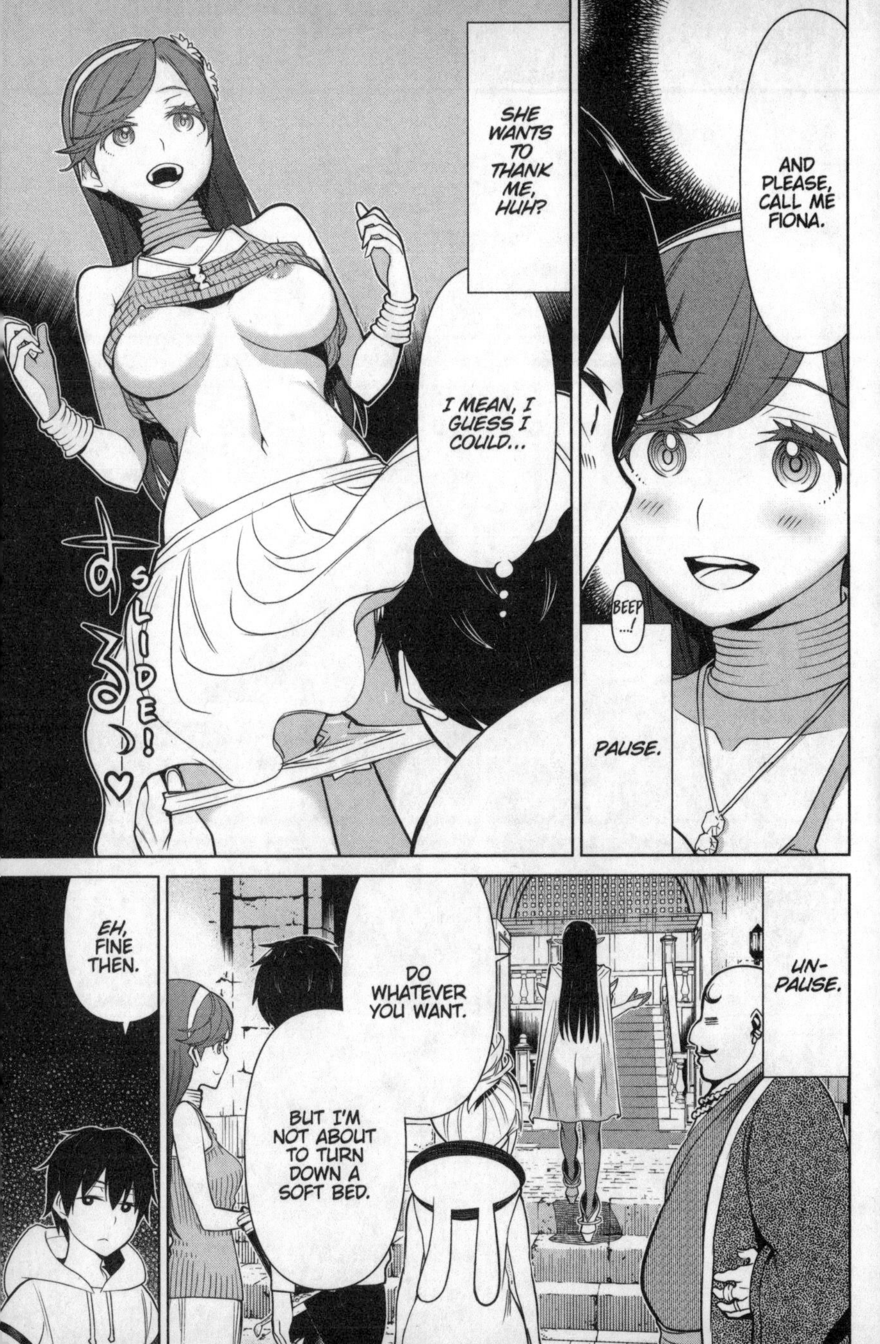
AND PLEASE, CALL ME FIONA.
BEEP ...!
PAUSE.
SHE WANTS TO THANK ME, HUH?
I MEAN, I GUESS I COULD...
SLIDE!
UN-PAUSE.
DO WHATEVER YOU WANT.
BUT I'M NOT ABOUT TO TURN DOWN A SOFT BED.
EH, FINE THEN.

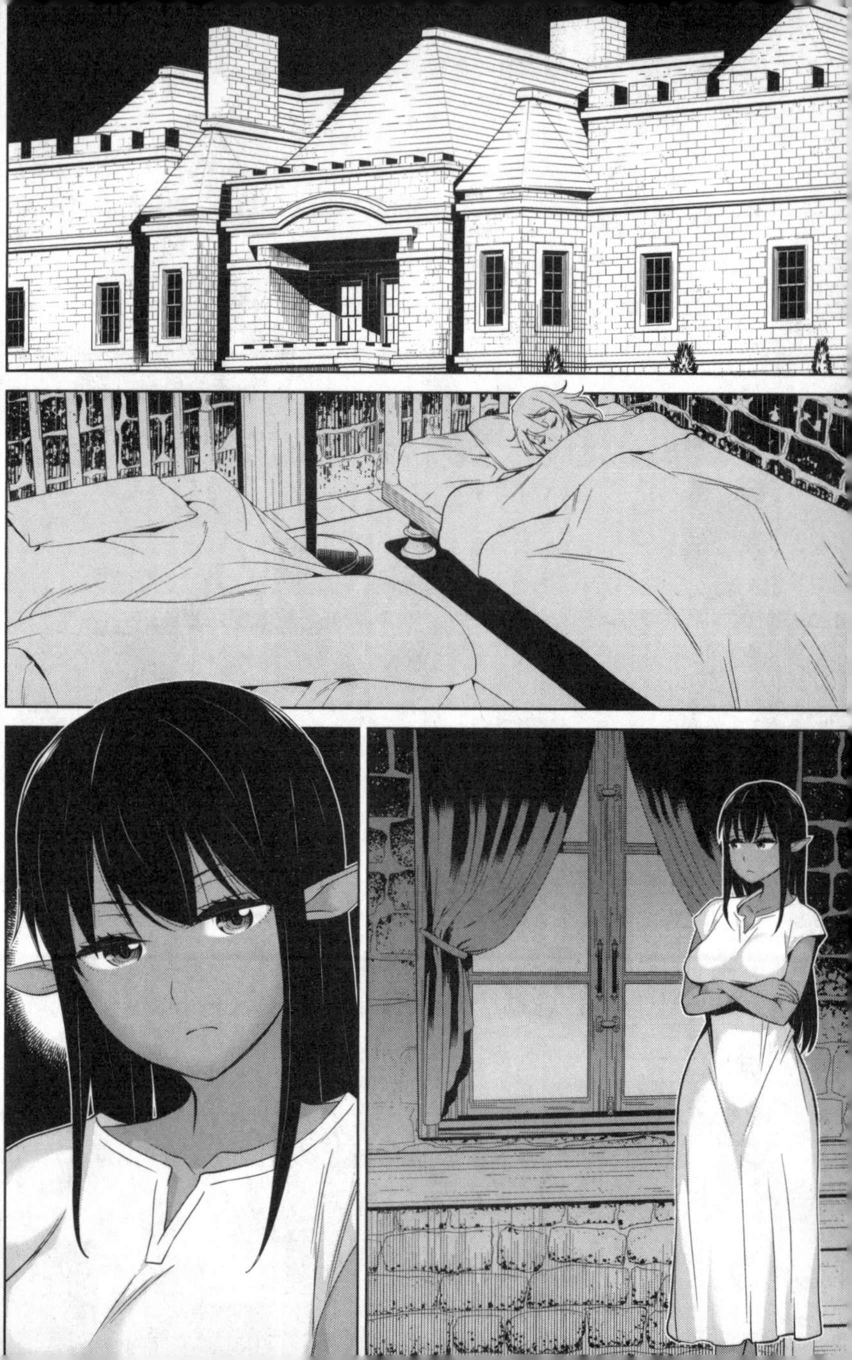

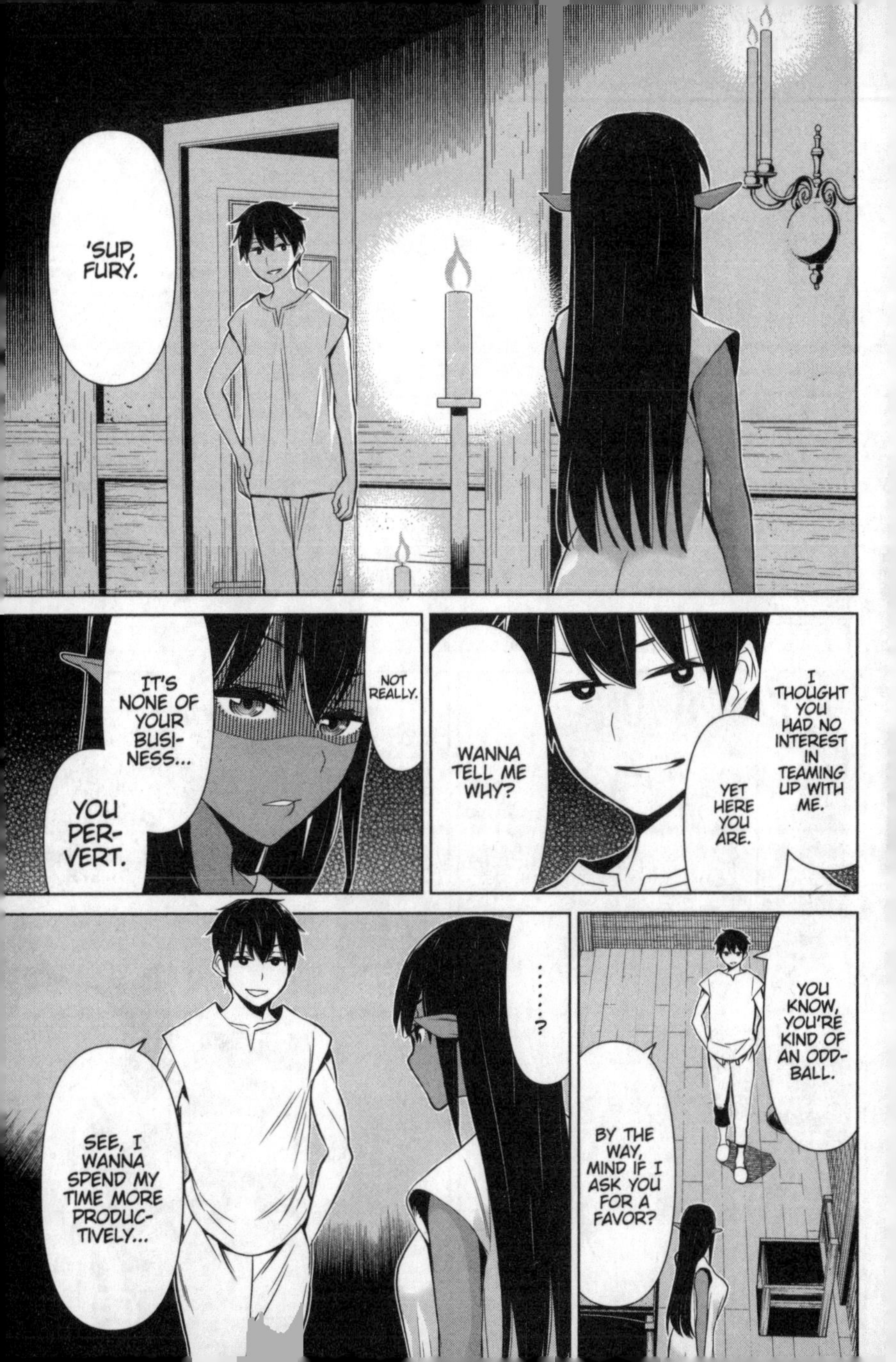
'SUP, FURY.
I THOUGHT YOU HAD NO INTEREST IN TEAMING UP WITH ME.
YET HERE YOU ARE.
WANNA TELL ME WHY?
NOT REALLY.
IT'S NONE OF YOUR BUSI-NESS...
YOU PER-VERT.
YOU KNOW, YOU'RE KIND OF AN ODD-BALL.
BY THE WAY, MIND IF I ASK YOU FOR A FAVOR?
......?
SEE, I WANNA SPEND MY TIME MORE PRODUC-TIVELY...

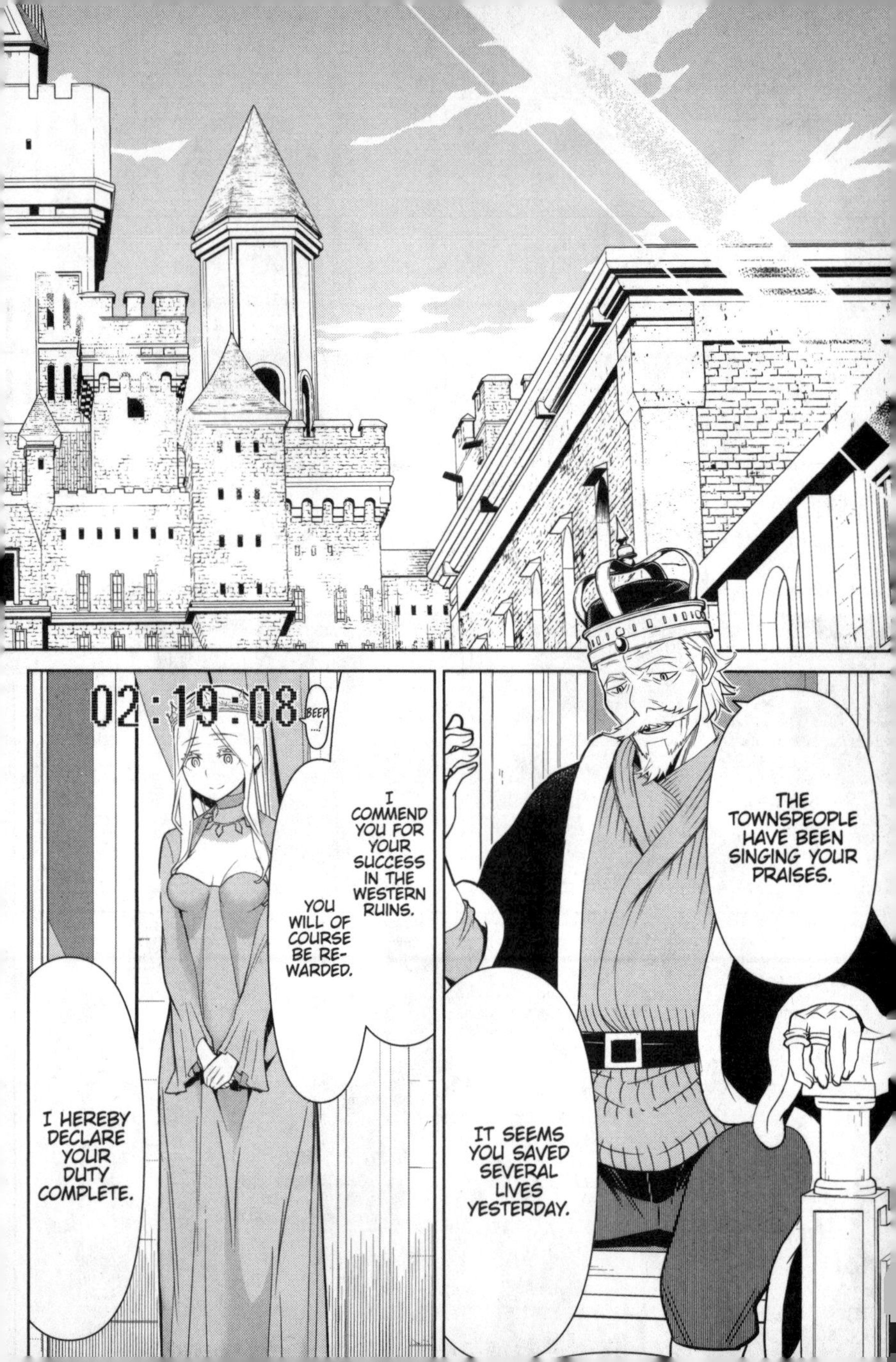
THE TOWNSPEOPLE HAVE BEEN SINGING YOUR PRAISES.
IT SEEMS YOU SAVED SEVERAL LIVES YESTERDAY.
02:19:08
BEEP...!
I COMMEND YOU FOR YOUR SUCCESS IN THE WESTERN RUINS.
YOU WILL OF COURSE BE RE-WARDED.
I HEREBY DECLARE YOUR DUTY COMPLETE.

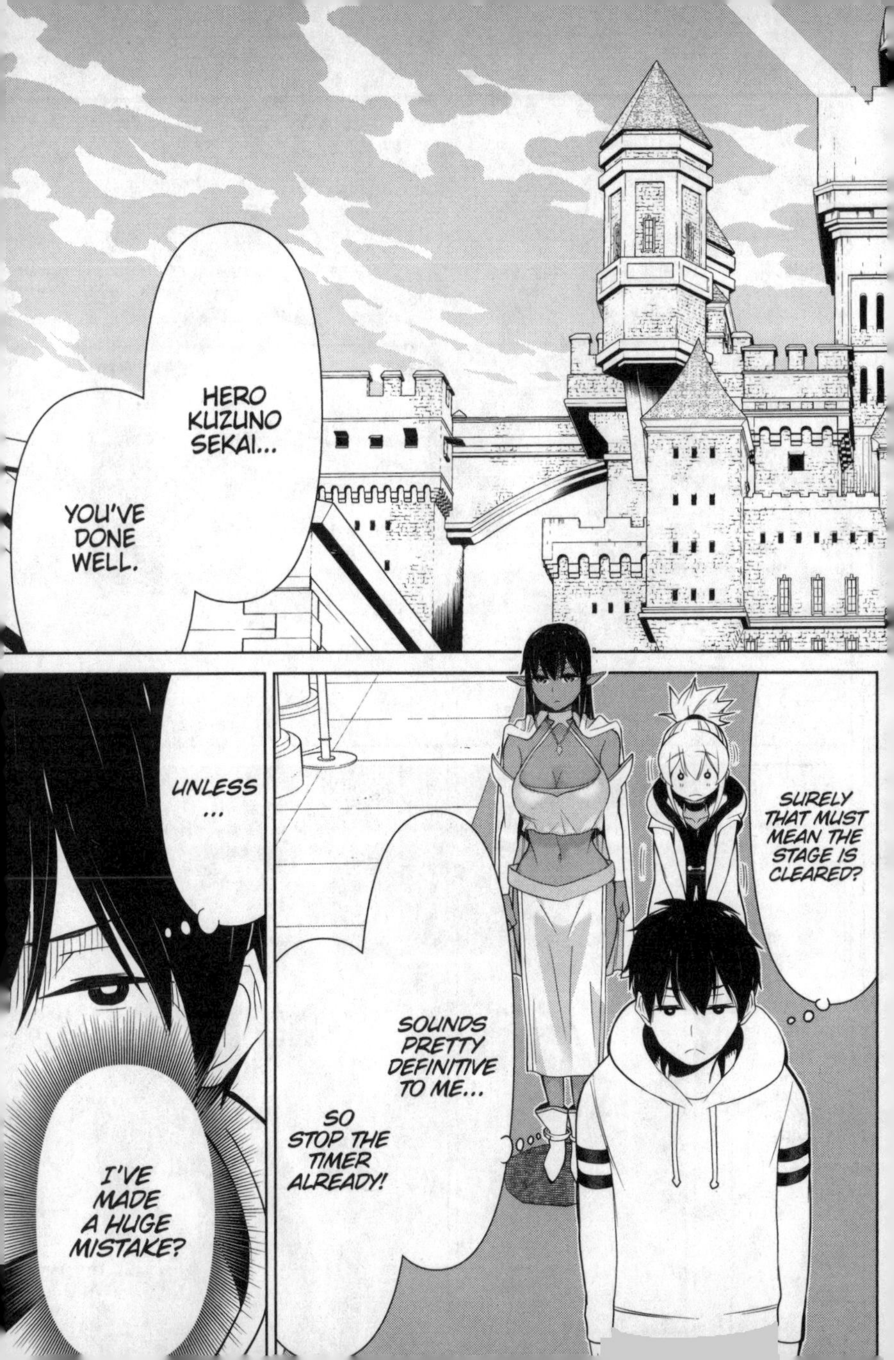
HERO KUZUNO SEKAI...
YOU'VE DONE WELL.
SURELY THAT MUST MEAN THE STAGE IS CLEARED?
SOUNDS PRETTY DEFINITIVE TO ME...
SO STOP THE TIMER ALREADY!
UNLESS...
I'VE MADE A HUGE MISTAKE?

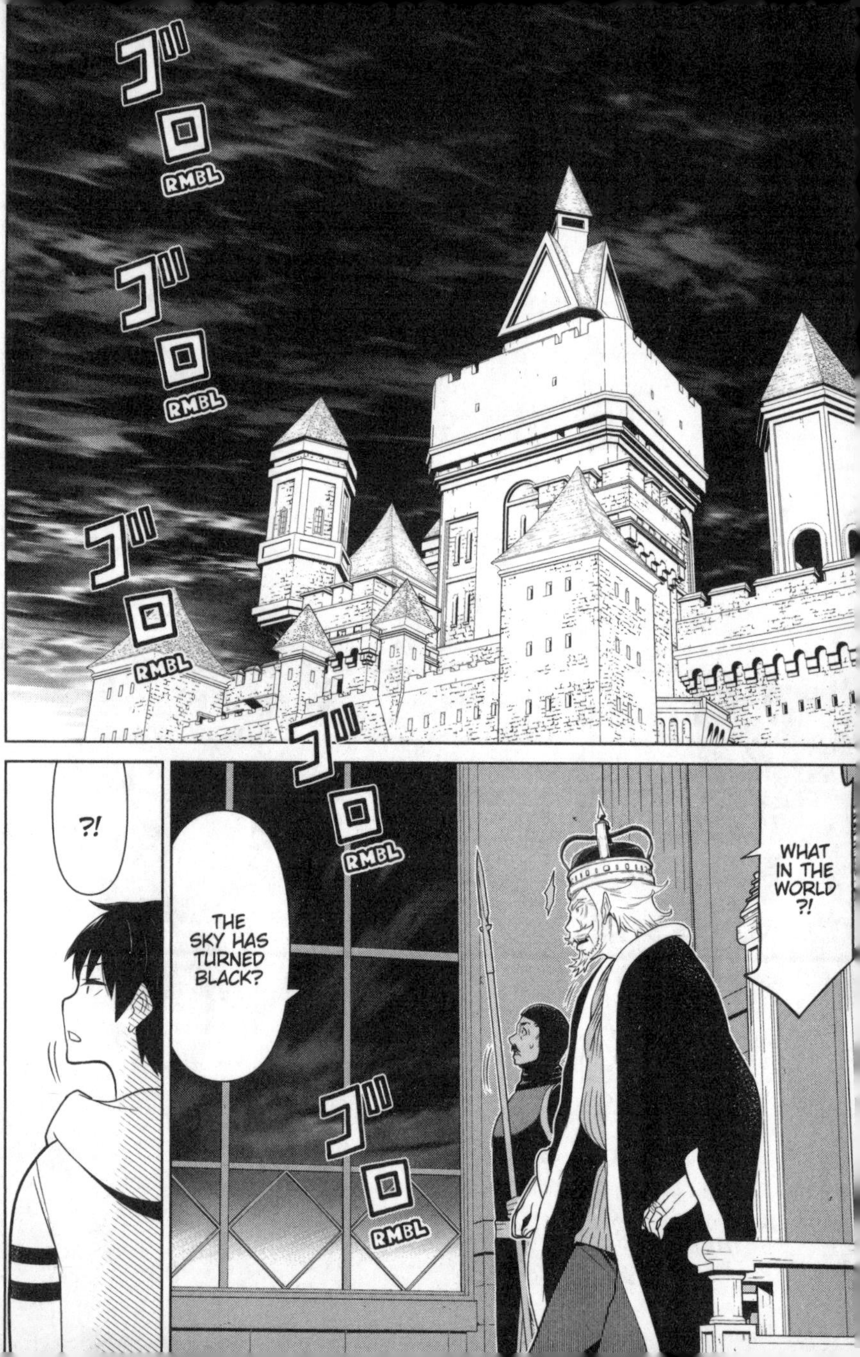
ゴロ
RMBL
ゴロ
RMBL
ゴロ
RMBL
ゴロ
RMBL
WHAT IN THE WORLD ?!
THE SKY HAS TURNED BLACK?
ゴロ
RMBL
?!

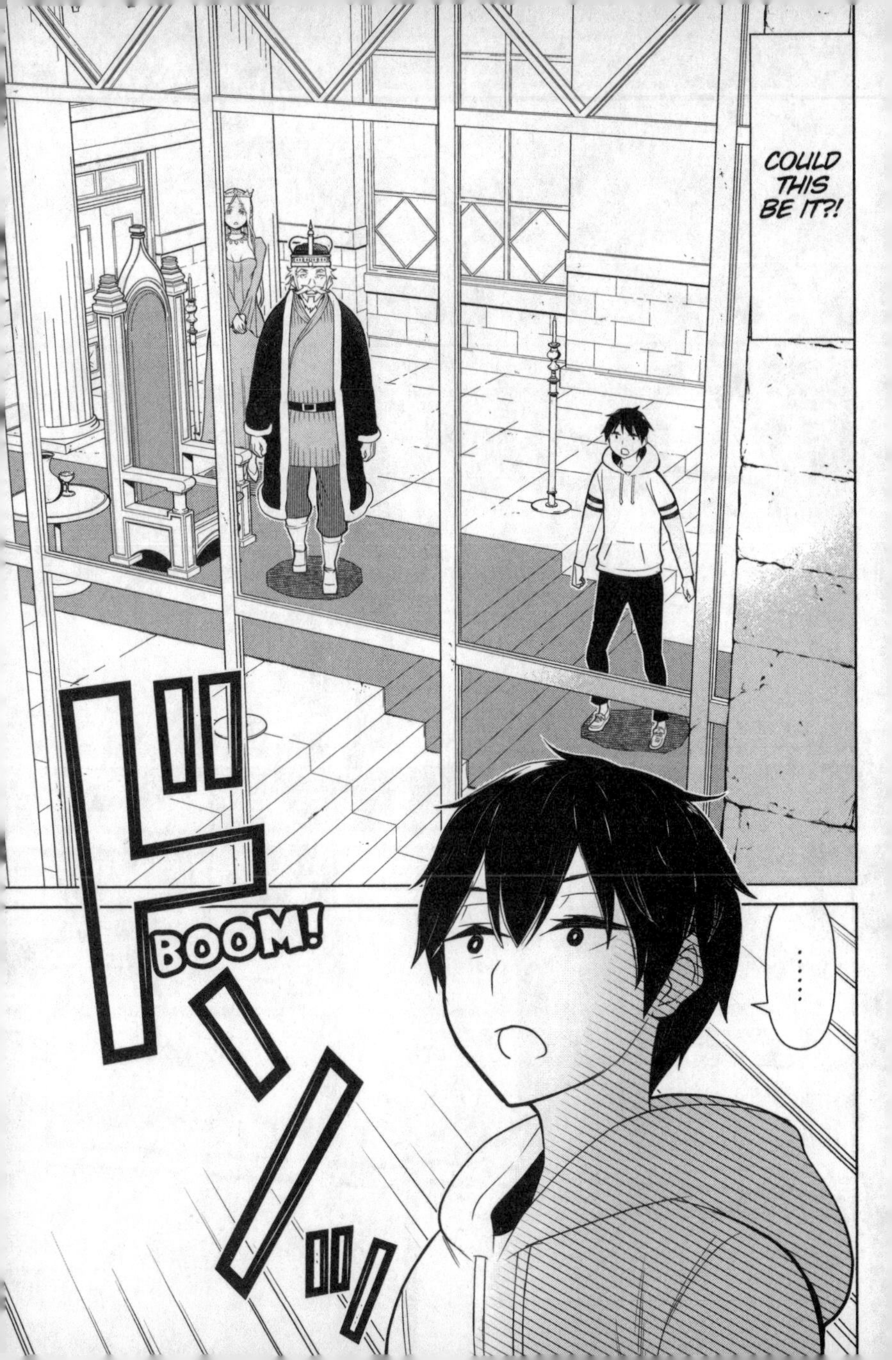
COULD THIS BE IT?!
BOOM!
......

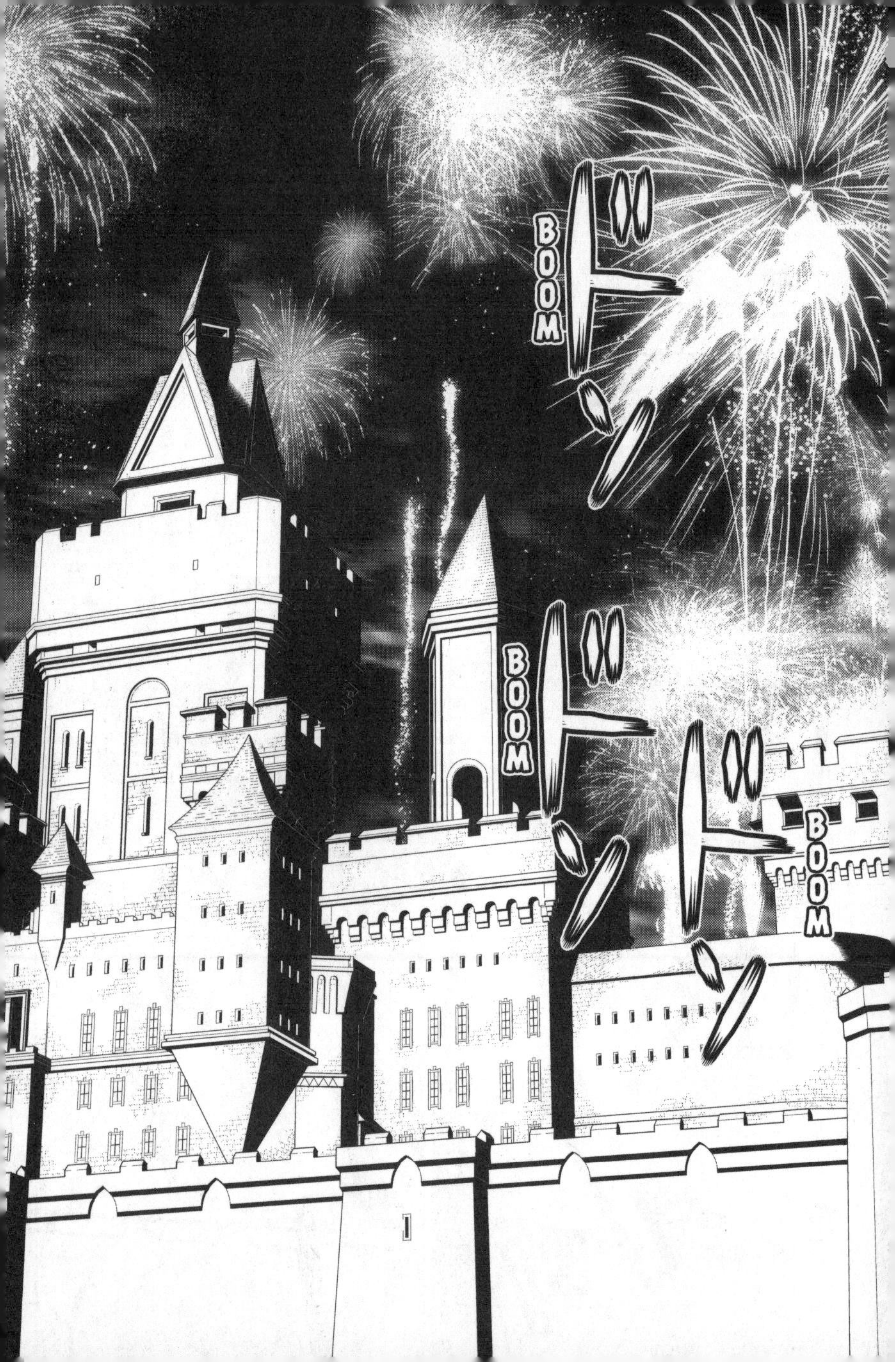
BOOM
BOOM
BOOM

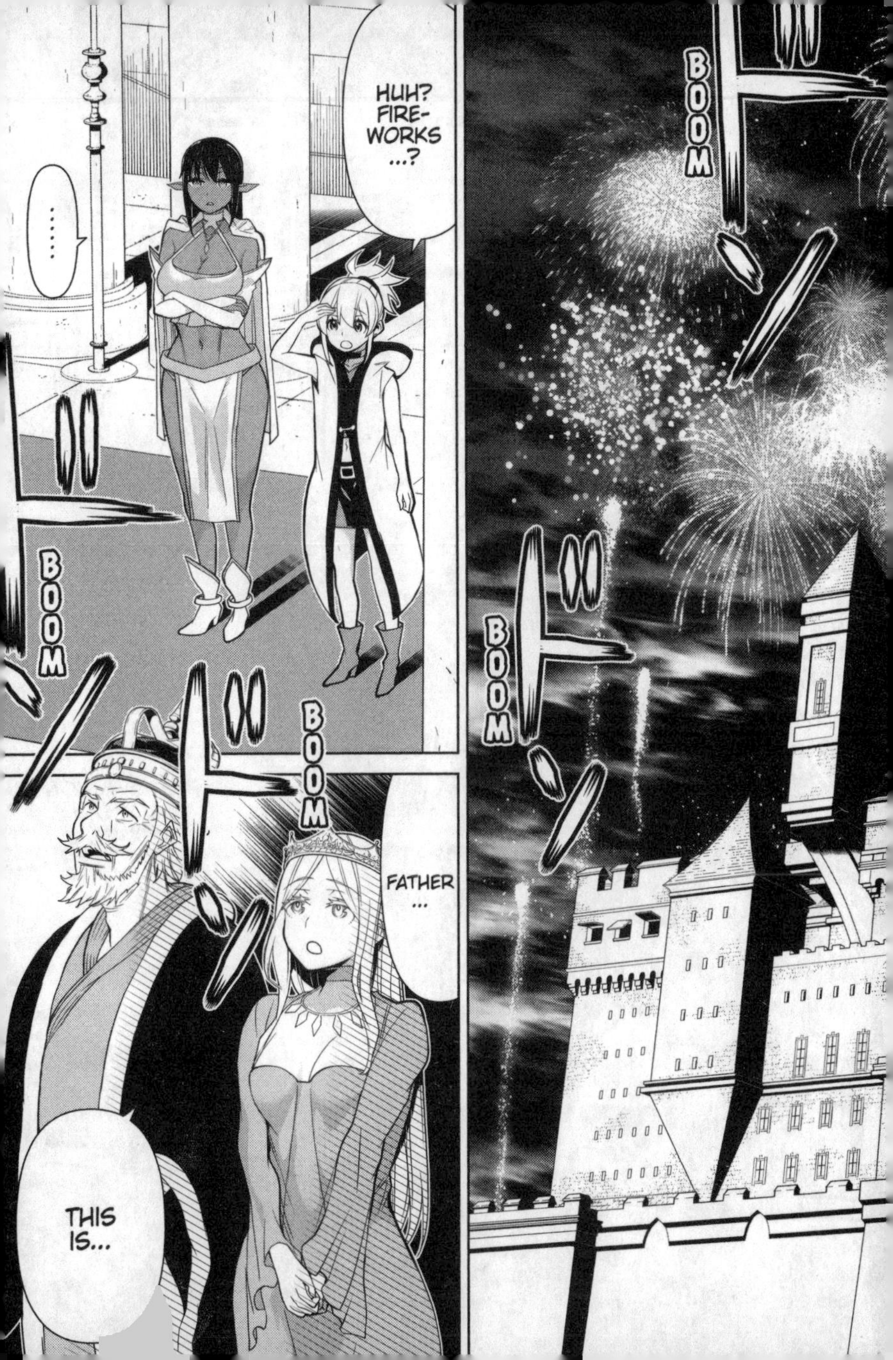
BOOM
BOOM
HUH? FIRE-WORKS ...?
......
BOOM
BOOM
FATHER ...
THIS IS...

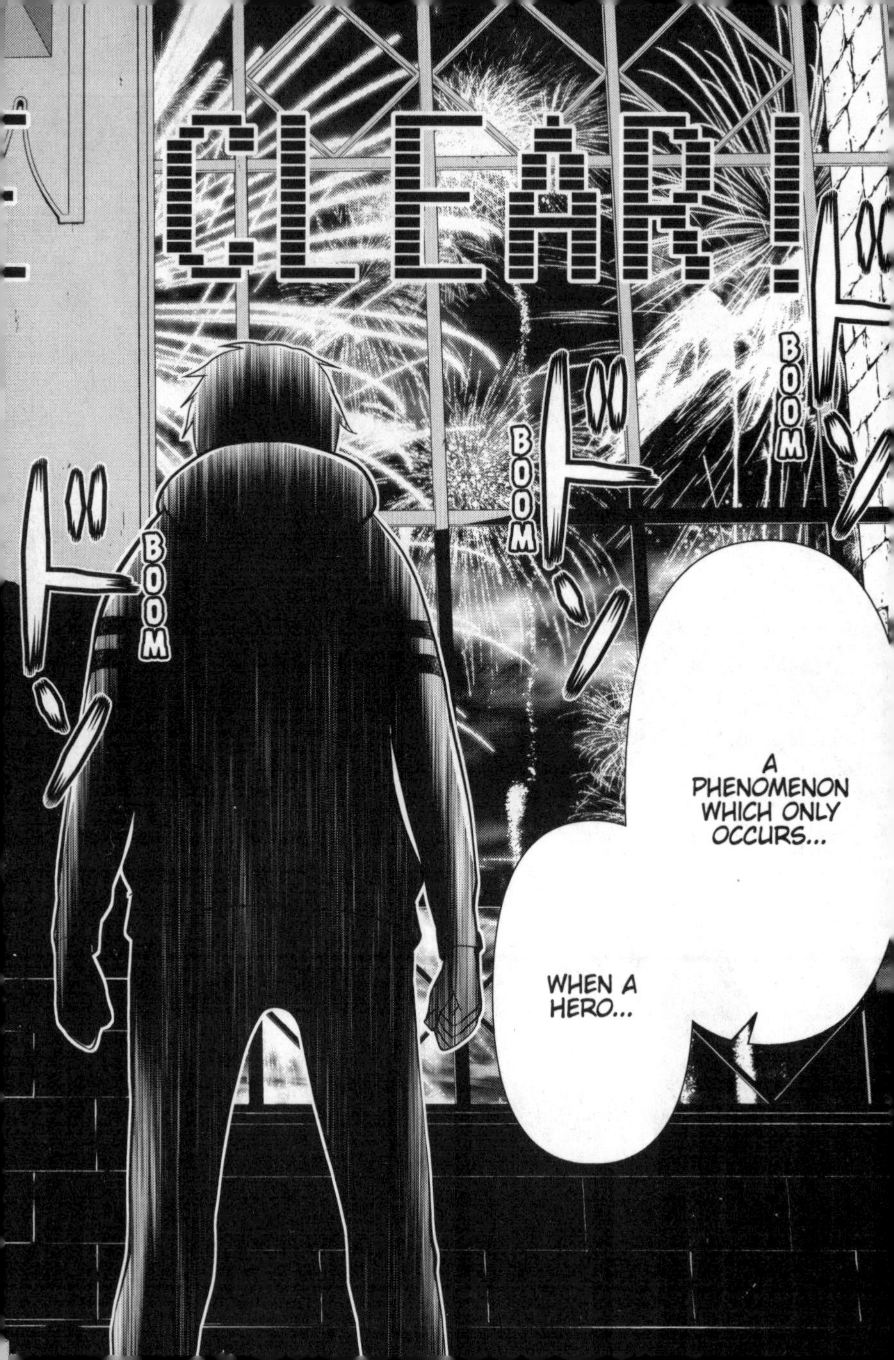
CLEAR!!
BOOM
BOOM
BOOM
A PHENOMENON WHICH ONLY OCCURS...
WHEN A HERO...

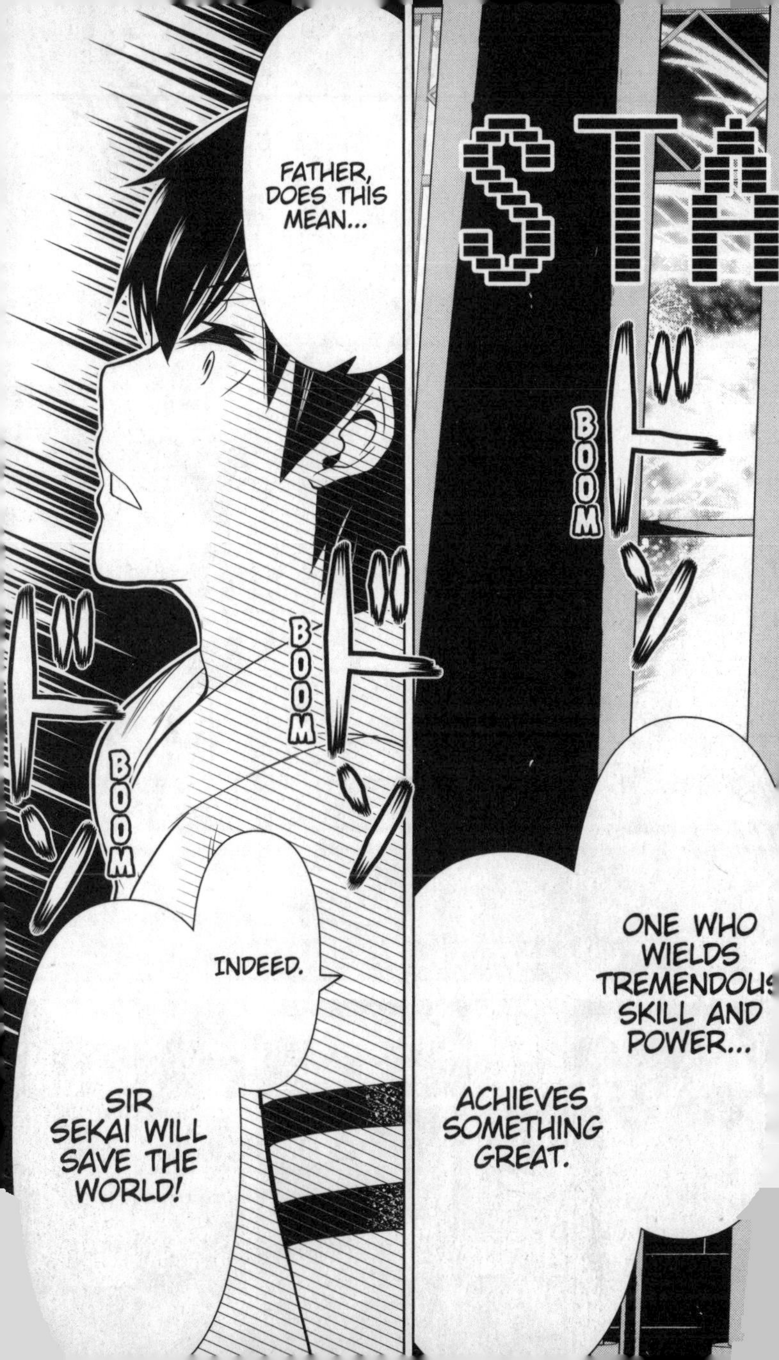
STA
BOOM
ONE WHO WIELDS TREMENDOUS SKILL AND POWER...
ACHIEVES SOMETHING GREAT.
FATHER, DOES THIS MEAN...
BOOM
BOOM
INDEED.
SIR SEKAI WILL SAVE THE WORLD!

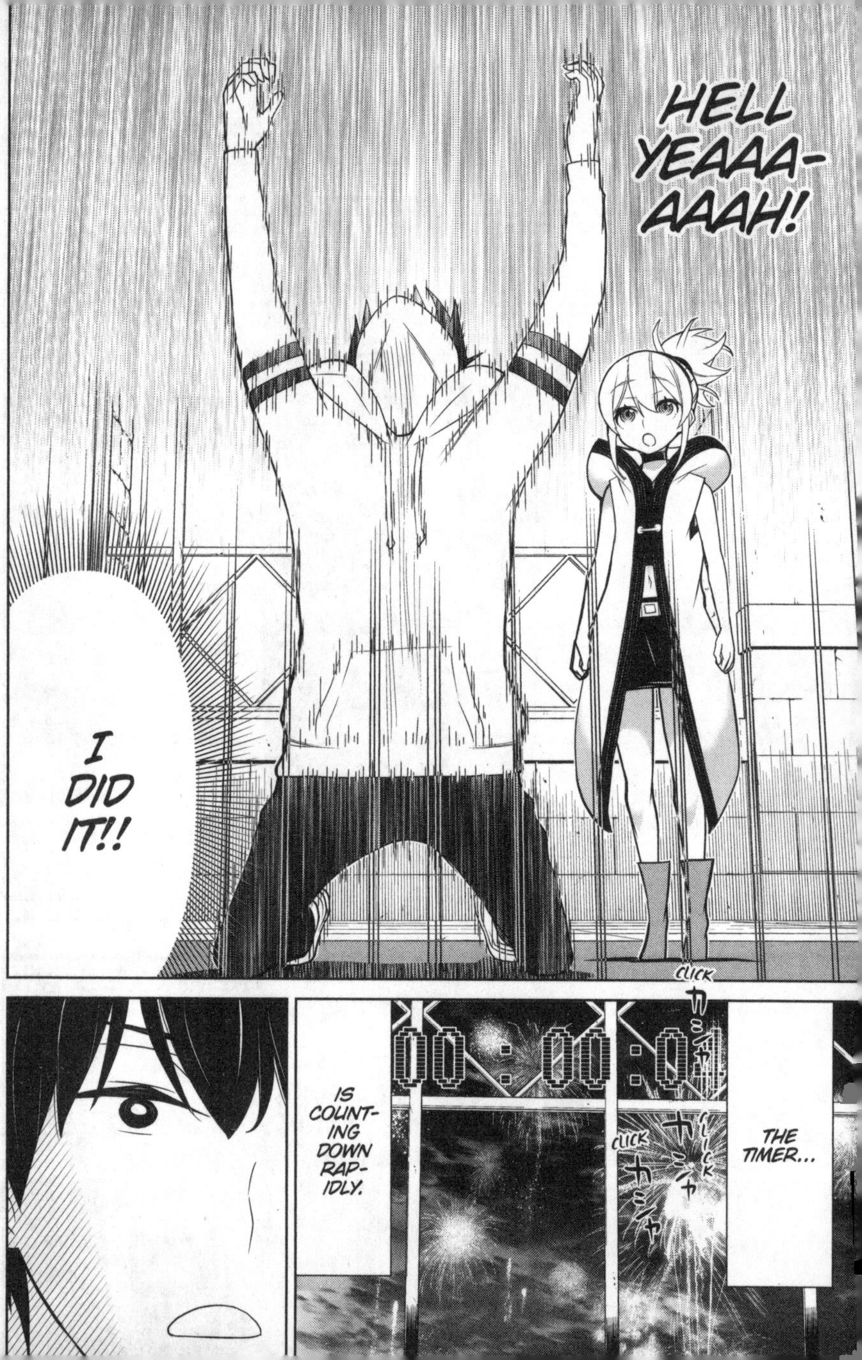
HELL YEAAAA-AAAAH!
I DID IT!!
CLICK
カシャ
THE TIMER...
CLICK
カシャ
CLICK
カシャ
00:00:01
IS COUNTING DOWN RAPIDLY.

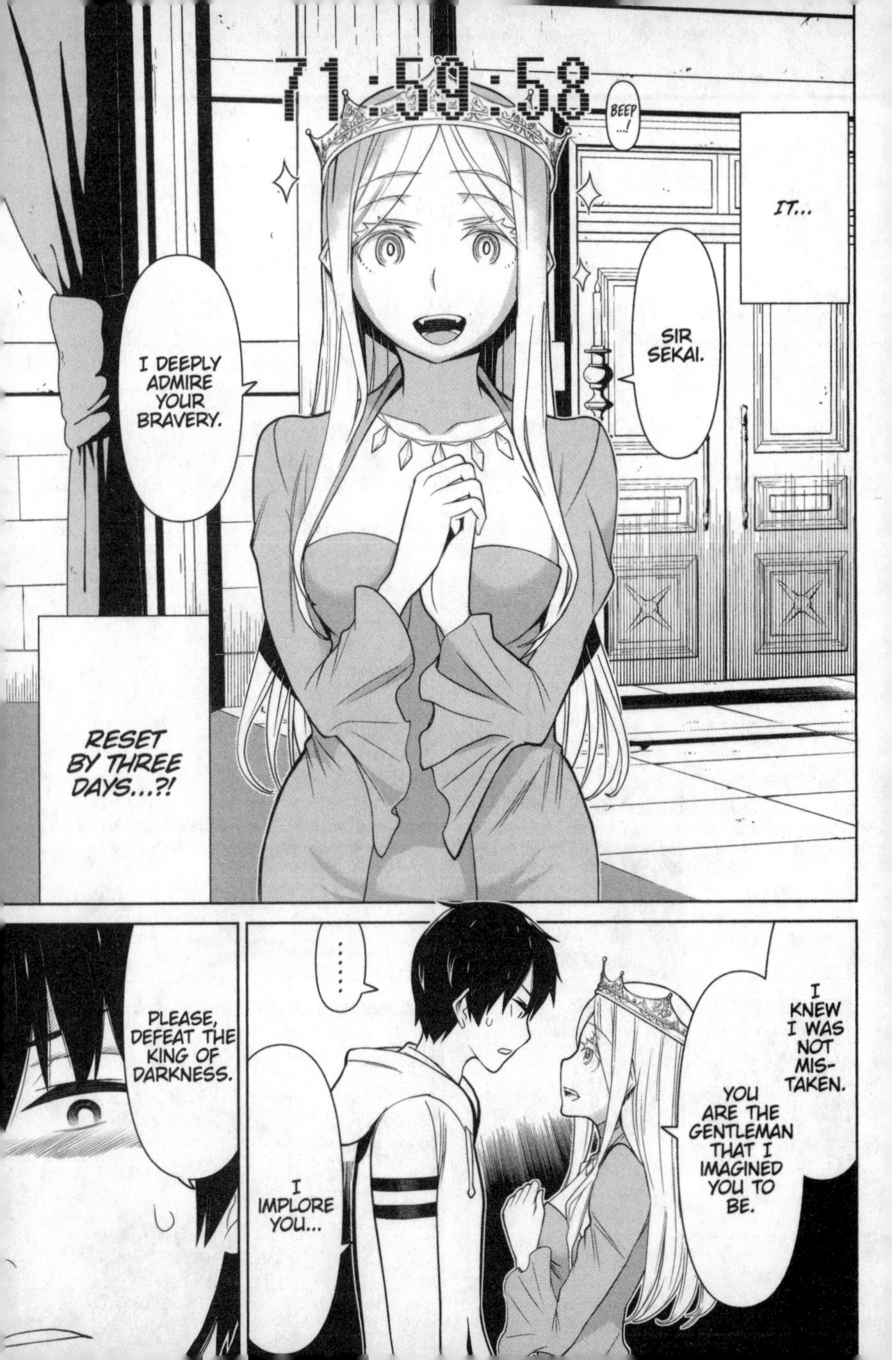

71:59:58
BEEP...!
IT...
SIR SEKAI.
I DEEPLY ADMIRE YOUR BRAVERY.
RESET BY THREE DAYS...?!
I KNEW I WAS NOT MIS-TAKEN.
YOU ARE THE GENTLEMAN THAT I IMAGINED YOU TO BE.
......
I IMPLORE YOU...
PLEASE, DEFEAT THE KING OF DARKNESS.

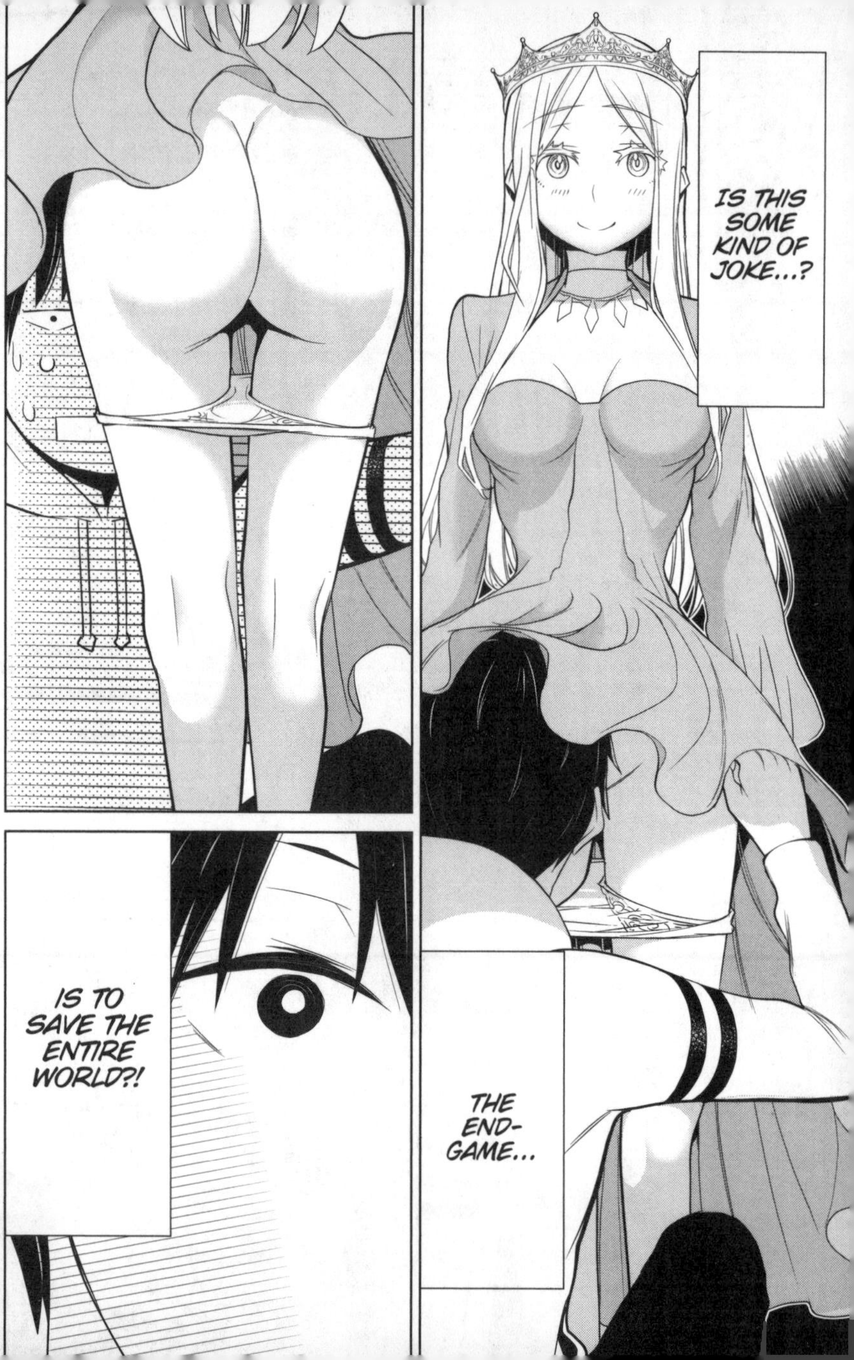
IS THIS SOME KIND OF JOKE...?
THE END-GAME...
IS TO SAVE THE ENTIRE WORLD?!

Chapter 4 - End

2 3 4 5 6 7

START
▶ PAUSE

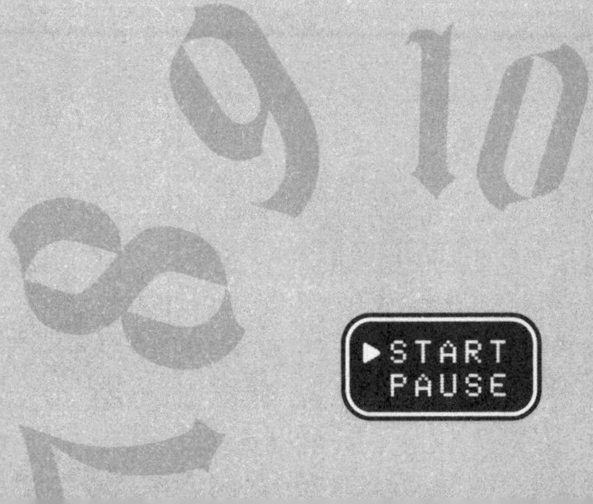
8 9 10
▶START
PAUSE

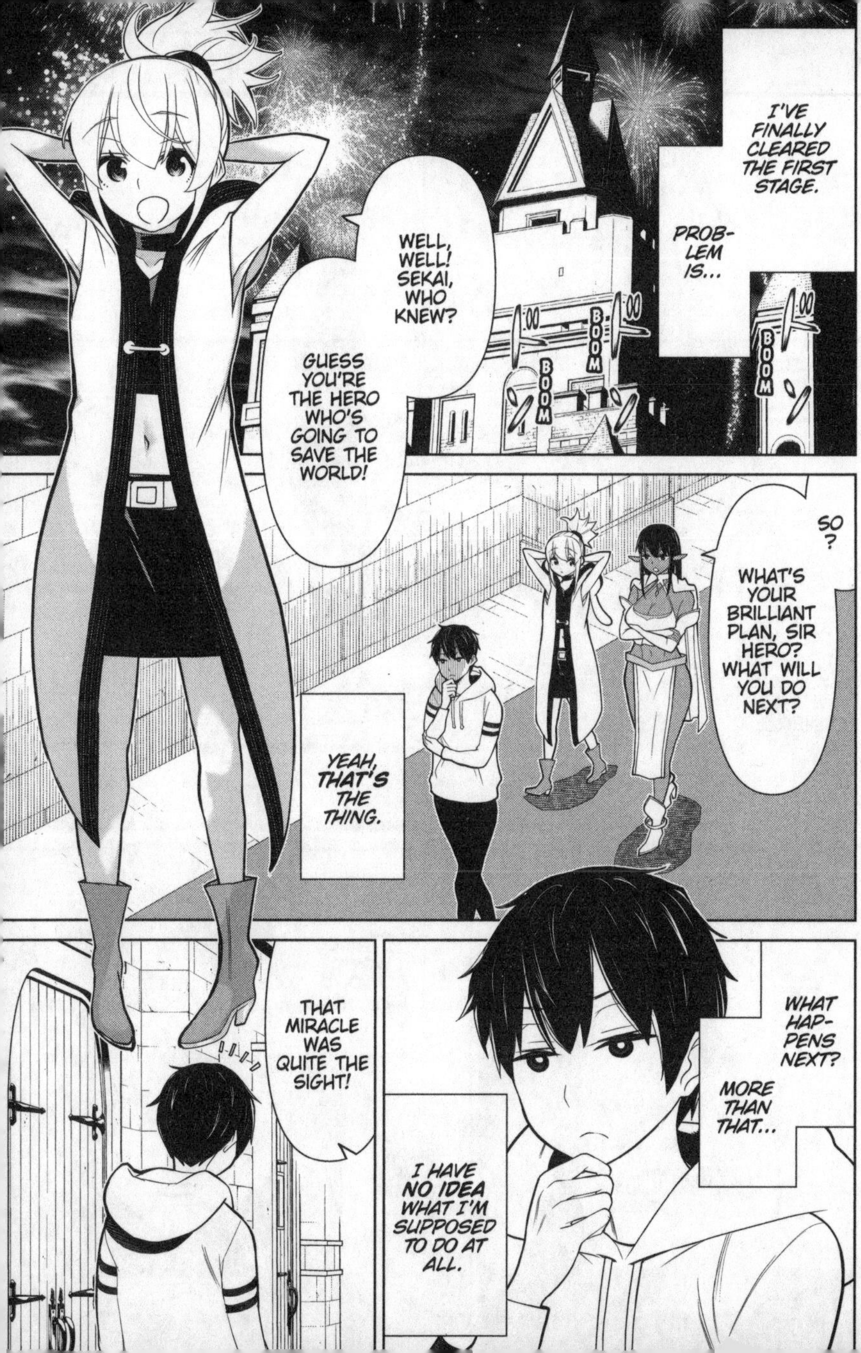

I'VE FINALLY CLEARED THE FIRST STAGE.
PROB-LEM IS...
BOOM
BOOM
BOOM
WELL, WELL! SEKAI, WHO KNEW?
GUESS YOU'RE THE HERO WHO'S GOING TO SAVE THE WORLD!
SO?
WHAT'S YOUR BRILLIANT PLAN, SIR HERO? WHAT WILL YOU DO NEXT?
YEAH, THAT'S THE THING.
WHAT HAP-PENS NEXT?
MORE THAN THAT...
I HAVE NO IDEA WHAT I'M SUPPOSED TO DO AT ALL.
THAT MIRACLE WAS QUITE THE SIGHT!

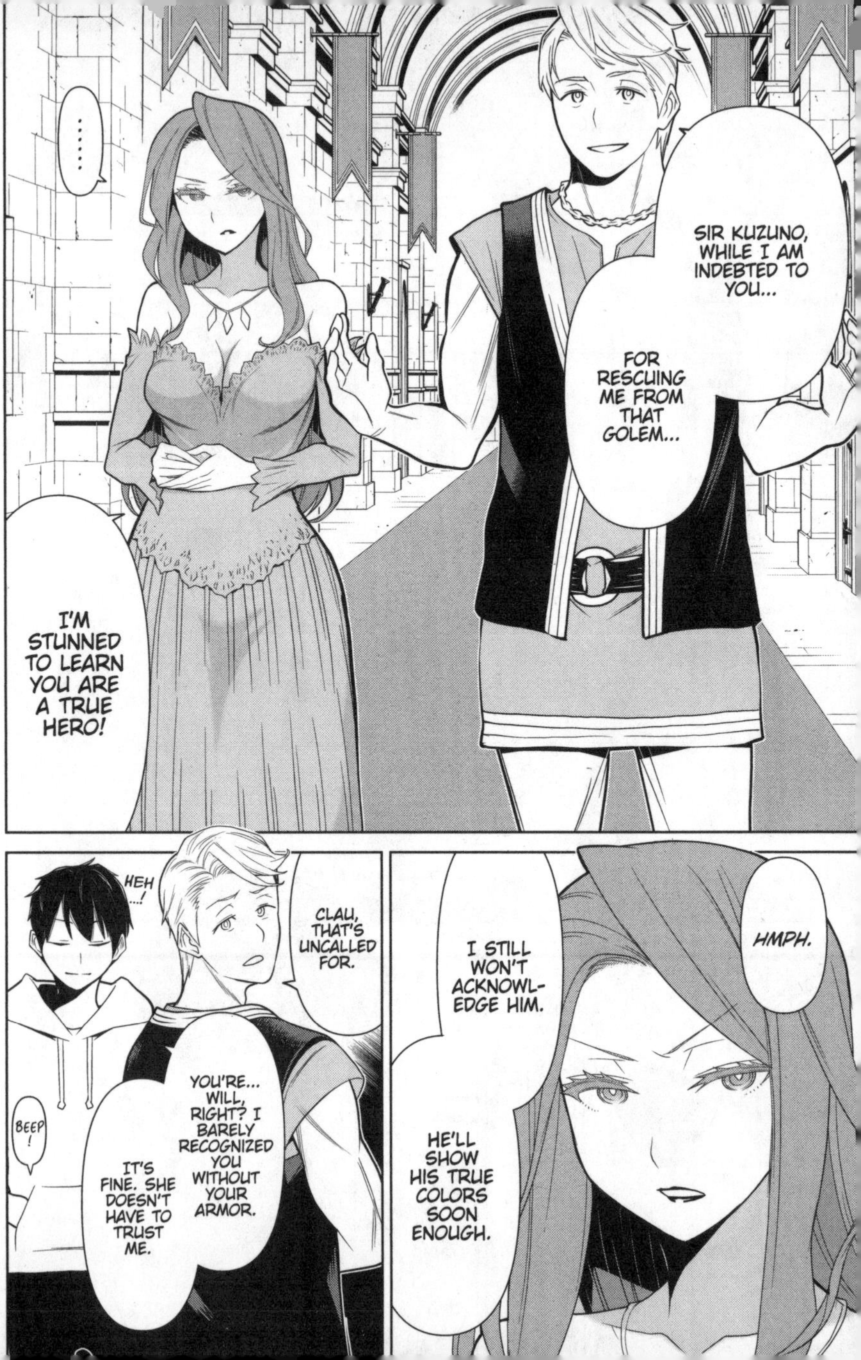
SIR KUZUNO, WHILE I AM INDEBTED TO YOU...
FOR RESCUING ME FROM THAT GOLEM...
......
I'M STUNNED TO LEARN YOU ARE A TRUE HERO!
HMPH.
I STILL WON'T ACKNOWL-EDGE HIM.
HE'LL SHOW HIS TRUE COLORS SOON ENOUGH.
CLAU, THAT'S UNCALLED FOR.
HEH ...!
YOU'RE... WILL, RIGHT? I BARELY RECOGNIZED YOU WITHOUT YOUR ARMOR.
IT'S FINE. SHE DOESN'T HAVE TO TRUST ME.
BEEP!

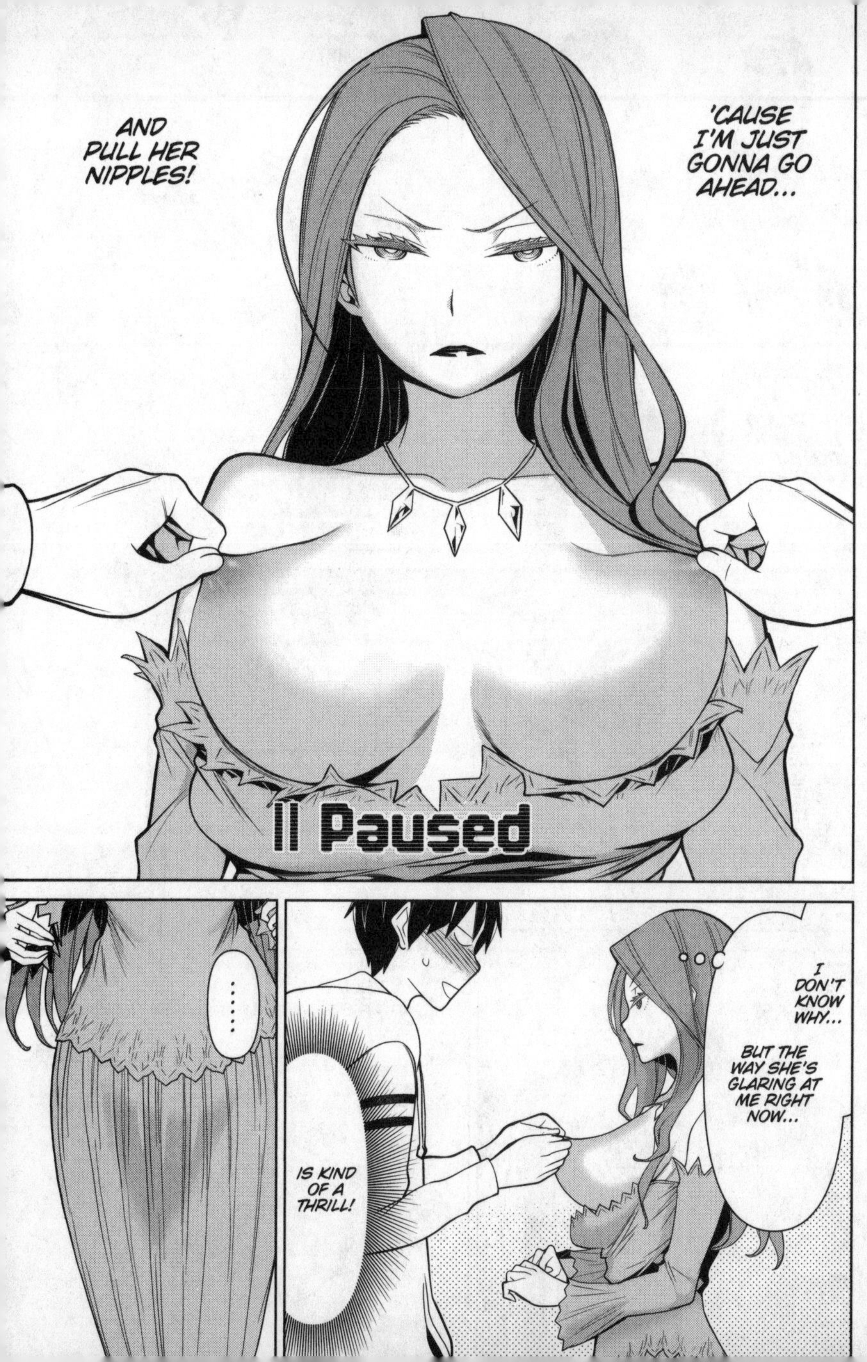
'CAUSE I'M JUST GONNA GO AHEAD...
AND PULL HER NIPPLES!
II Paused
I DON'T KNOW WHY...
BUT THE WAY SHE'S GLARING AT ME RIGHT NOW...
IS KIND OF A THRILL!
......

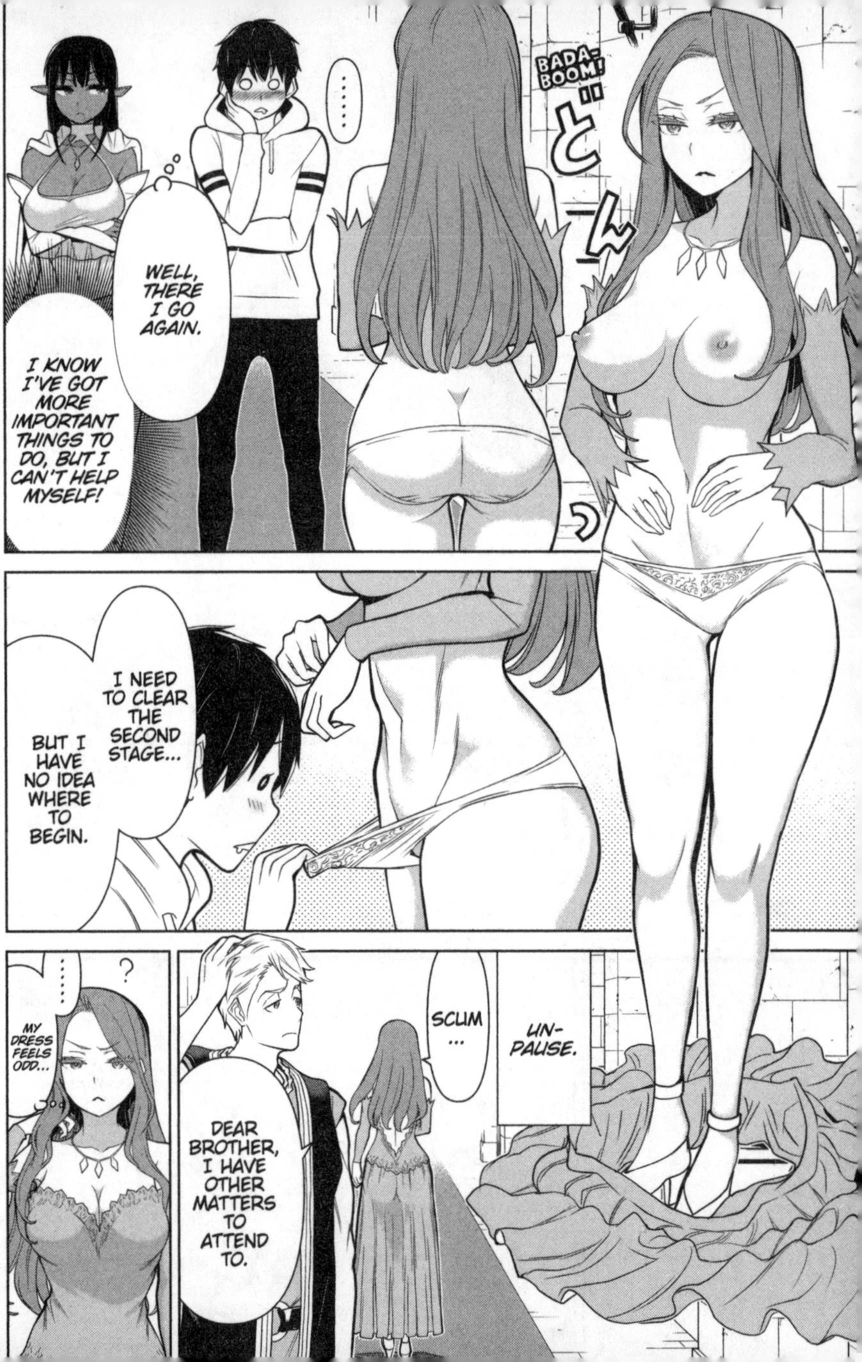

BADA-BOOM!
とん
......
WELL, THERE I GO AGAIN.
I KNOW I'VE GOT MORE IMPORTANT THINGS TO DO, BUT I CAN'T HELP MYSELF!
I NEED TO CLEAR THE SECOND STAGE...
BUT I HAVE NO IDEA WHERE TO BEGIN.
UN-PAUSE.
SCUM...
DEAR BROTHER, I HAVE OTHER MATTERS TO ATTEND TO.
......
?
MY DRESS FEELS ODD...

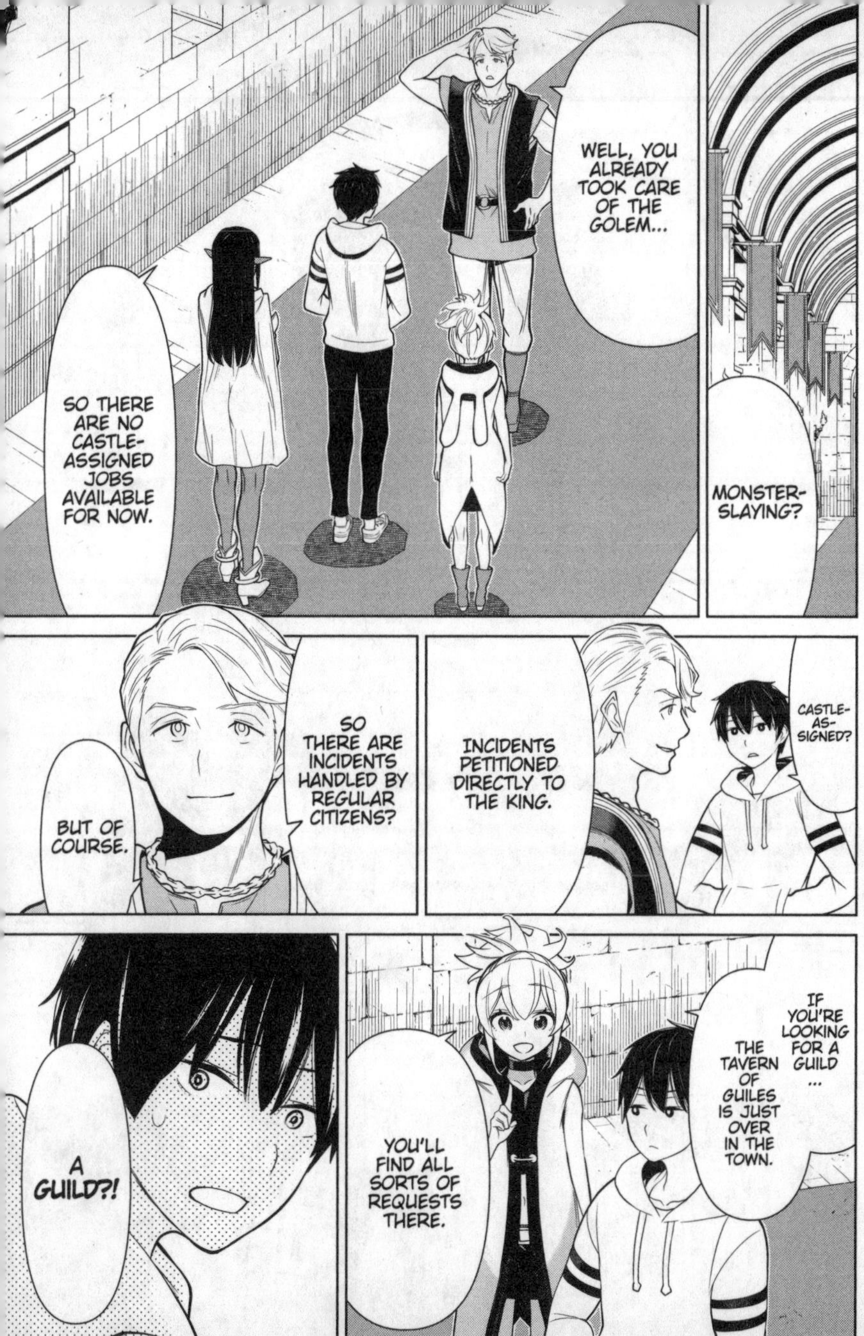
MONSTER-SLAYING?
WELL, YOU ALREADY TOOK CARE OF THE GOLEM...
SO THERE ARE NO CASTLE-ASSIGNED JOBS AVAILABLE FOR NOW.
CASTLE-AS-SIGNED?
INCIDENTS PETITIONED DIRECTLY TO THE KING.
SO THERE ARE INCIDENTS HANDLED BY REGULAR CITIZENS?
BUT OF COURSE.
IF YOU'RE LOOKING FOR A GUILD...
THE TAVERN OF GUILES IS JUST OVER IN THE TOWN.
YOU'LL FIND ALL SORTS OF REQUESTS THERE.
A GUILD?!

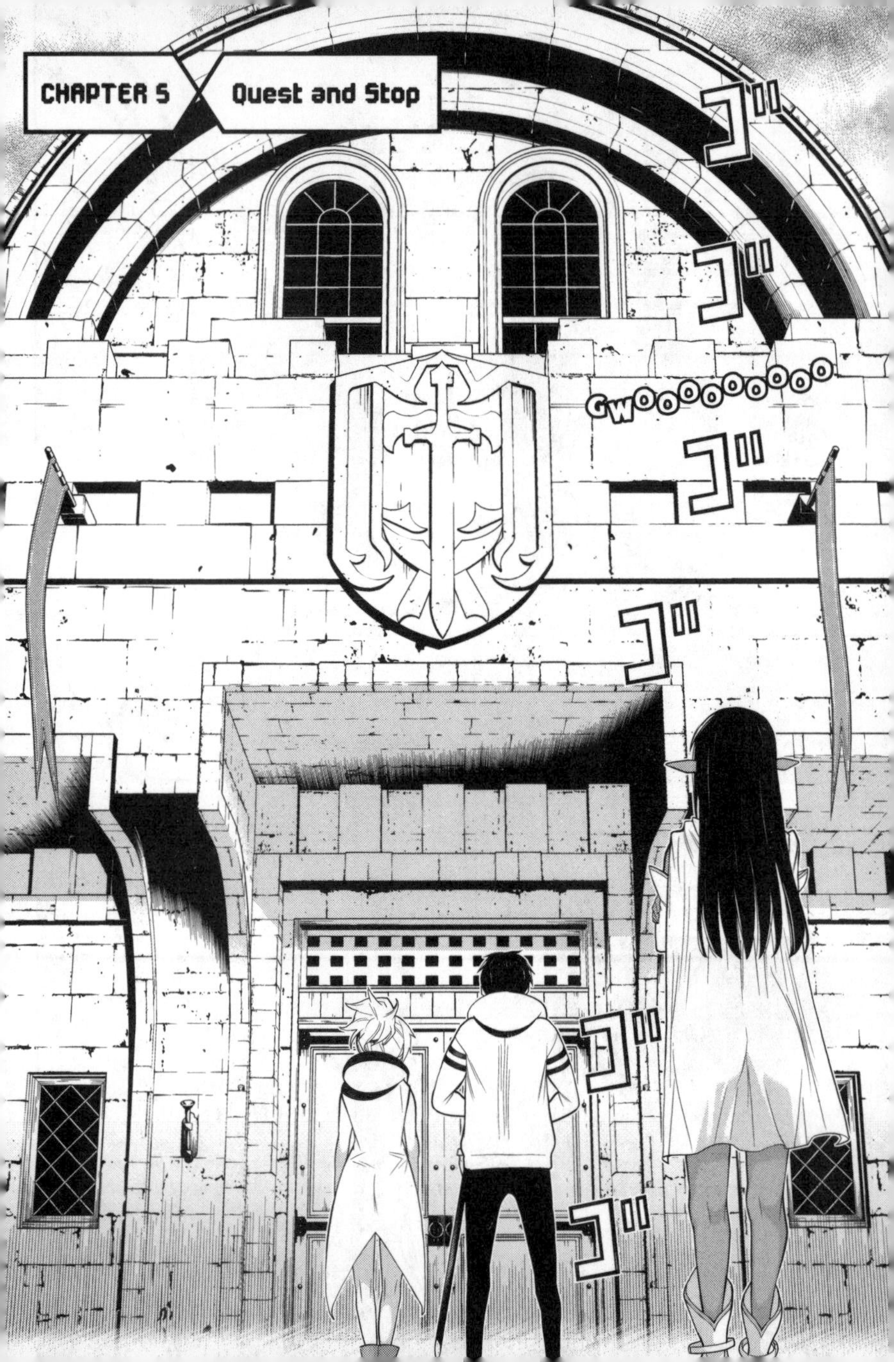
CHAPTER 5
Quest and Stop
ゴ
ゴ
GWOOOOOOOOOO
ゴ
ゴ
ゴ
ゴ

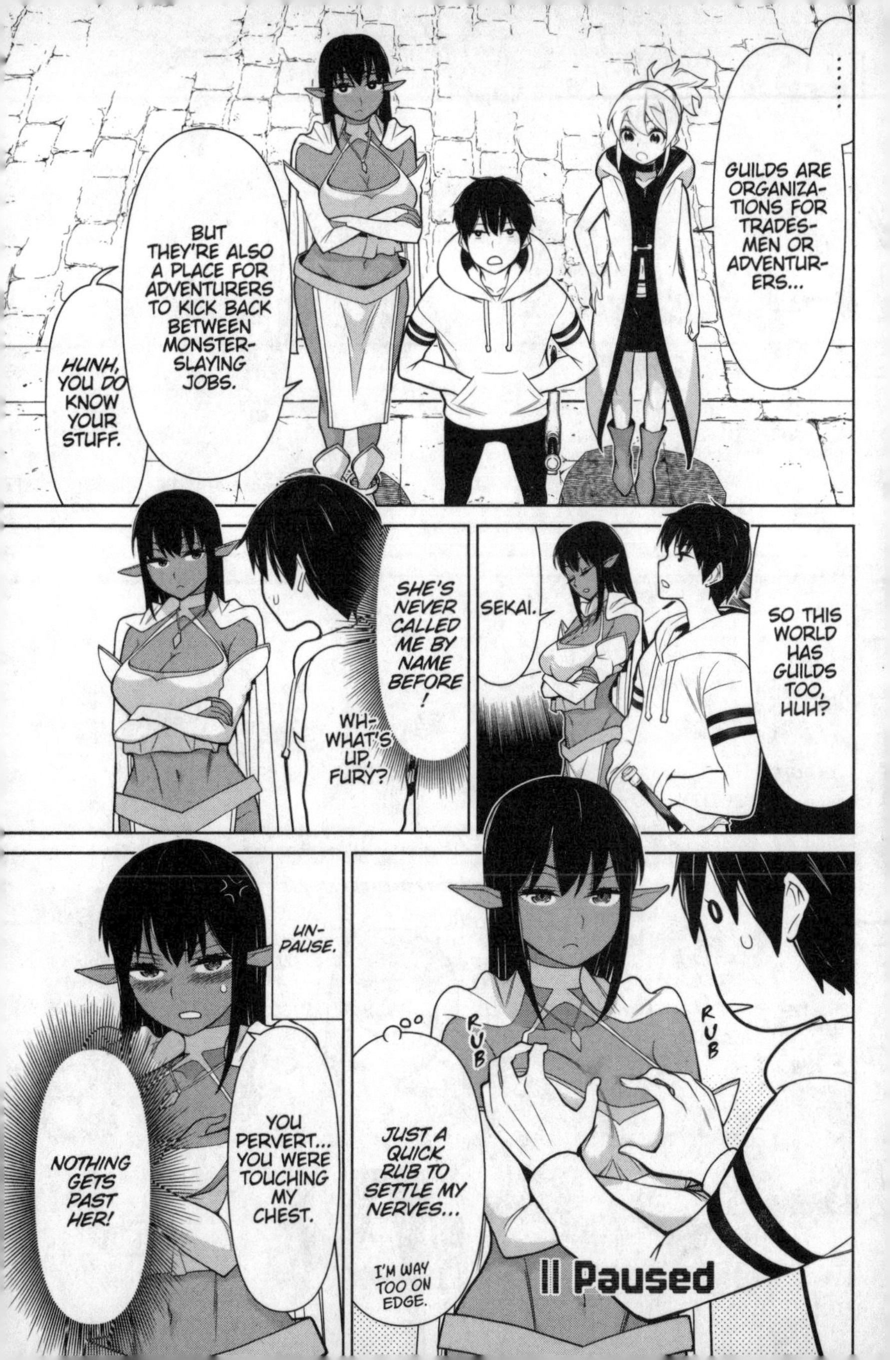
...
GUILDS ARE ORGANIZATIONS FOR TRADESMEN OR ADVENTURERS...
BUT THEY'RE ALSO A PLACE FOR ADVENTURERS TO KICK BACK BETWEEN MONSTER-SLAYING JOBS.
HUNH, YOU DO KNOW YOUR STUFF.
SO THIS WORLD HAS GUILDS TOO, HUH?
SEKAI.
SHE'S NEVER CALLED ME BY NAME BEFORE!
WH-WHAT'S UP, FURY?
RUB
RUB
JUST A QUICK RUB TO SETTLE MY NERVES...
I'M WAY TOO ON EDGE.
II Paused
UN-PAUSE.
YOU PERVERT... YOU WERE TOUCHING MY CHEST.
NOTHING GETS PAST HER!

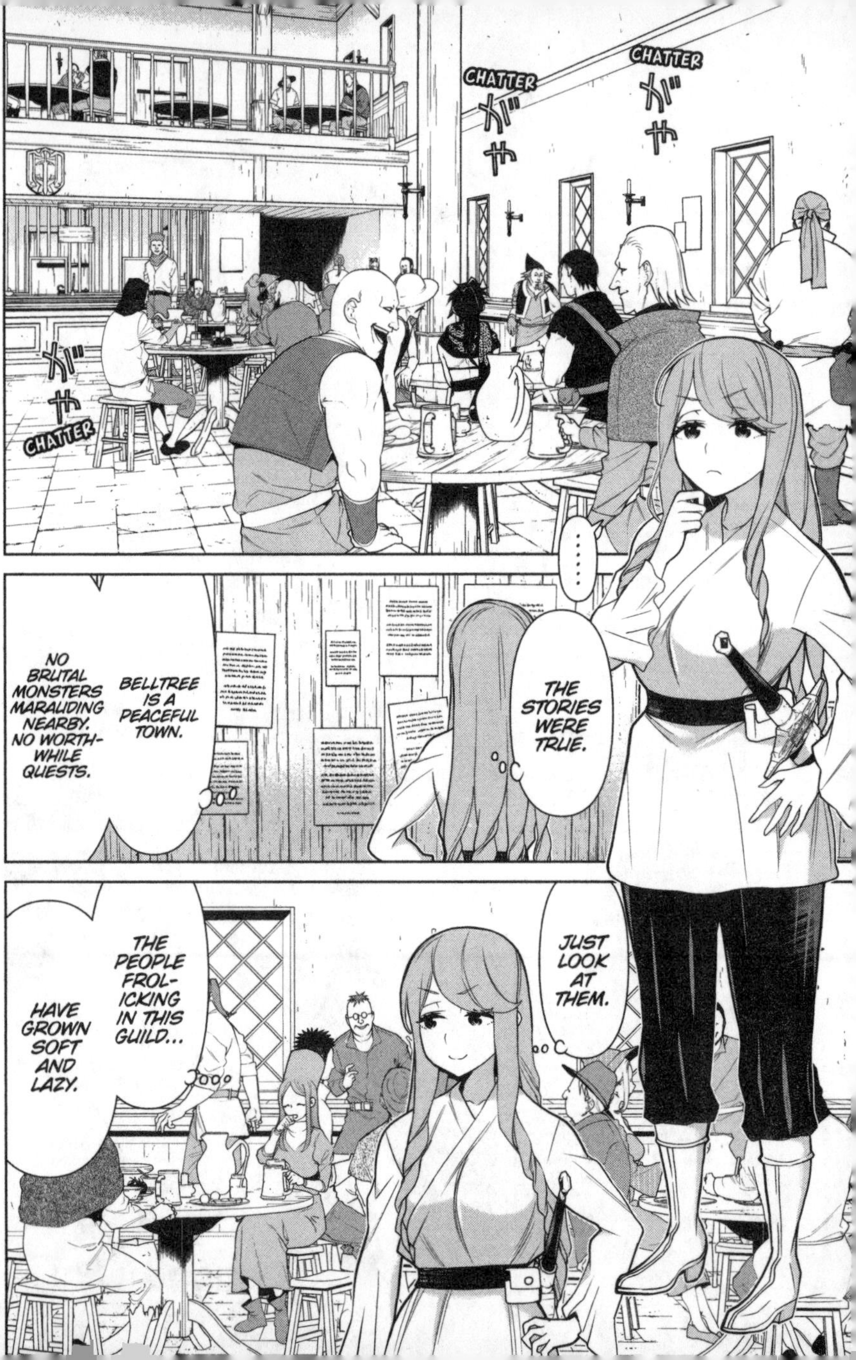
CHATTER
ガヤ
CHATTER
ガヤ
ガヤ
CHATTER
......
THE STORIES WERE TRUE.
BELLTREE IS A PEACEFUL TOWN.
NO BRUTAL MONSTERS MARAUDING NEARBY. NO WORTH-WHILE QUESTS.
JUST LOOK AT THEM.
THE PEOPLE FROL-ICKING IN THIS GUILD...
HAVE GROWN SOFT AND LAZY.

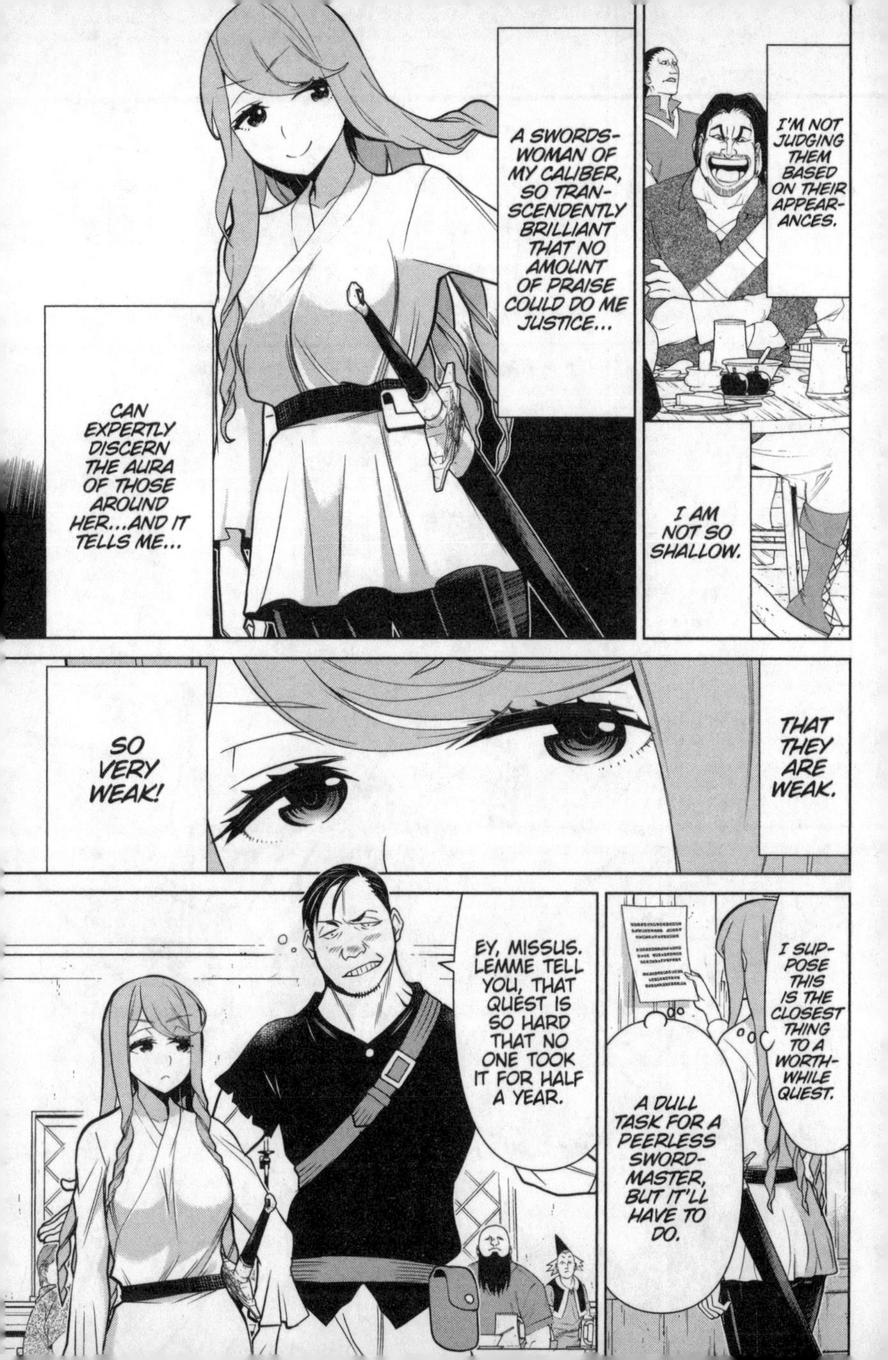
I'M NOT JUDGING THEM BASED ON THEIR APPEAR-ANCES.
I AM NOT SO SHALLOW.
A SWORDS-WOMAN OF MY CALIBER, SO TRAN-SCENDENTLY BRILLIANT THAT NO AMOUNT OF PRAISE COULD DO ME JUSTICE...
CAN EXPERTLY DISCERN THE AURA OF THOSE AROUND HER...AND IT TELLS ME...
THAT THEY ARE WEAK.
SO VERY WEAK!
I SUP-POSE THIS IS THE CLOSEST THING TO A WORTH-WHILE QUEST.
A DULL TASK FOR A PEERLESS SWORD-MASTER, BUT IT'LL HAVE TO DO.
EY, MISSUS. LEMME TELL YOU, THAT QUEST IS SO HARD THAT NO ONE TOOK IT FOR HALF A YEAR.

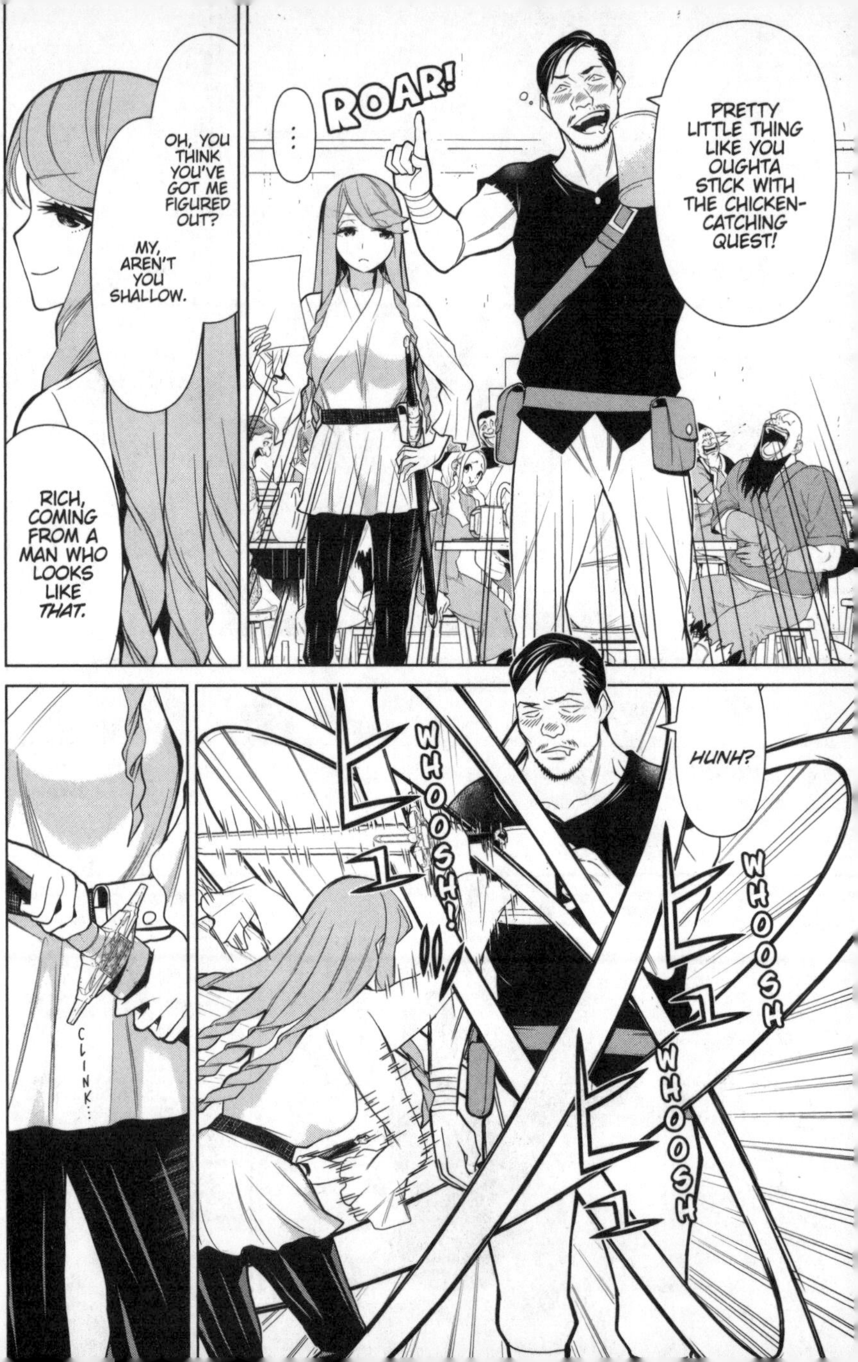
PRETTY LITTLE THING LIKE YOU OUGHTA STICK WITH THE CHICKEN-CATCHING QUEST!
ROAR!
...
OH, YOU THINK YOU'VE GOT ME FIGURED OUT?
MY, AREN'T YOU SHALLOW.
RICH, COMING FROM A MAN WHO LOOKS LIKE *THAT*.
HUNH?
WHOOSH
WHOOSH
WHOOSH!
CLINK...

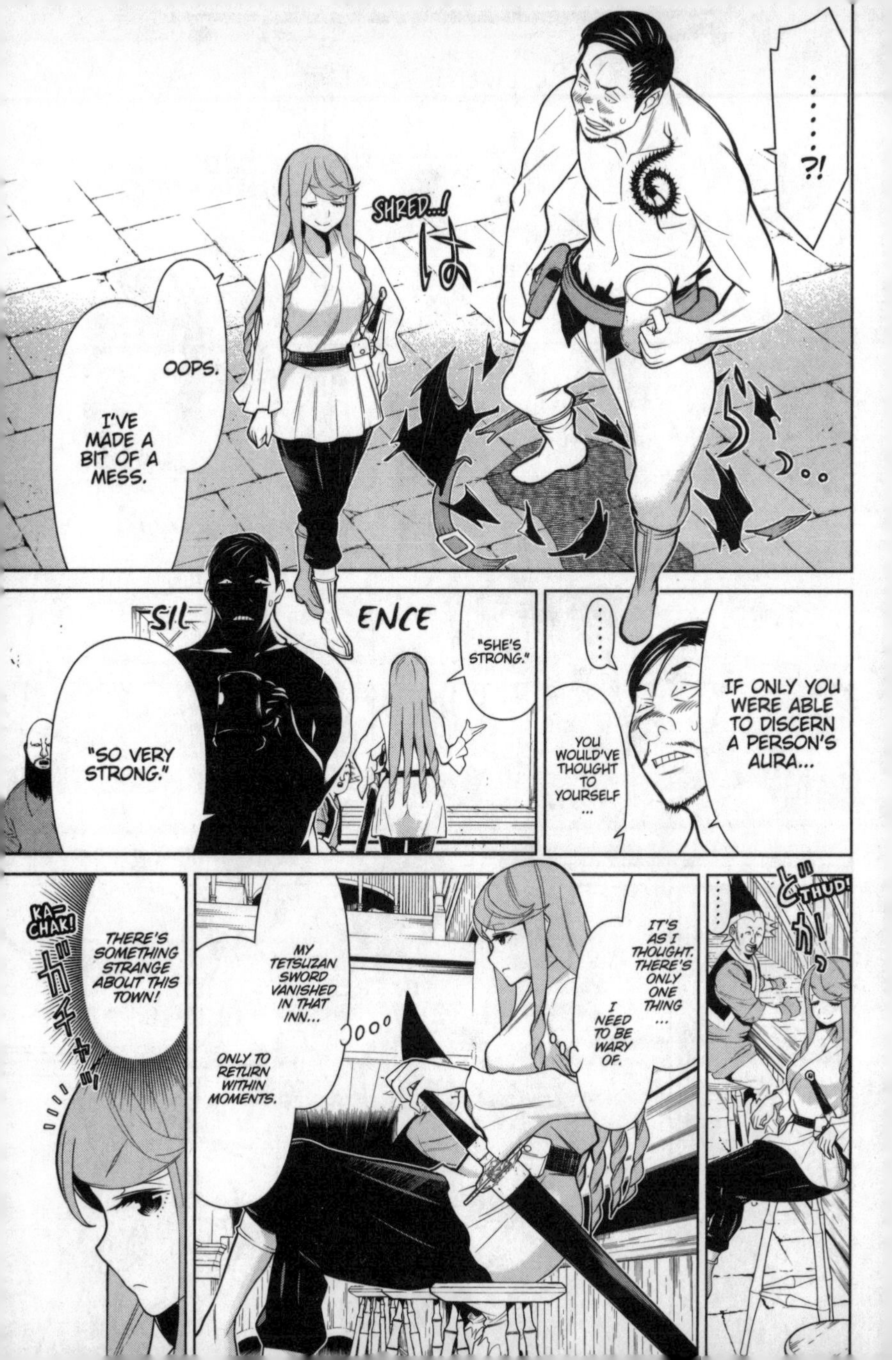
......?!
SHRED...!
は
OOPS.
I'VE MADE A BIT OF A MESS.
IF ONLY YOU WERE ABLE TO DISCERN A PERSON'S AURA...
......
YOU WOULD'VE THOUGHT TO YOURSELF ...
SILENCE
"SHE'S STRONG."
"SO VERY STRONG."
THUD!
どかッ
IT'S AS I THOUGHT. THERE'S ONLY ONE THING ...
I NEED TO BE WARY OF.
MY TETSUZAN SWORD VANISHED IN THAT INN...
ONLY TO RETURN WITHIN MOMENTS.
KA-CHAK!
ガチャッ
THERE'S SOMETHING STRANGE ABOUT THIS TOWN!

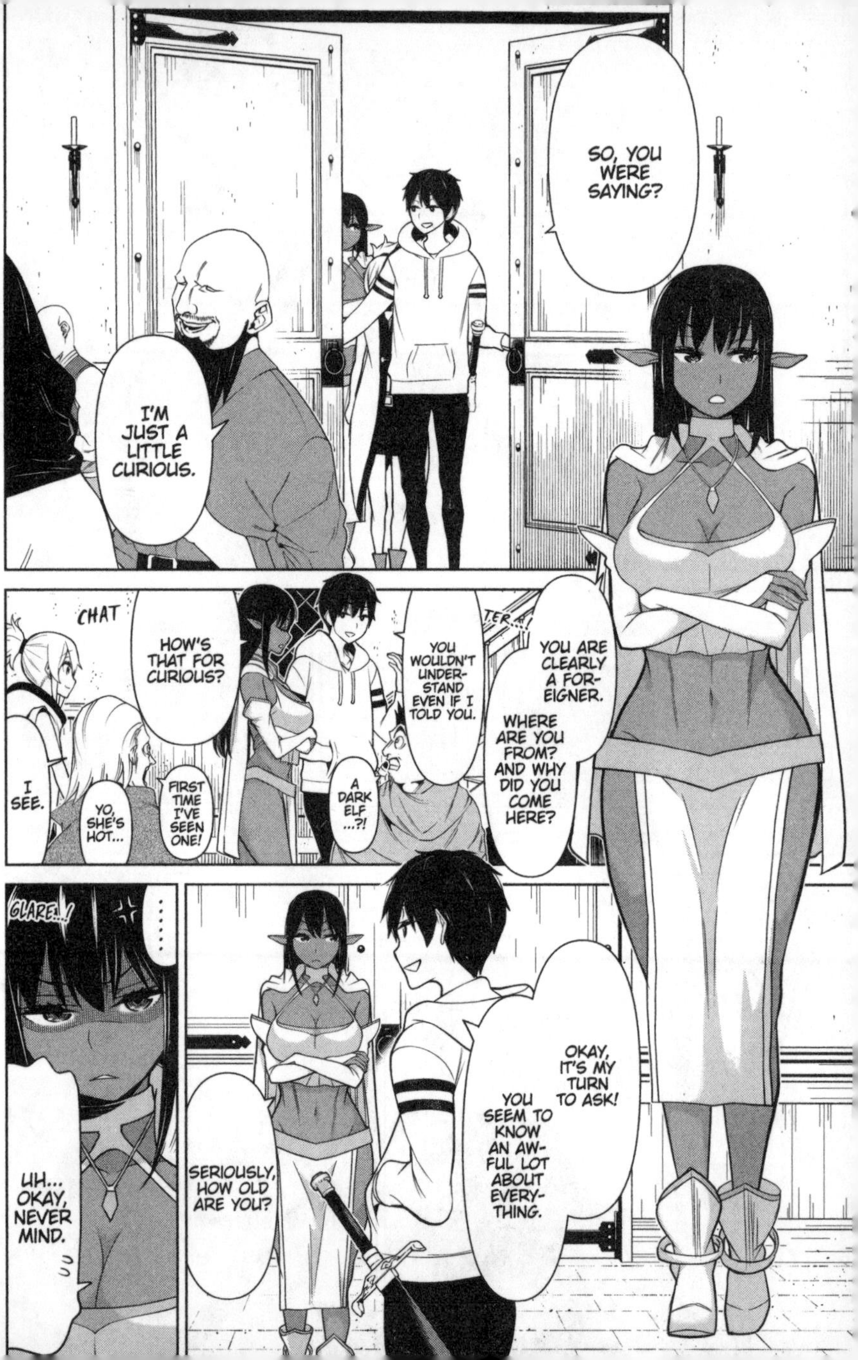
SO, YOU WERE SAYING?
I'M JUST A LITTLE CURIOUS.
YOU ARE CLEARLY A FOR-EIGNER.
WHERE ARE YOU FROM? AND WHY DID YOU COME HERE?
YOU WOULDN'T UNDER-STAND EVEN IF I TOLD YOU.
HOW'S THAT FOR CURIOUS?
CHAT
A DARK ELF ...?!
FIRST TIME I'VE SEEN ONE!
YO, SHE'S HOT...
I SEE.
OKAY, IT'S MY TURN TO ASK!
YOU SEEM TO KNOW AN AW-FUL LOT ABOUT EVERY-THING.
SERIOUSLY, HOW OLD ARE YOU?
GLARE...!
......
UH... OKAY, NEVER MIND.

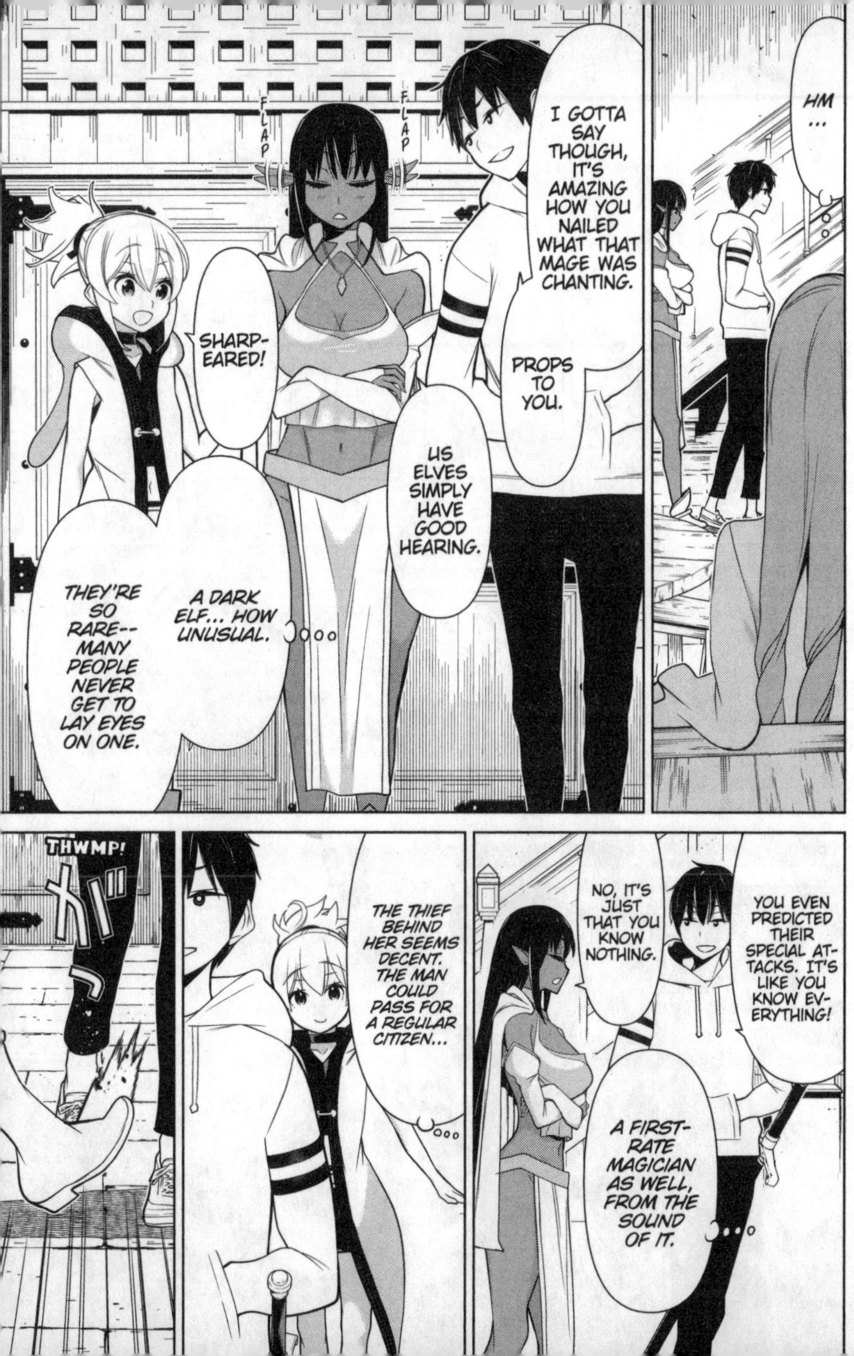
HM...
I GOTTA SAY THOUGH, IT'S AMAZING HOW YOU NAILED WHAT THAT MAGE WAS CHANTING.
PROPS TO YOU.
FLAP FLAP
SHARP-EARED!
US ELVES SIMPLY HAVE GOOD HEARING.
A DARK ELF... HOW UNUSUAL.
THEY'RE SO RARE--MANY PEOPLE NEVER GET TO LAY EYES ON ONE.
YOU EVEN PREDICTED THEIR SPECIAL AT-TACKS. IT'S LIKE YOU KNOW EV-ERYTHING!
NO, IT'S JUST THAT YOU KNOW NOTHING.
A FIRST-RATE MAGICIAN AS WELL, FROM THE SOUND OF IT.
THE THIEF BEHIND HER SEEMS DECENT. THE MAN COULD PASS FOR A REGULAR CITIZEN...
THWMP!

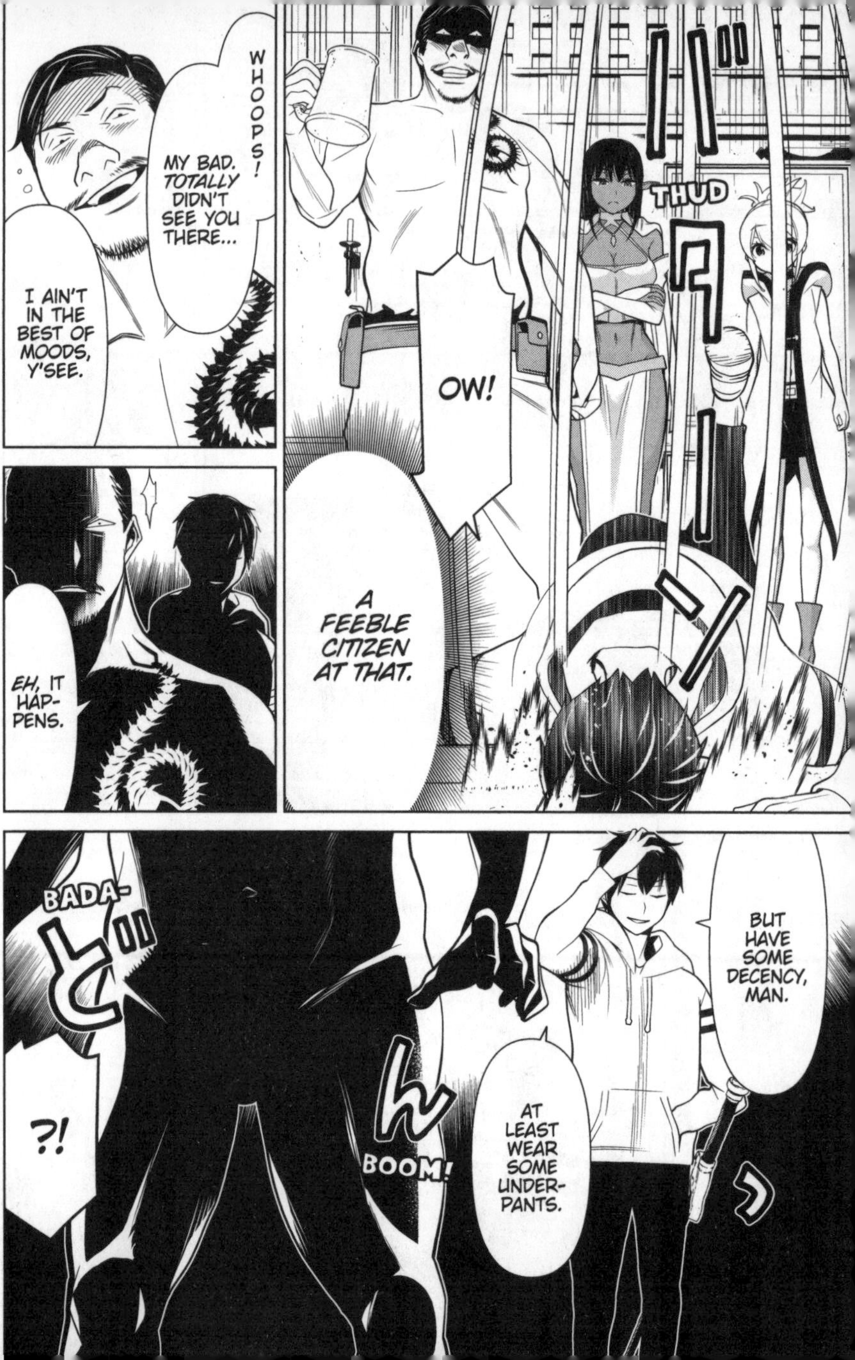
THUD
OW!
A FEEBLE CITIZEN AT THAT.
WHOOPS!
MY BAD. TOTALLY DIDN'T SEE YOU THERE...
I AIN'T IN THE BEST OF MOODS, Y'SEE.
EH, IT HAPPENS.
BUT HAVE SOME DECENCY, MAN.
AT LEAST WEAR SOME UNDERPANTS.
BOOM!
BADA-
?!

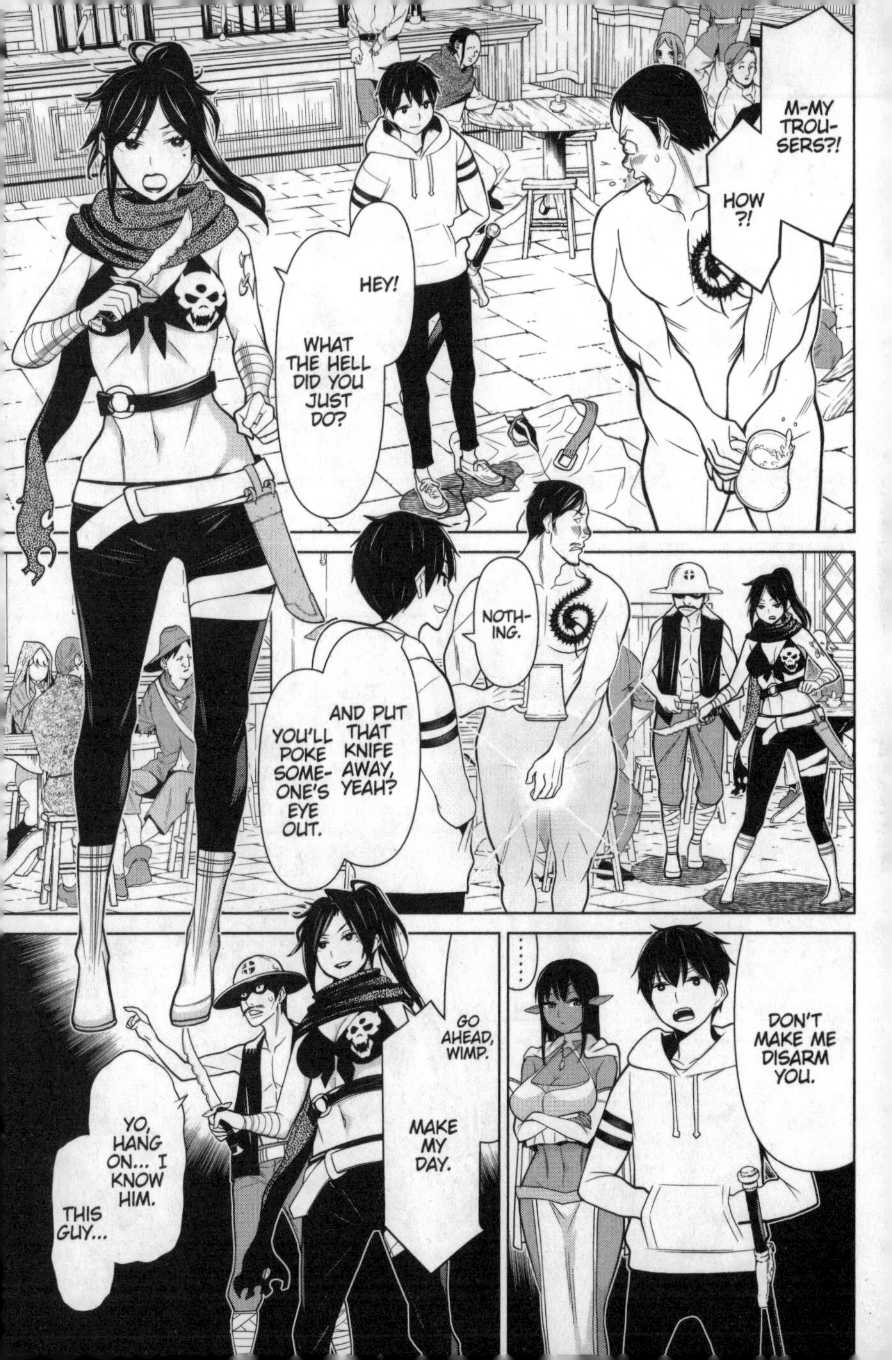
M-MY TROUSERS?!
HOW?!
HEY!
WHAT THE HELL DID YOU JUST DO?
NOTHING.
AND PUT THAT KNIFE AWAY, YEAH?
YOU'LL POKE SOMEONE'S EYE OUT.
DON'T MAKE ME DISARM YOU.
......
GO AHEAD, WIMP.
MAKE MY DAY.
YO, HANG ON... I KNOW HIM.
THIS GUY...

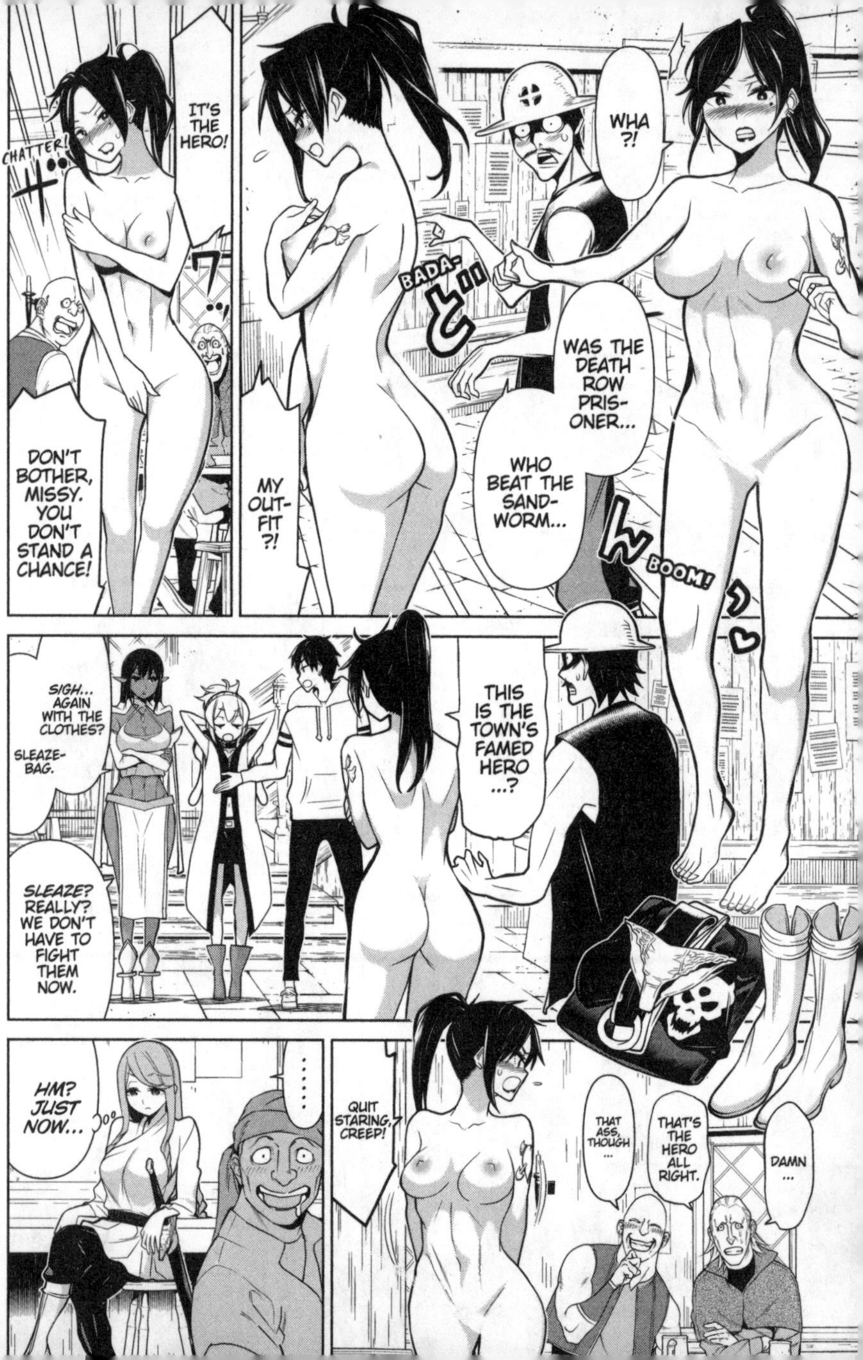
WHA ?!
WAS THE DEATH ROW PRISONER...
WHO BEAT THE SANDWORM...
BOOM!
BADA-
MY OUTFIT ?!
IT'S THE HERO!
CHATTER!
DON'T BOTHER, MISSY. YOU DON'T STAND A CHANCE!
THIS IS THE TOWN'S FAMED HERO ...?
SIGH... AGAIN WITH THE CLOTHES?
SLEAZEBAG.
SLEAZE? REALLY? WE DON'T HAVE TO FIGHT THEM NOW.
DAMN ...
THAT'S THE HERO ALL RIGHT.
THAT ASS, THOUGH ...
QUIT STARING, CREEP!
......
HM? JUST NOW...

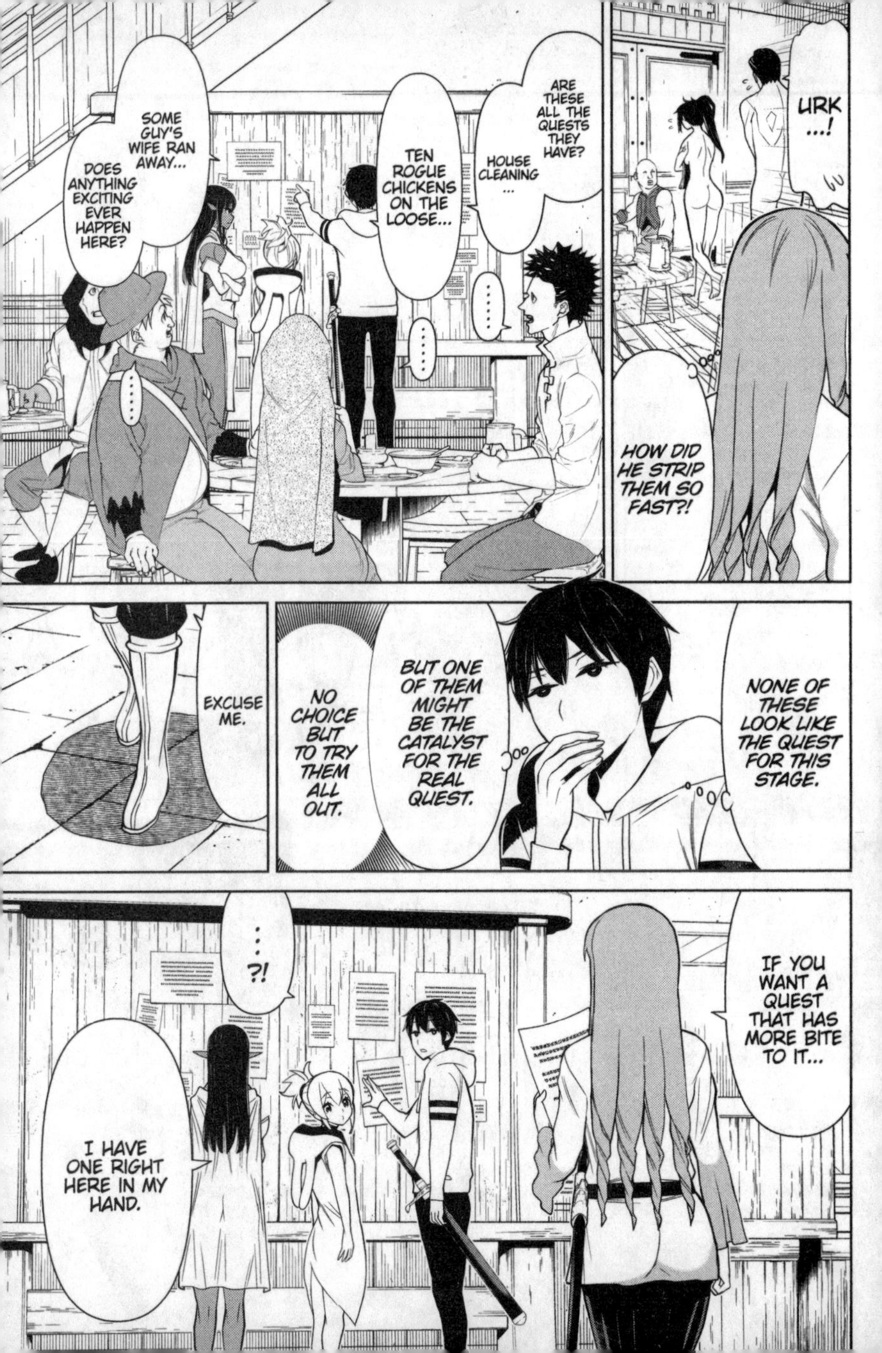
URK ...!
HOW DID HE STRIP THEM SO FAST?!
ARE THESE ALL THE QUESTS THEY HAVE?
HOUSE CLEANING ...
TEN ROGUE CHICKENS ON THE LOOSE...
SOME GUY'S WIFE RAN AWAY...
DOES ANYTHING EXCITING EVER HAPPEN HERE?
......
......
......
NONE OF THESE LOOK LIKE THE QUEST FOR THIS STAGE.
BUT ONE OF THEM MIGHT BE THE CATALYST FOR THE REAL QUEST.
NO CHOICE BUT TO TRY THEM ALL OUT.
EXCUSE ME.
IF YOU WANT A QUEST THAT HAS MORE BITE TO IT...
...?!
I HAVE ONE RIGHT HERE IN MY HAND.

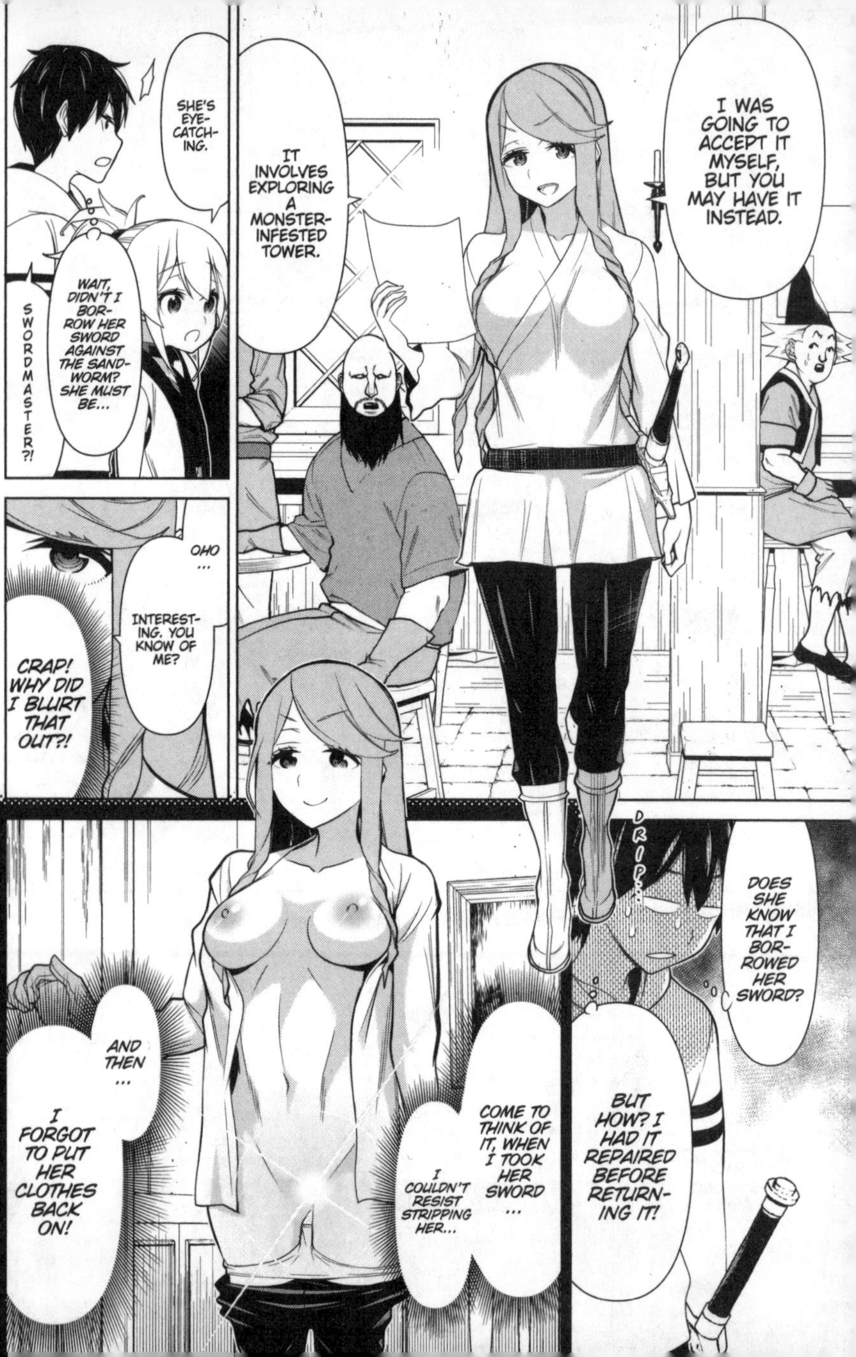
I WAS GOING TO ACCEPT IT MYSELF, BUT YOU MAY HAVE IT INSTEAD.
IT INVOLVES EXPLORING A MONSTER-INFESTED TOWER.
SHE'S EYE-CATCHING.
WAIT, DIDN'T I BORROW HER SWORD AGAINST THE SANDWORM? SHE MUST BE...
SWORDMASTER?!
OHO... INTERESTING. YOU KNOW OF ME?
CRAP! WHY DID I BLURT THAT OUT?!
DRIP...
DOES SHE KNOW THAT I BORROWED HER SWORD?
BUT HOW? I HAD IT REPAIRED BEFORE RETURNING IT!
COME TO THINK OF IT, WHEN I TOOK HER SWORD...
I COULDN'T RESIST STRIPPING HER...
AND THEN... I FORGOT TO PUT HER CLOTHES BACK ON!

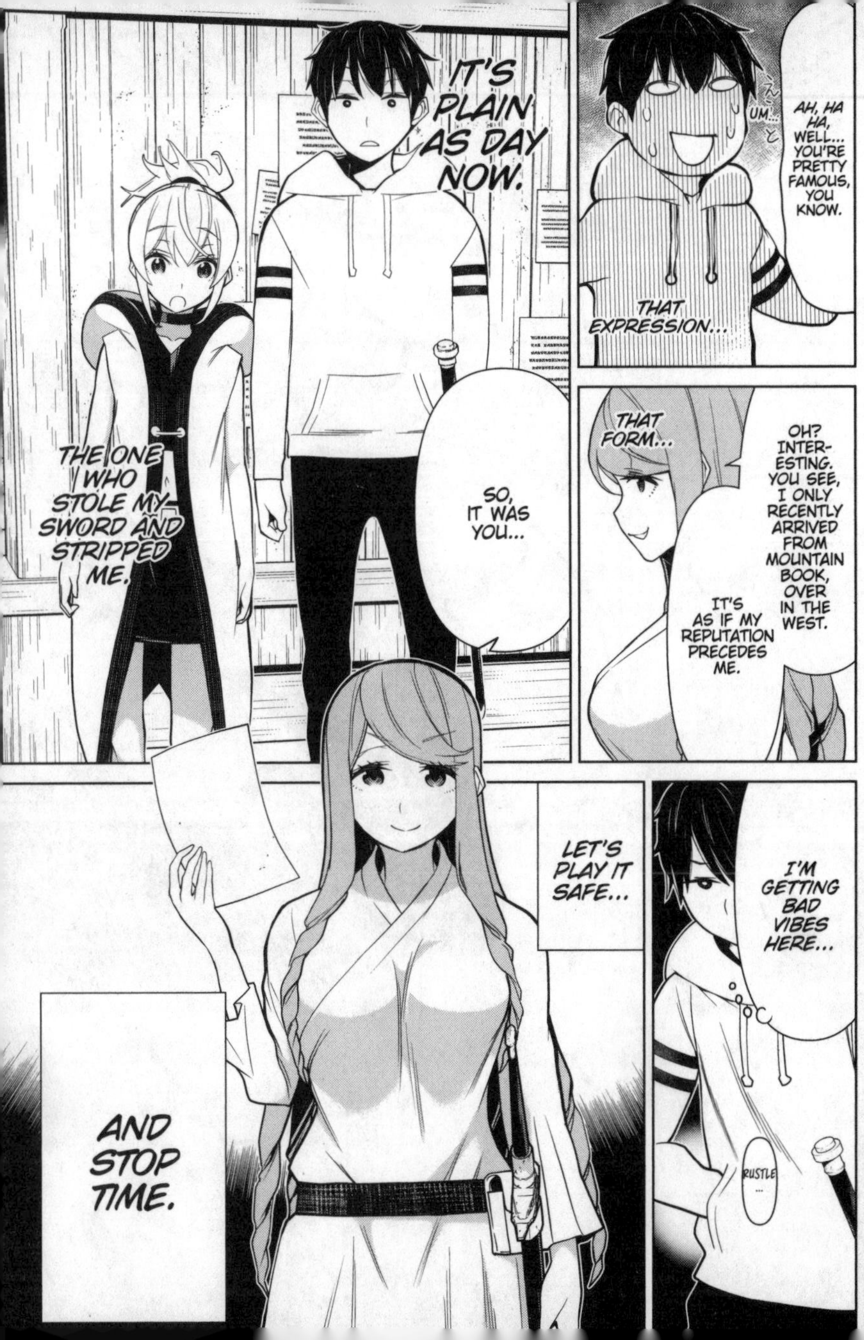
UM...
AH, HA HA, WELL... YOU'RE PRETTY FAMOUS, YOU KNOW.
THAT EXPRESSION...
OH? INTERESTING. YOU SEE, I ONLY RECENTLY ARRIVED FROM MOUNTAIN BOOK, OVER IN THE WEST.
THAT FORM...
IT'S AS IF MY REPUTATION PRECEDES ME.
IT'S PLAIN AS DAY NOW.
SO, IT WAS YOU...
THE ONE WHO STOLE MY SWORD AND STRIPPED ME.
I'M GETTING BAD VIBES HERE...
RUSTLE...
LET'S PLAY IT SAFE...
AND STOP TIME.

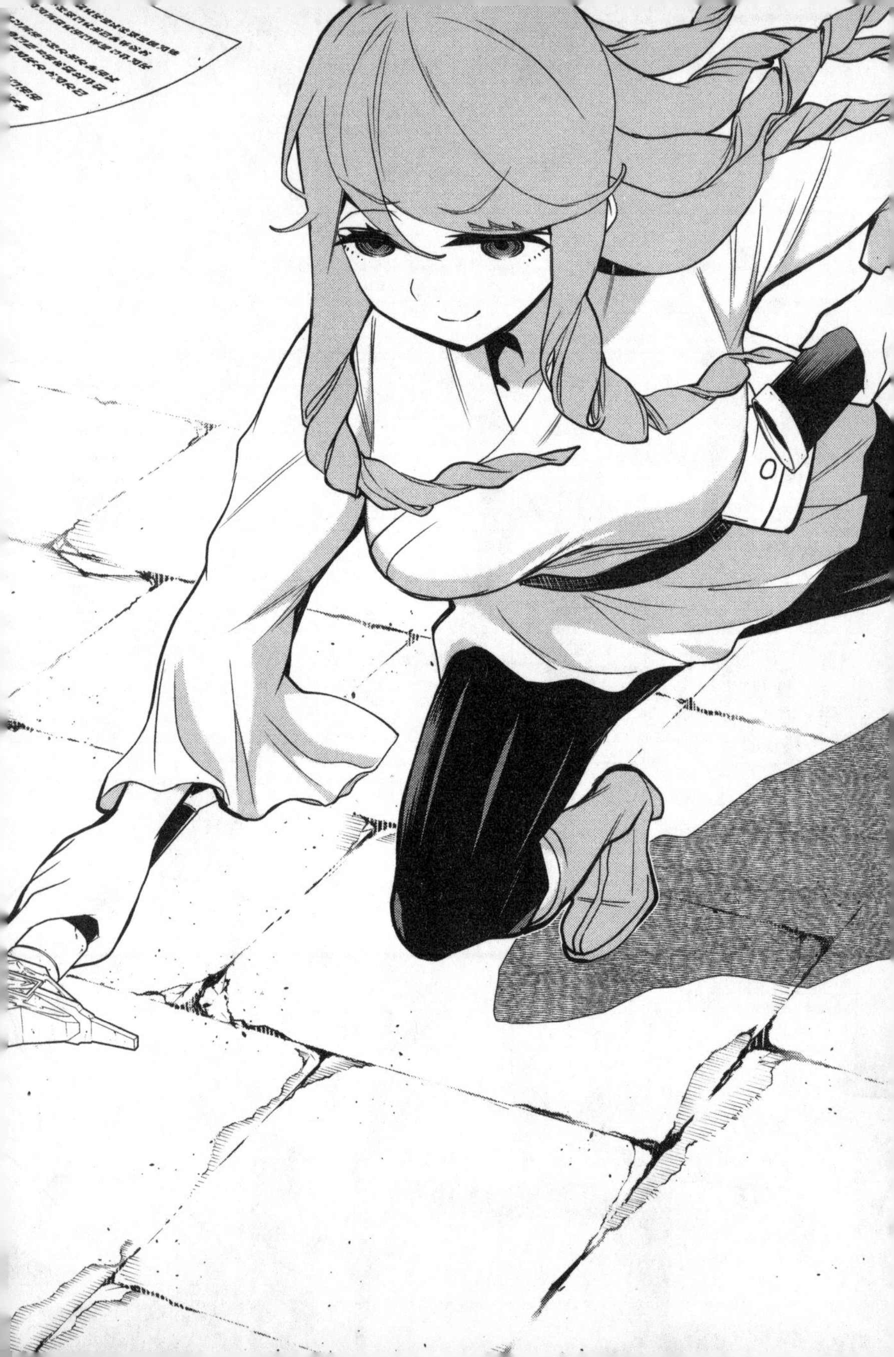

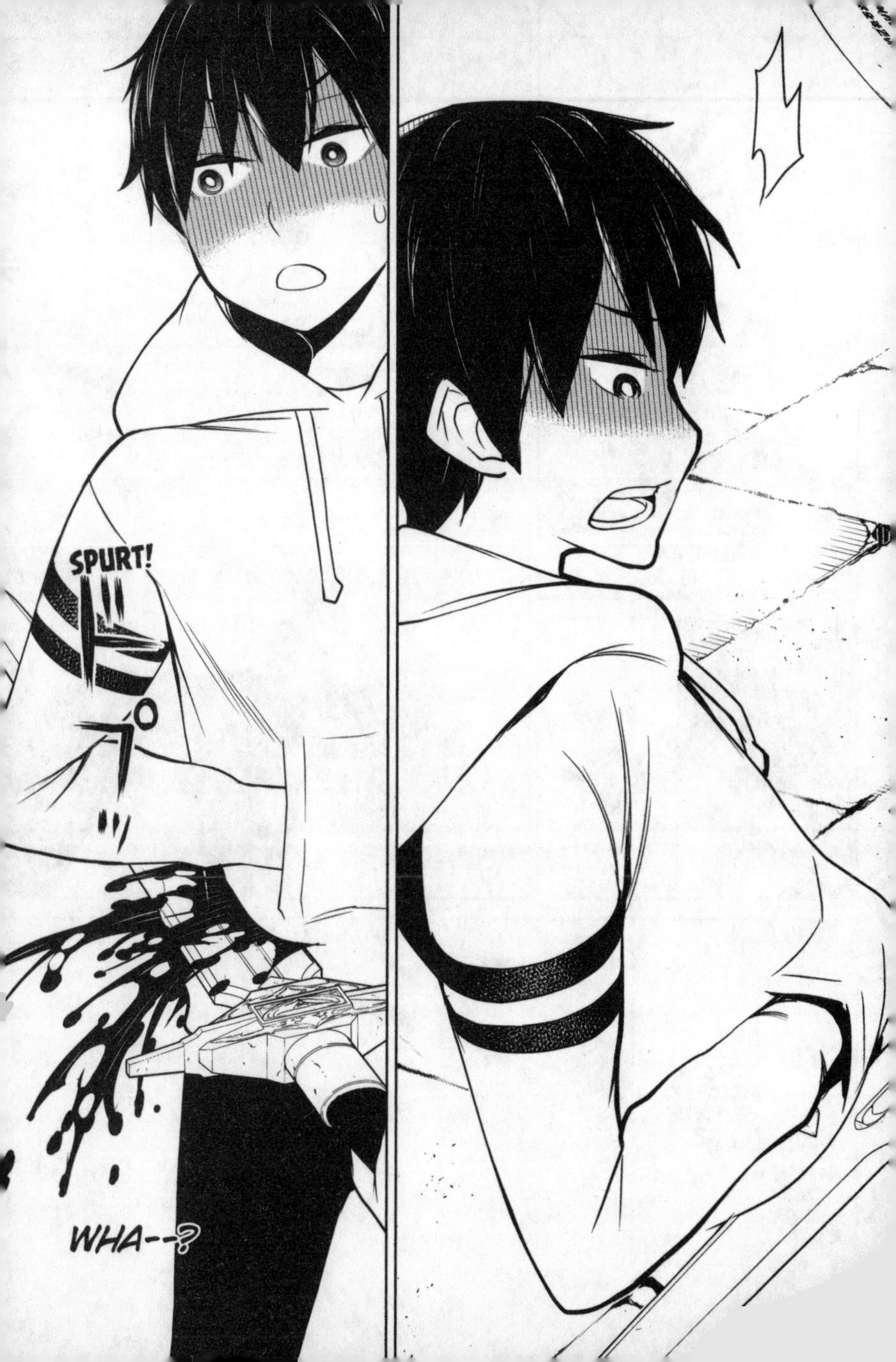
SPURT!
WHA--?

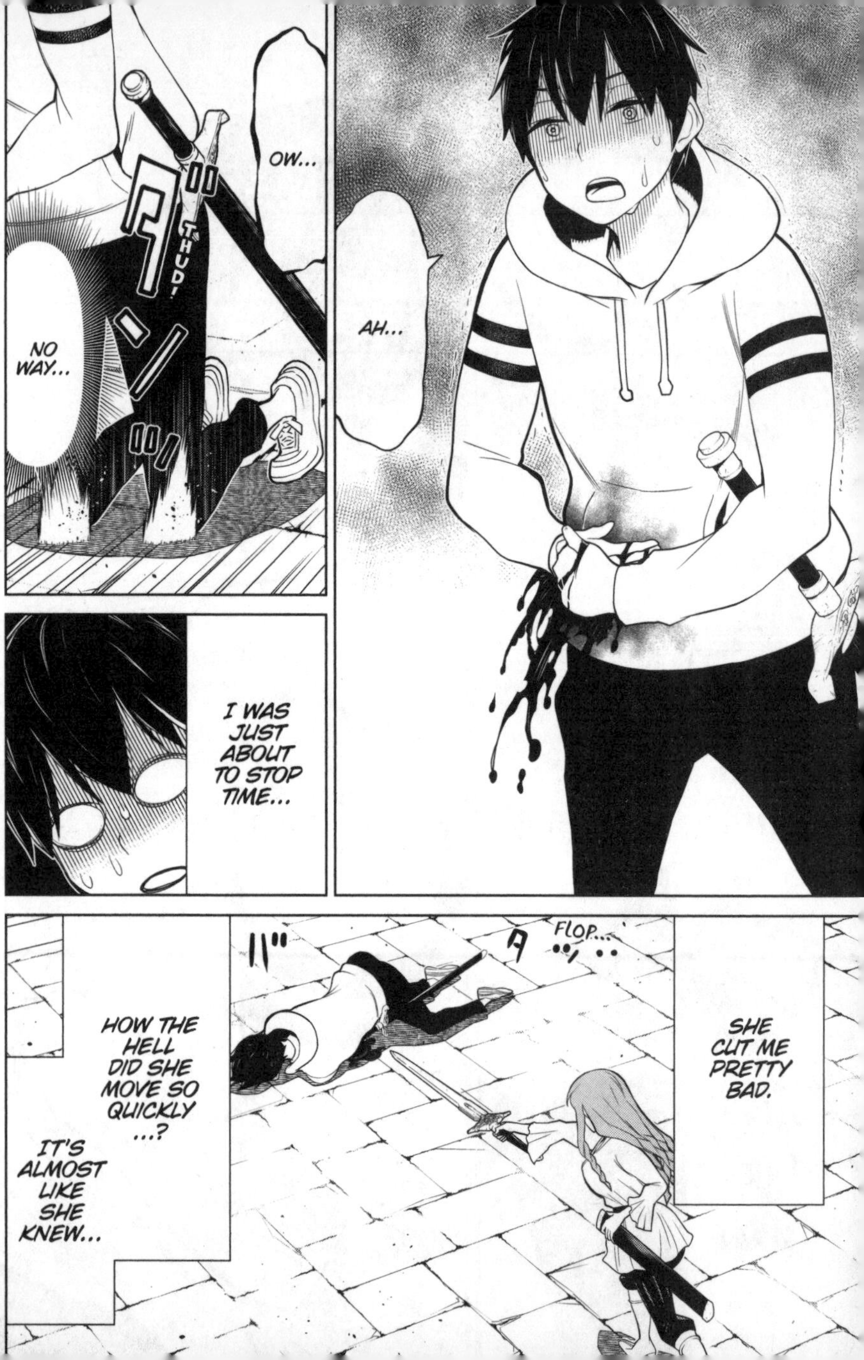
OW...
AH...
THUD!
NO WAY...
I WAS JUST ABOUT TO STOP TIME...
SHE CUT ME PRETTY BAD.
FLOP...
HOW THE HELL DID SHE MOVE SO QUICKLY ...?
IT'S ALMOST LIKE SHE KNEW...

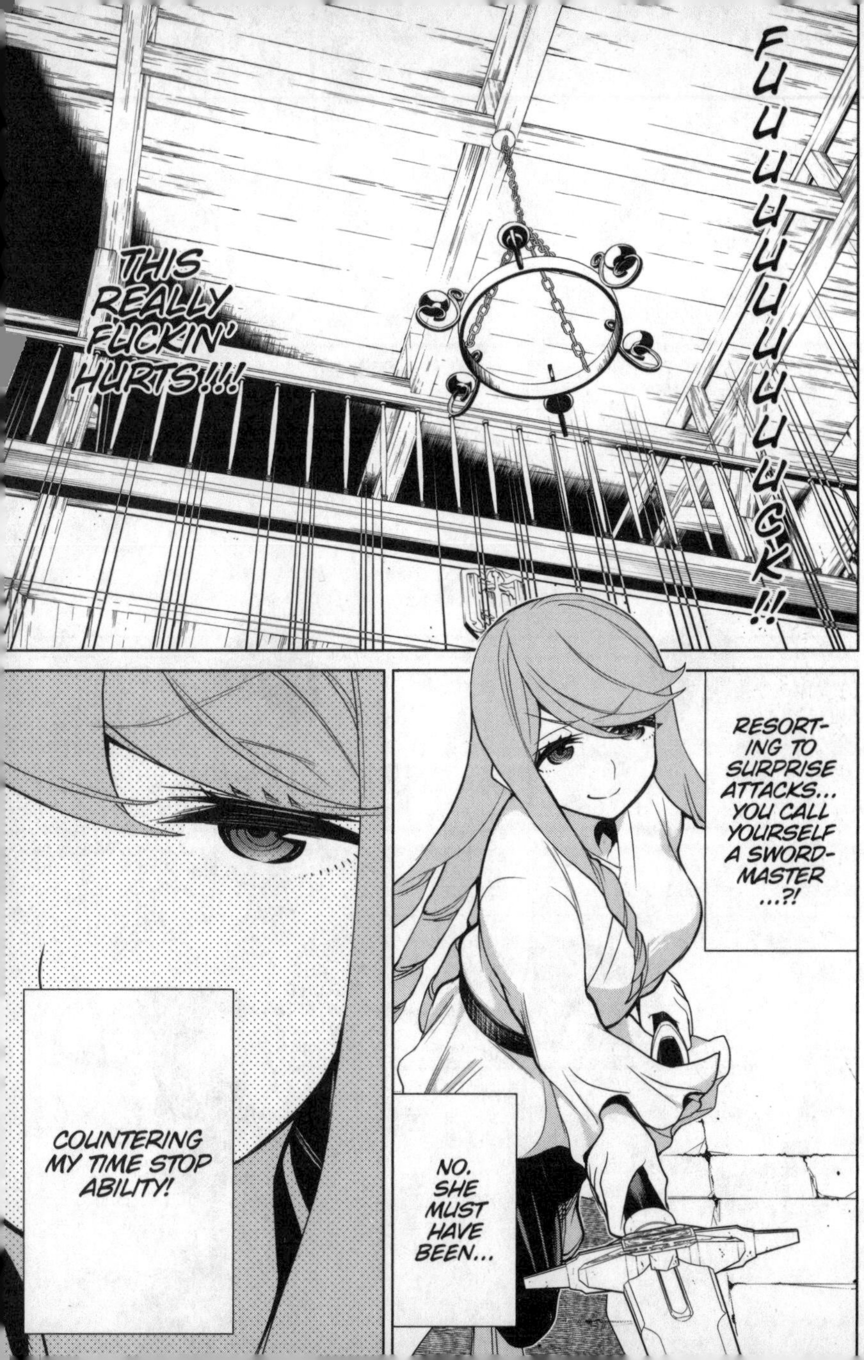
FUUUUUUUUUCK!!
THIS REALLY FUCKIN' HURTS!!!
RESORTING TO SURPRISE ATTACKS... YOU CALL YOURSELF A SWORD-MASTER ...?!
NO. SHE MUST HAVE BEEN...
COUNTERING MY TIME STOP ABILITY!

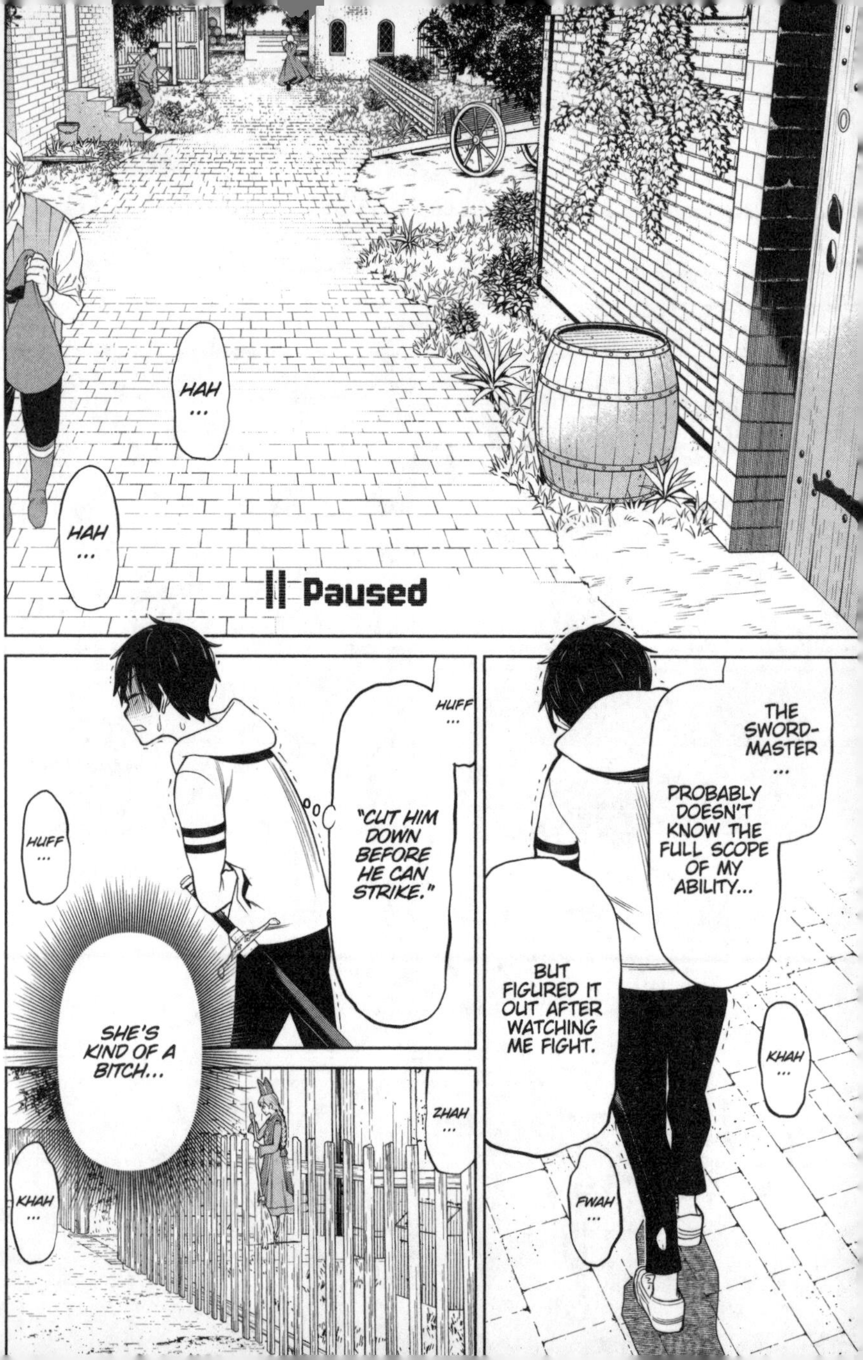
HAH ...
HAH ...
|| Paused
THE SWORD-MASTER ...
PROBABLY DOESN'T KNOW THE FULL SCOPE OF MY ABILITY...
BUT FIGURED IT OUT AFTER WATCHING ME FIGHT.
KHAH ...
FWAH ...
HUFF ...
"CUT HIM DOWN BEFORE HE CAN STRIKE."
HUFF ...
SHE'S KIND OF A BITCH...
ZHAH ...
KHAH ...

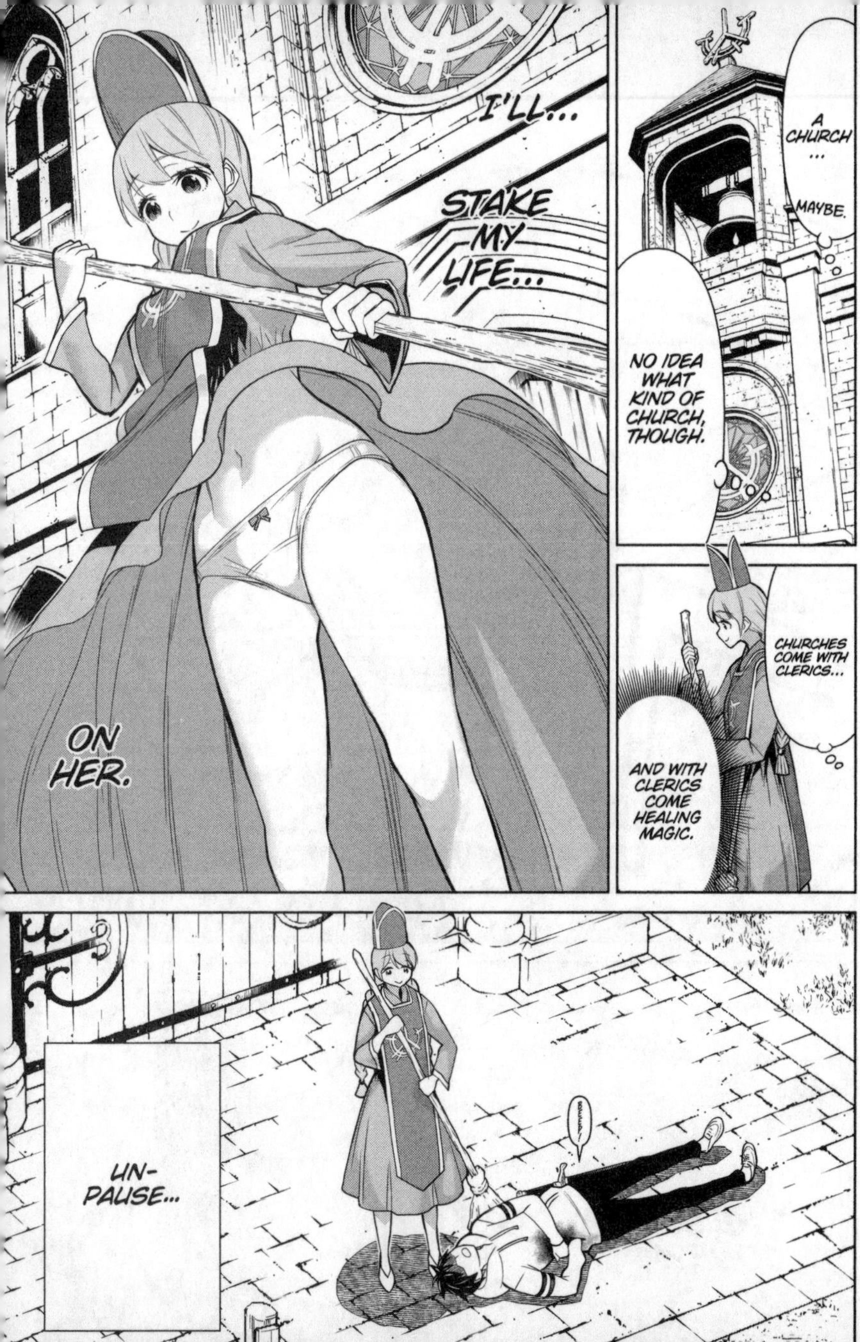
A CHURCH ...
MAYBE.
NO IDEA WHAT KIND OF CHURCH, THOUGH.
CHURCHES COME WITH CLERICS...
AND WITH CLERICS COME HEALING MAGIC.
I'LL...
STAKE MY LIFE...
ON HER.
UN-PAUSE...

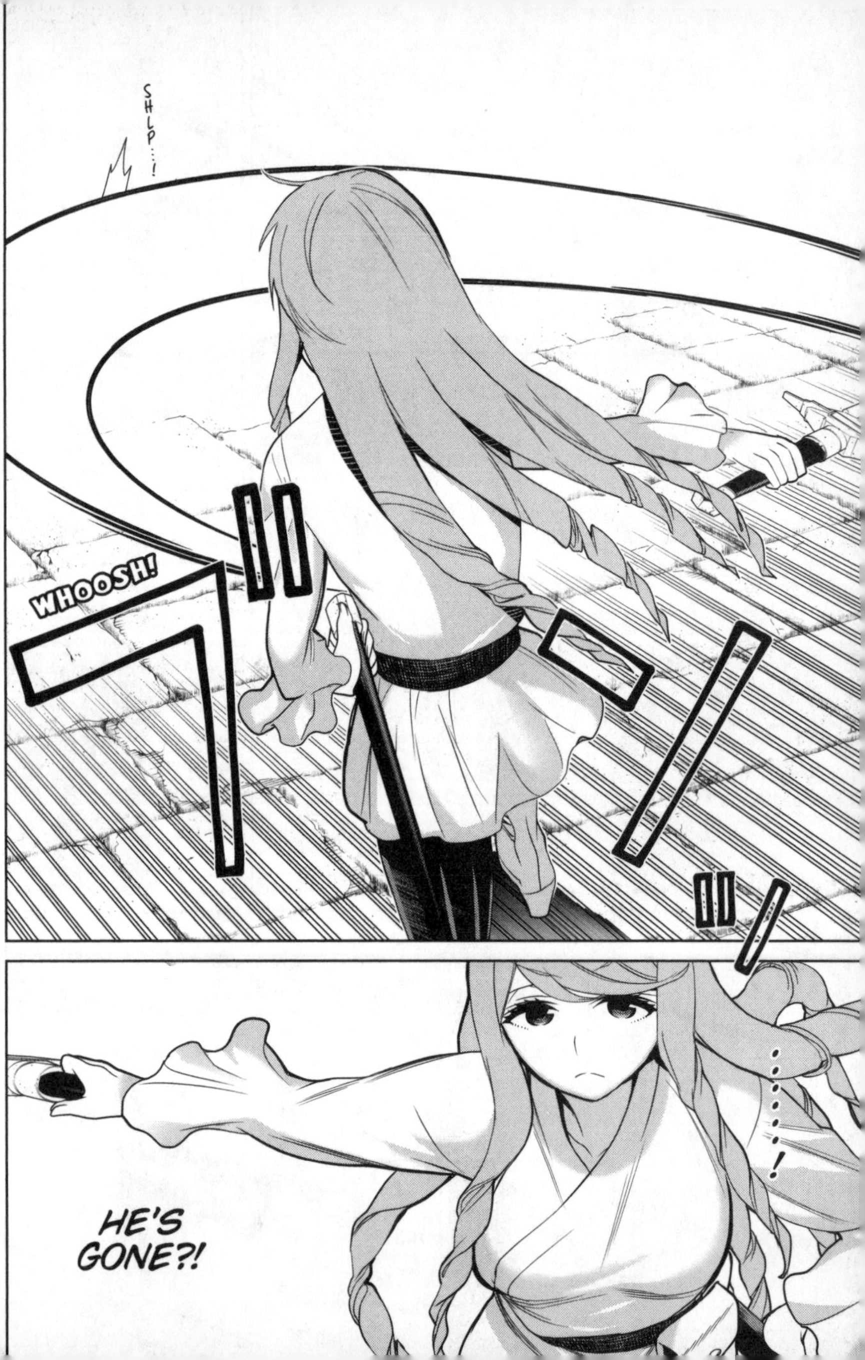
SHLP...!
WHOOSH!
......!
HE'S GONE?!

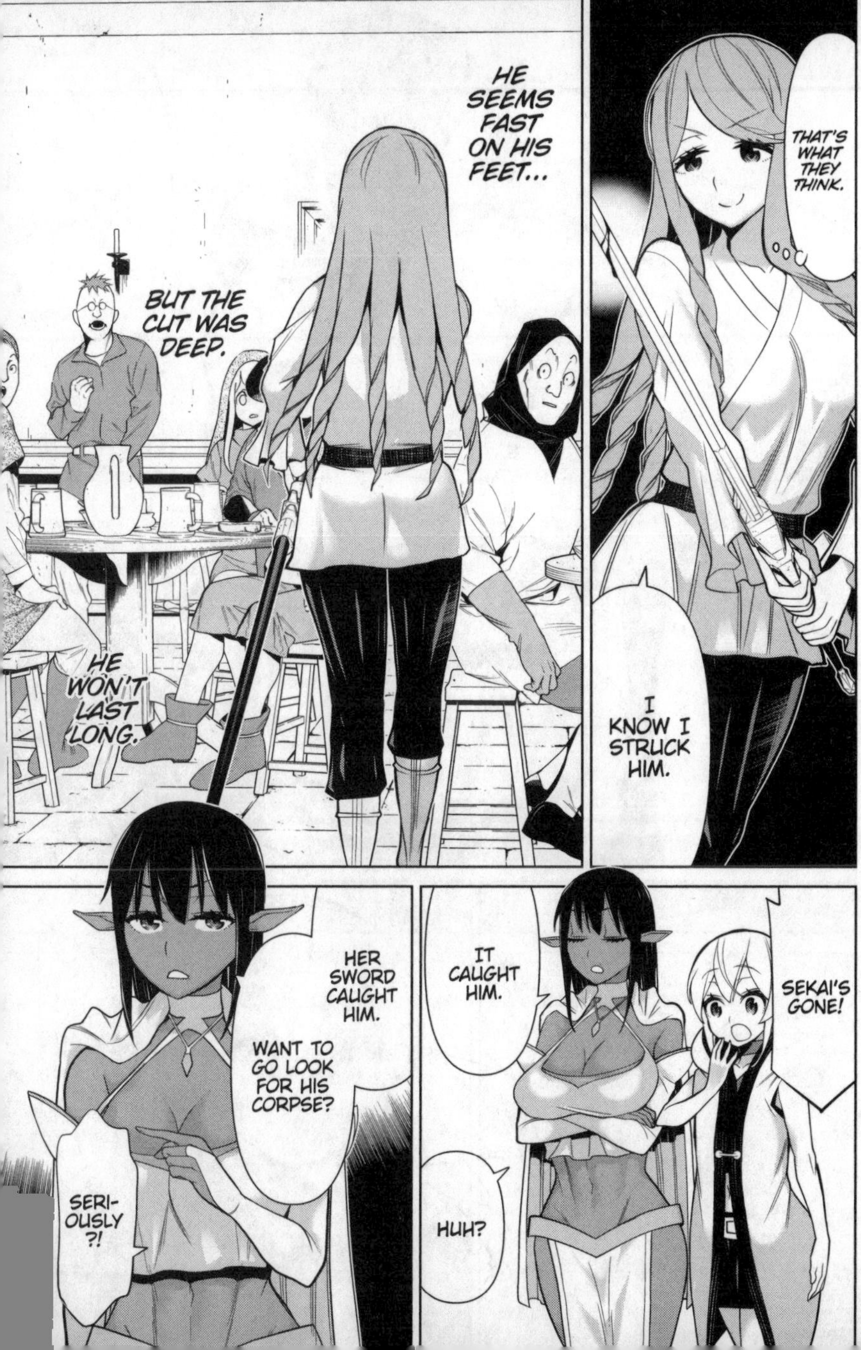
THAT'S WHAT THEY THINK.
I KNOW I STRUCK HIM.
HE SEEMS FAST ON HIS FEET...
BUT THE CUT WAS DEEP.
HE WON'T LAST LONG.
SEKAI'S GONE!
IT CAUGHT HIM.
HUH?
HER SWORD CAUGHT HIM.
WANT TO GO LOOK FOR HIS CORPSE?
SERI-OUSLY ?!

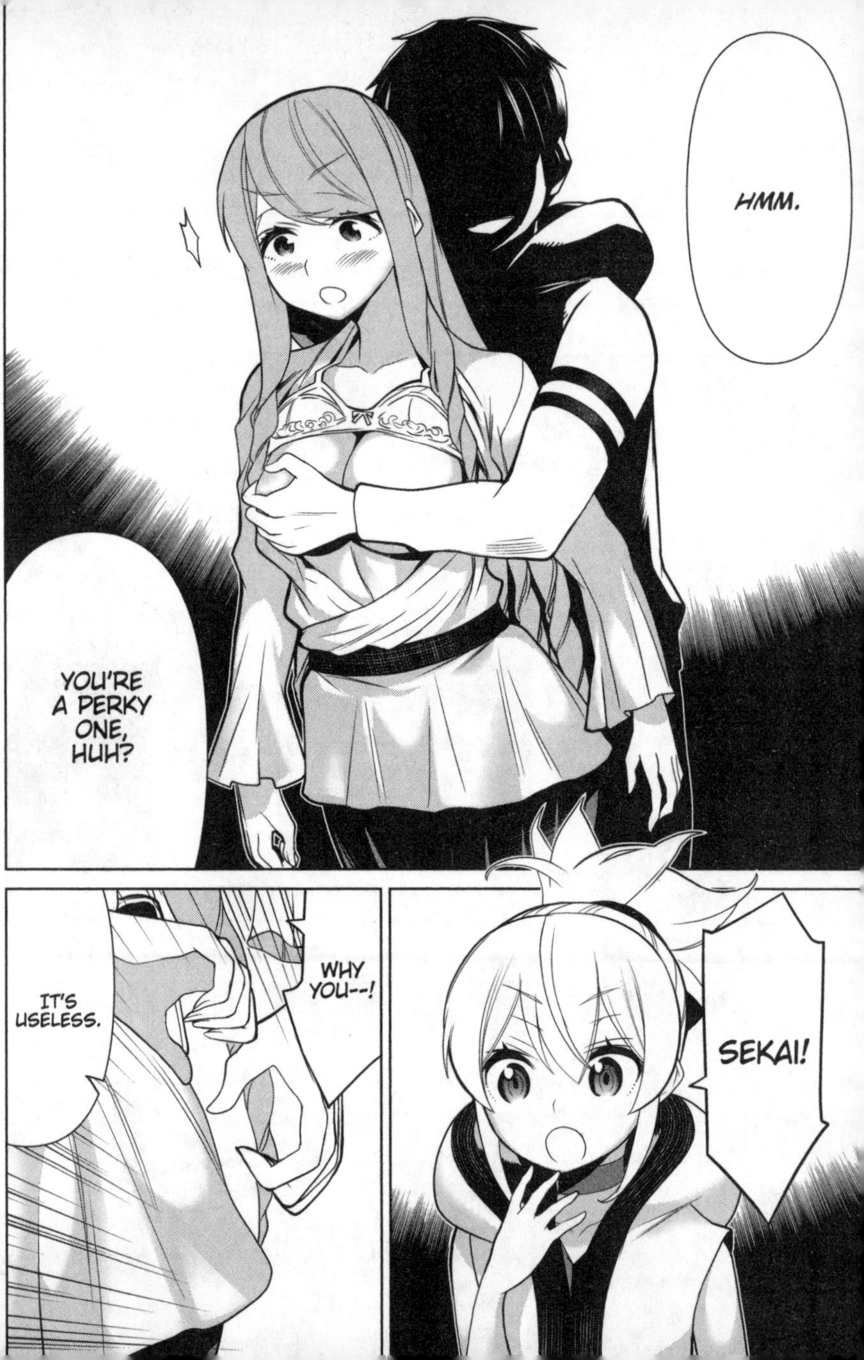
HMM.
YOU'RE A PERKY ONE, HUH?
SEKAI!
WHY YOU--!
IT'S USELESS.

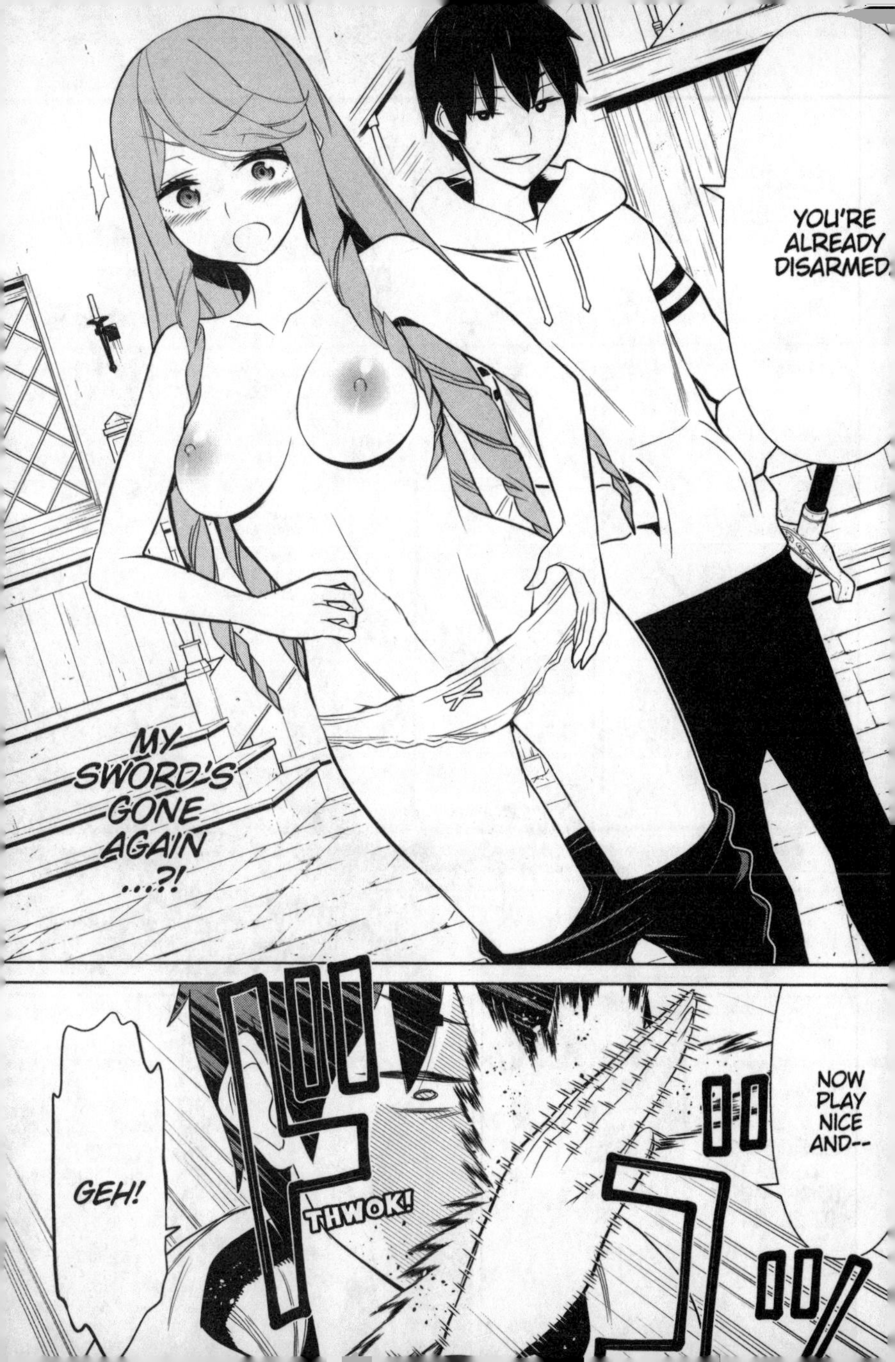
YOU'RE ALREADY DISARMED.
MY SWORD'S GONE AGAIN ...?!
NOW PLAY NICE AND--
THWOK!
GEH!

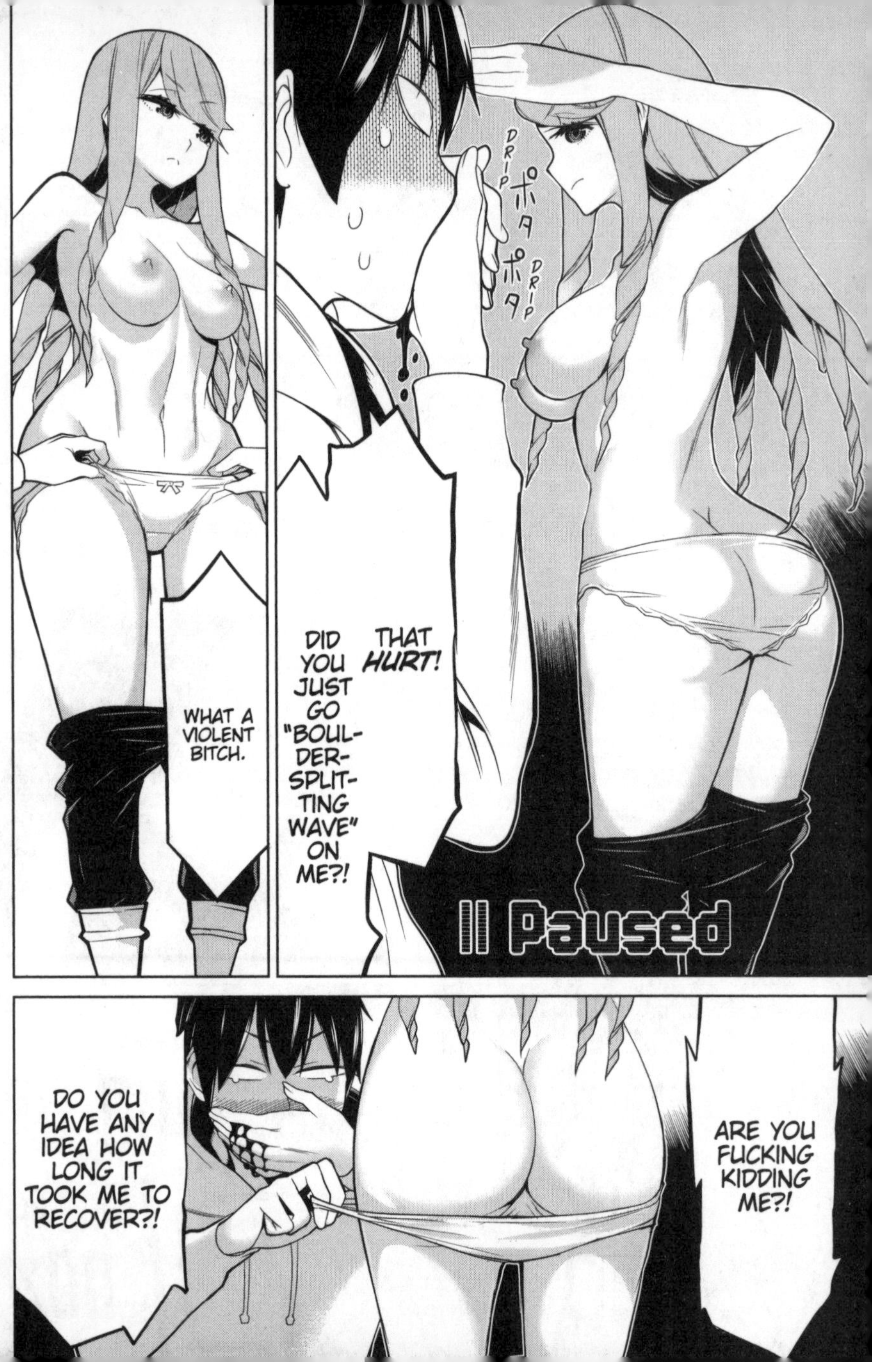
DRIP
ポタポタ
DRIP
THAT HURT!
DID YOU JUST GO "BOULDER-SPLITTING WAVE" ON ME?!
II Paused
WHAT A VIOLENT BITCH.
ARE YOU FUCKING KIDDING ME?!
DO YOU HAVE ANY IDEA HOW LONG IT TOOK ME TO RECOVER?!

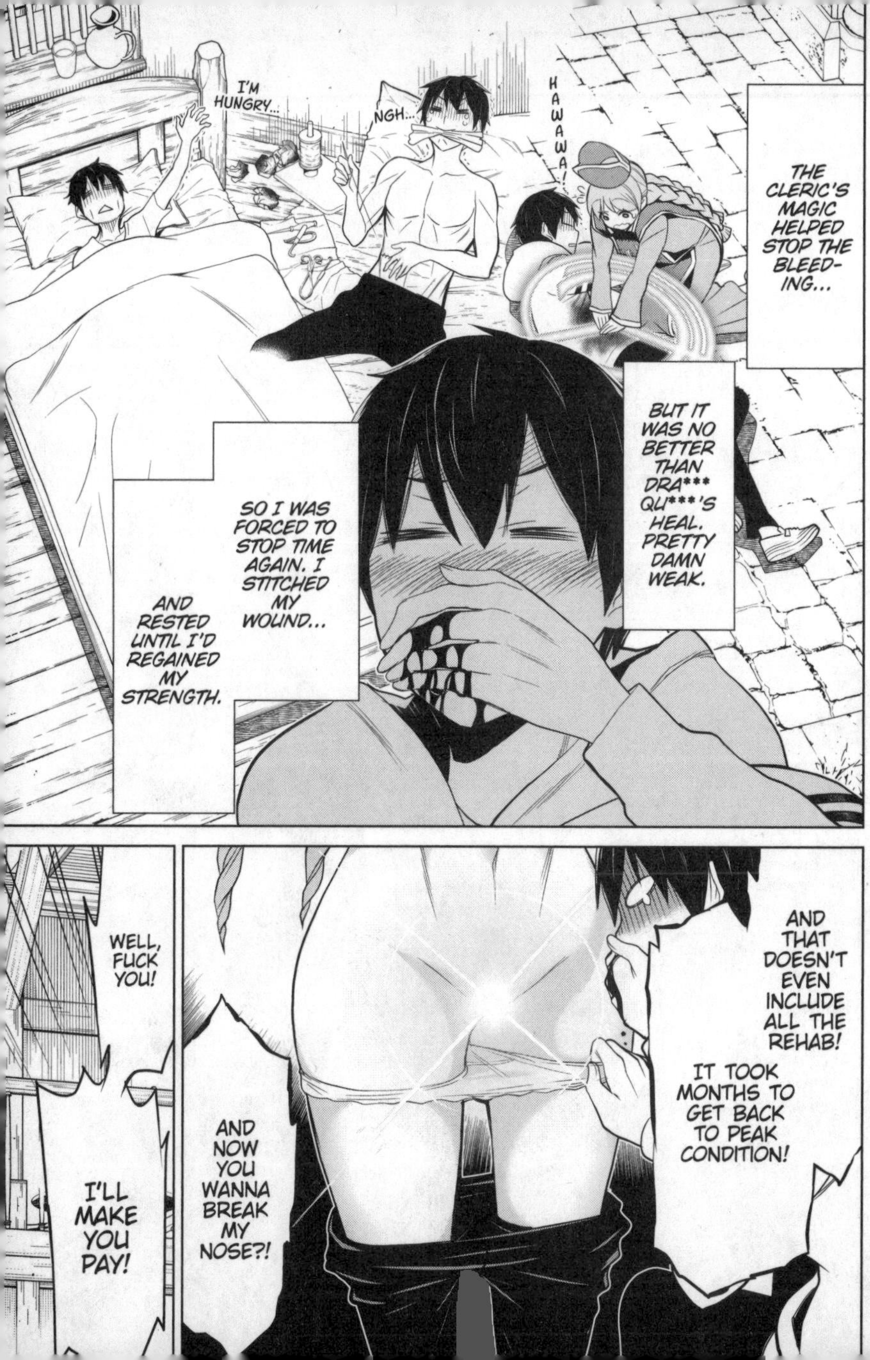
THE CLERIC'S MAGIC HELPED STOP THE BLEED-ING...
HAWAWA!
NGH...
I'M HUNGRY...
BUT IT WAS NO BETTER THAN DRA*** QU***'S HEAL. PRETTY DAMN WEAK.
SO I WAS FORCED TO STOP TIME AGAIN. I STITCHED MY WOUND...
AND RESTED UNTIL I'D REGAINED MY STRENGTH.
AND THAT DOESN'T EVEN INCLUDE ALL THE REHAB!
IT TOOK MONTHS TO GET BACK TO PEAK CONDITION!
AND NOW YOU WANNA BREAK MY NOSE?!
WELL, FUCK YOU!
I'LL MAKE YOU PAY!

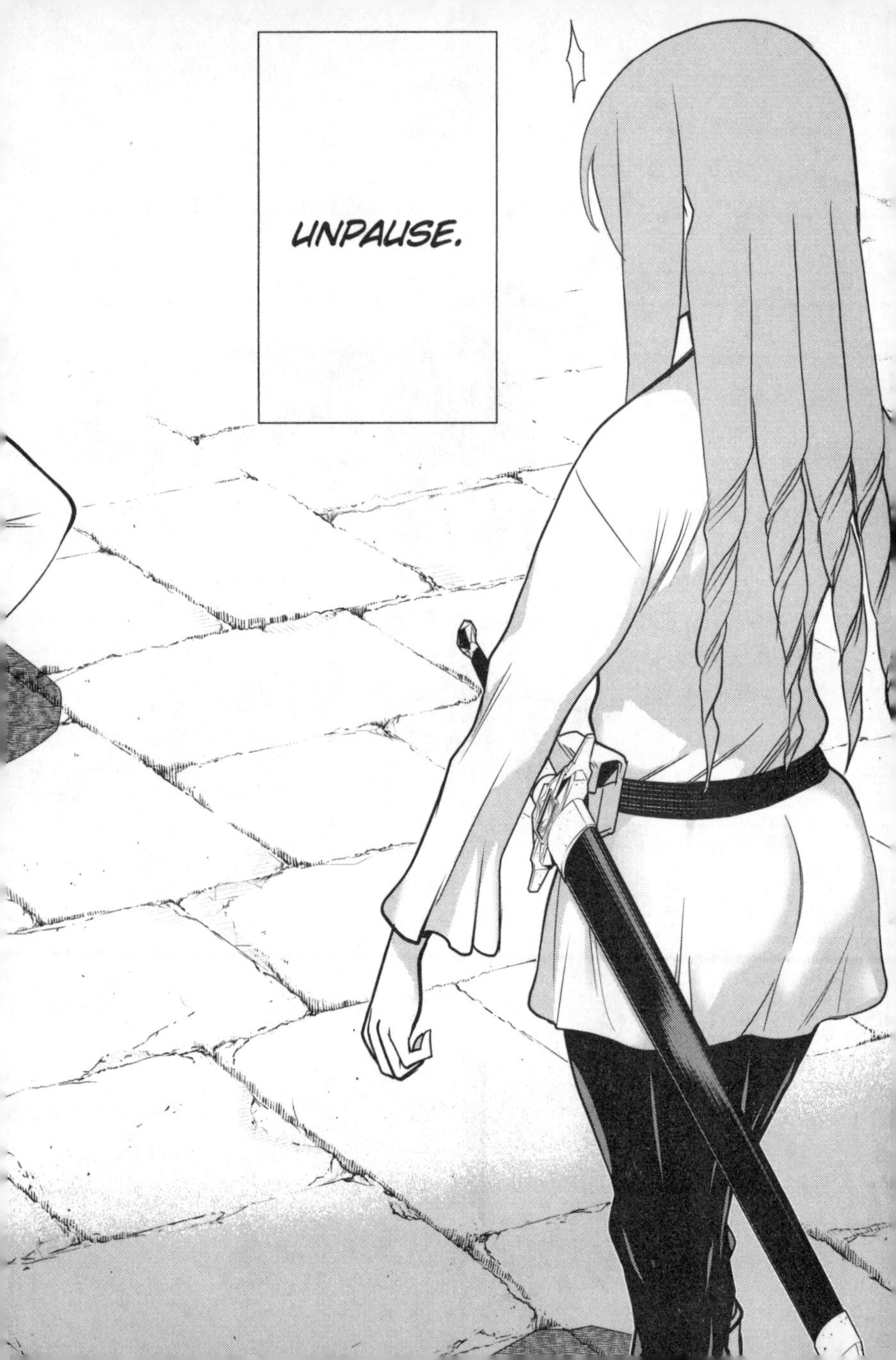
UNPAUSE.

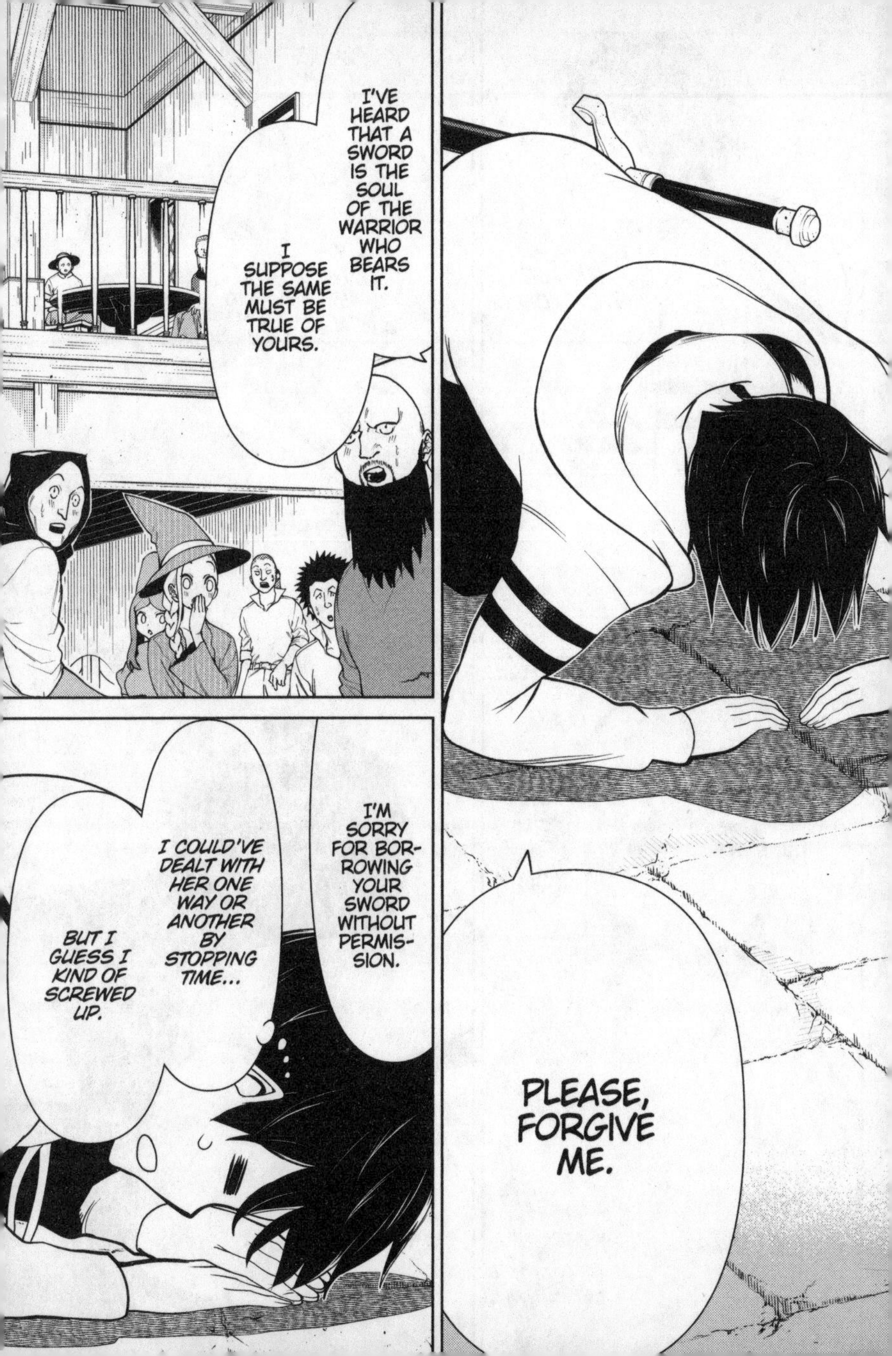
PLEASE, FORGIVE ME.
I'VE HEARD THAT A SWORD IS THE SOUL OF THE WARRIOR WHO BEARS IT.
I SUPPOSE THE SAME MUST BE TRUE OF YOURS.
I'M SORRY FOR BOR-ROWING YOUR SWORD WITHOUT PERMIS-SION.
I COULD'VE DEALT WITH HER ONE WAY OR ANOTHER BY STOPPING TIME...
BUT I GUESS I KIND OF SCREWED UP.

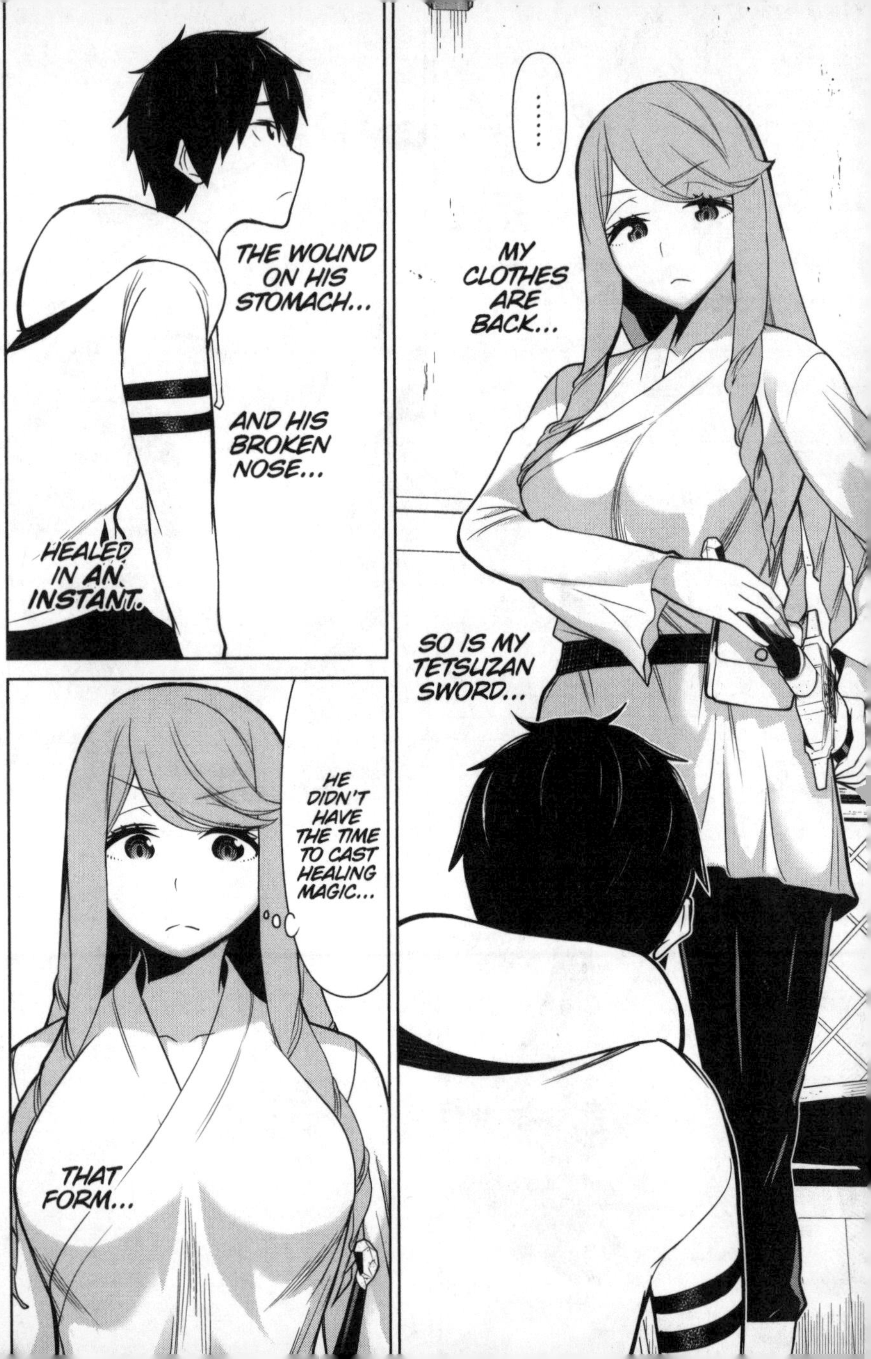
......
MY CLOTHES ARE BACK...
SO IS MY TETSUZAN SWORD...
THE WOUND ON HIS STOMACH...
AND HIS BROKEN NOSE...
HEALED IN AN INSTANT.
HE DIDN'T HAVE THE TIME TO CAST HEALING MAGIC...
THAT FORM...

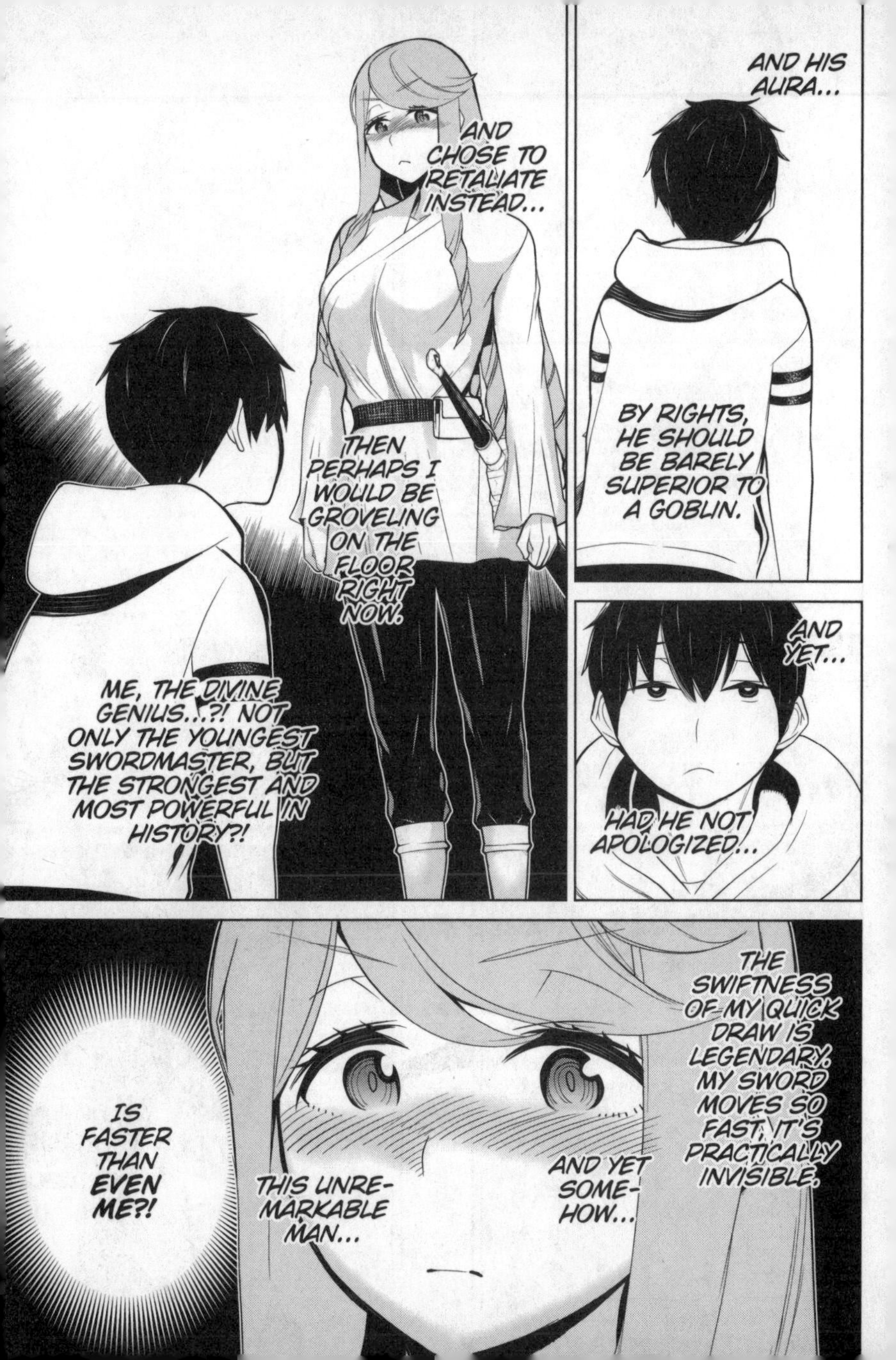
AND HIS AURA...
BY RIGHTS, HE SHOULD BE BARELY SUPERIOR TO A GOBLIN.
AND YET...
HAD HE NOT APOLOGIZED...
AND CHOSE TO RETALIATE INSTEAD...
THEN PERHAPS I WOULD BE GROVELING ON THE FLOOR RIGHT NOW.
ME, THE DIVINE GENIUS...?! NOT ONLY THE YOUNGEST SWORDMASTER, BUT THE STRONGEST AND MOST POWERFUL IN HISTORY?!
THE SWIFTNESS OF MY QUICK DRAW IS LEGENDARY. MY SWORD MOVES SO FAST, IT'S PRACTICALLY INVISIBLE.
AND YET SOME-HOW...
THIS UNRE-MARKABLE MAN...
IS FASTER THAN **EVEN ME?!**

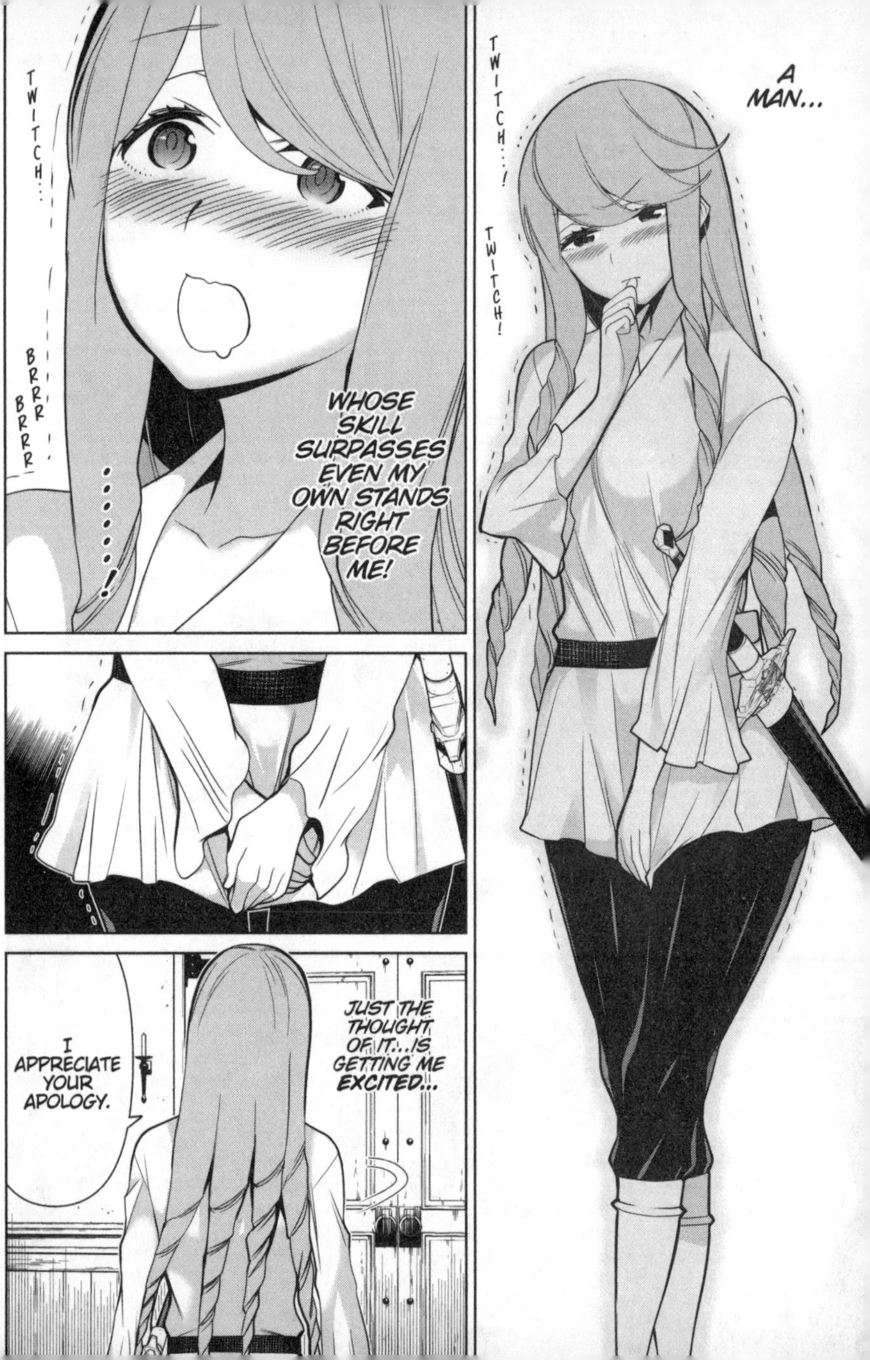
A MAN...
TWITCH...!
TWITCH!
WHOSE SKILL SURPASSES EVEN MY OWN STANDS RIGHT BEFORE ME!
TWITCH...!
BRRR
BRRR
......!
JUST THE THOUGHT OF IT...IS GETTING ME EXCITED...
I APPRECIATE YOUR APOLOGY.

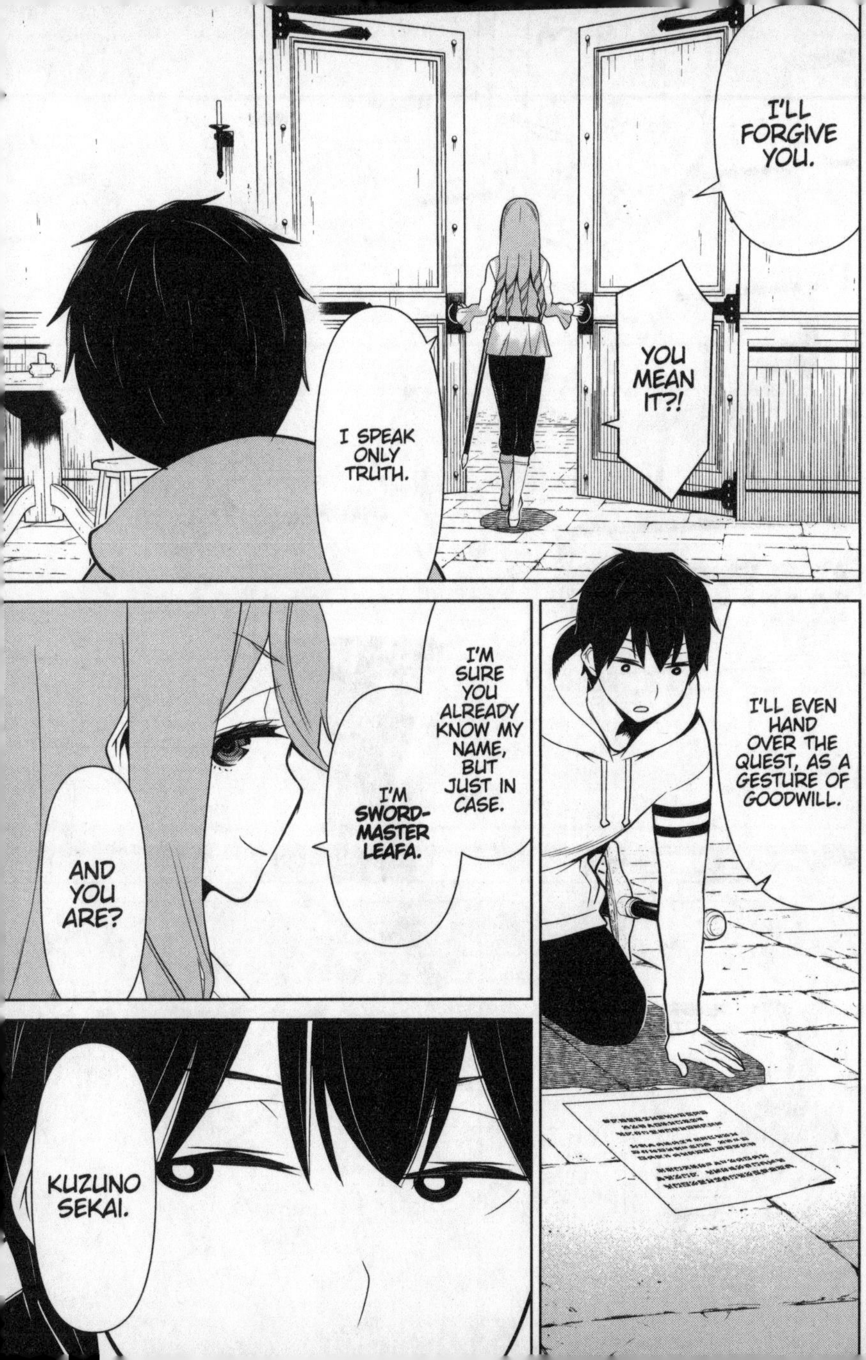
I'LL FORGIVE YOU.
YOU MEAN IT?!
I SPEAK ONLY TRUTH.
I'LL EVEN HAND OVER THE QUEST, AS A GESTURE OF GOODWILL.
I'M SURE YOU ALREADY KNOW MY NAME, BUT JUST IN CASE.
I'M SWORD-MASTER LEAFA.
AND YOU ARE?
KUZUNO SEKAI.

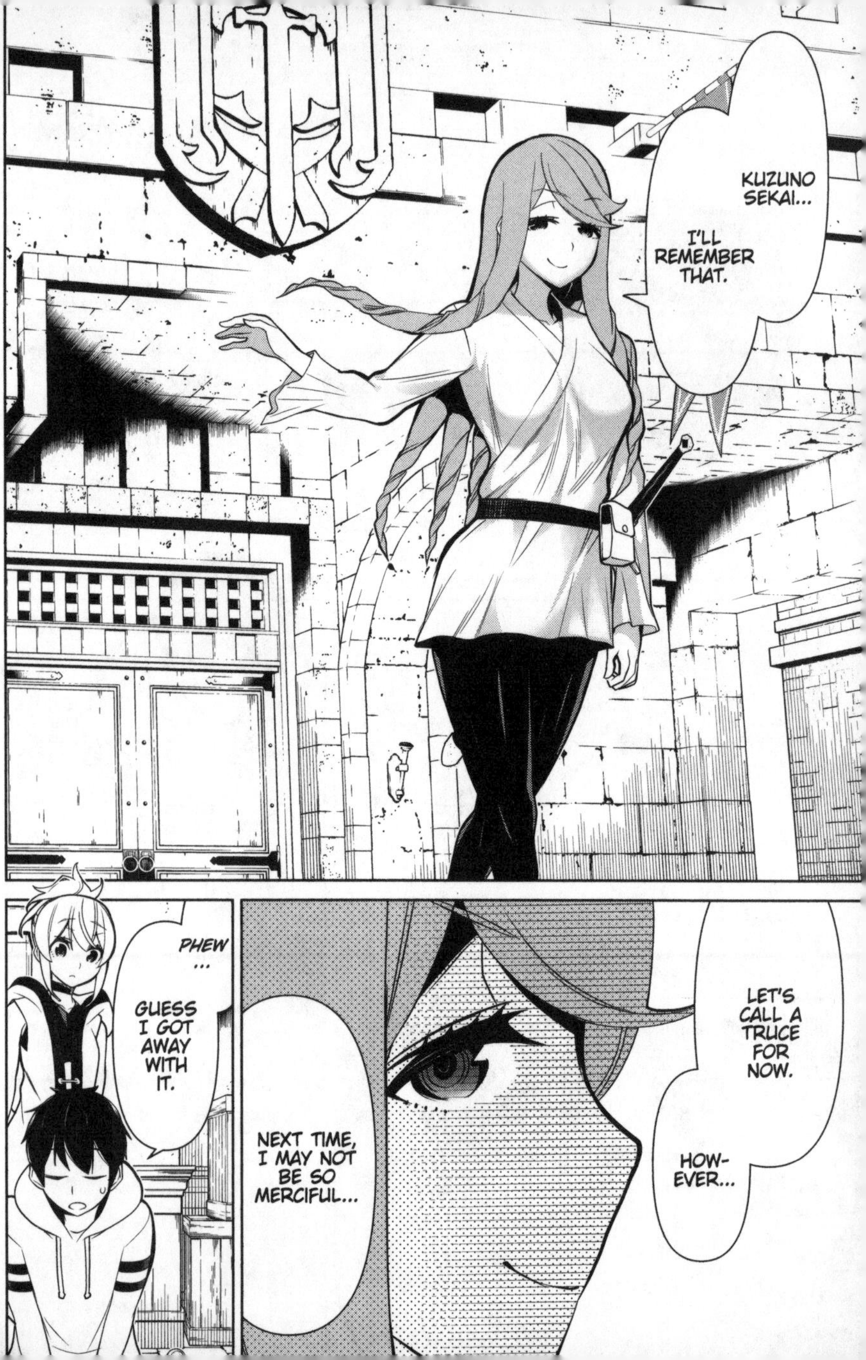
KUZUNO SEKAI...
I'LL REMEMBER THAT.
LET'S CALL A TRUCE FOR NOW.
HOW-EVER...
NEXT TIME, I MAY NOT BE SO MERCIFUL...
PHEW...
GUESS I GOT AWAY WITH IT.

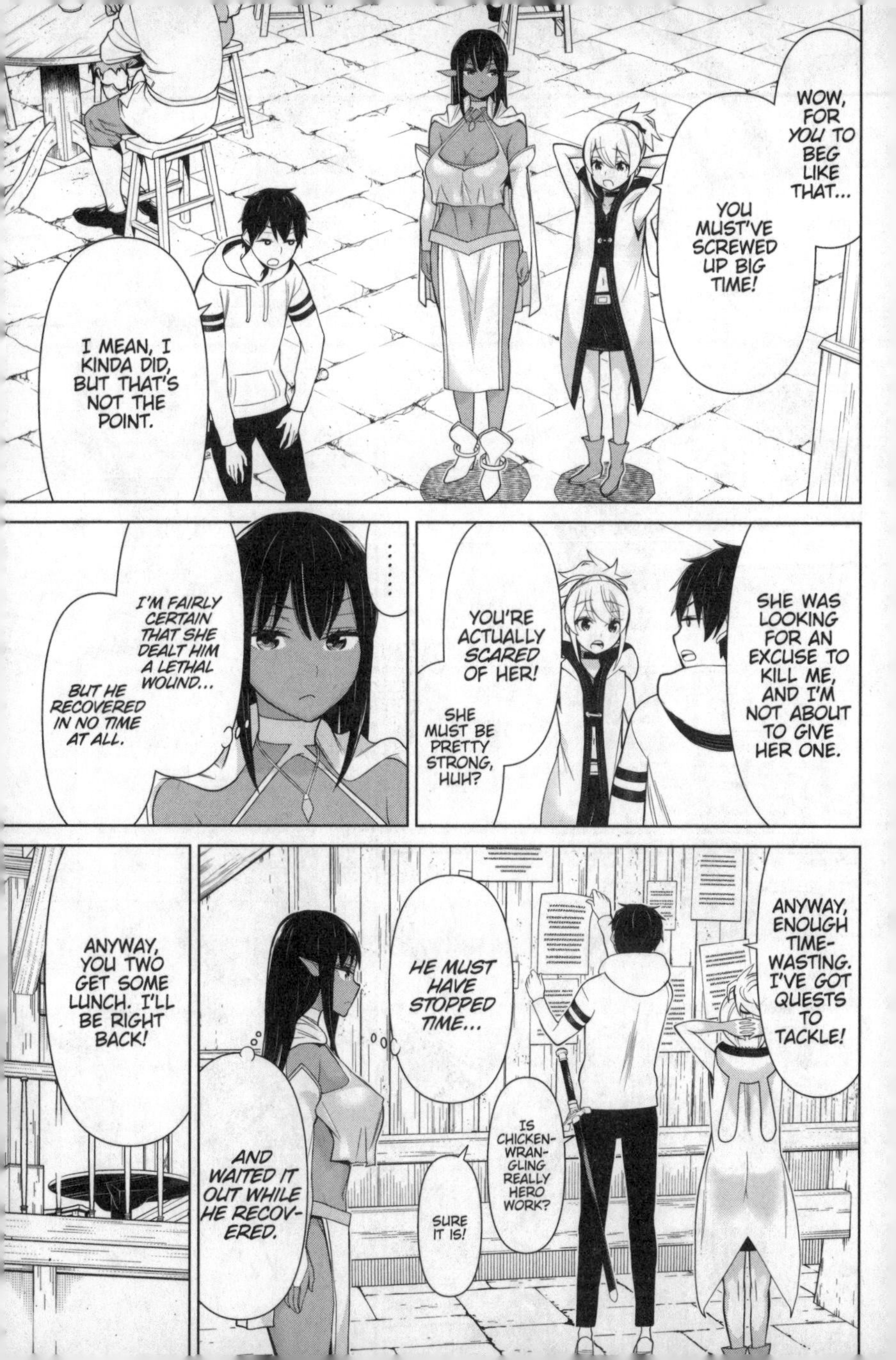
WOW, FOR *YOU* TO BEG LIKE THAT...
YOU MUST'VE SCREWED UP BIG TIME!
I MEAN, I KINDA DID, BUT THAT'S NOT THE POINT.
SHE WAS LOOKING FOR AN EXCUSE TO KILL ME, AND I'M NOT ABOUT TO GIVE HER ONE.
YOU'RE ACTUALLY SCARED OF HER!
SHE MUST BE PRETTY STRONG, HUH?
......
I'M FAIRLY CERTAIN THAT SHE DEALT HIM A LETHAL WOUND...
BUT HE RECOVERED IN NO TIME AT ALL.
ANYWAY, ENOUGH TIME-WASTING. I'VE GOT QUESTS TO TACKLE!
HE MUST HAVE STOPPED TIME...
IS CHICKEN-WRANGLING REALLY HERO WORK?
SURE IT IS!
AND WAITED IT OUT WHILE HE RECOVERED.
ANYWAY, YOU TWO GET SOME LUNCH. I'LL BE RIGHT BACK!

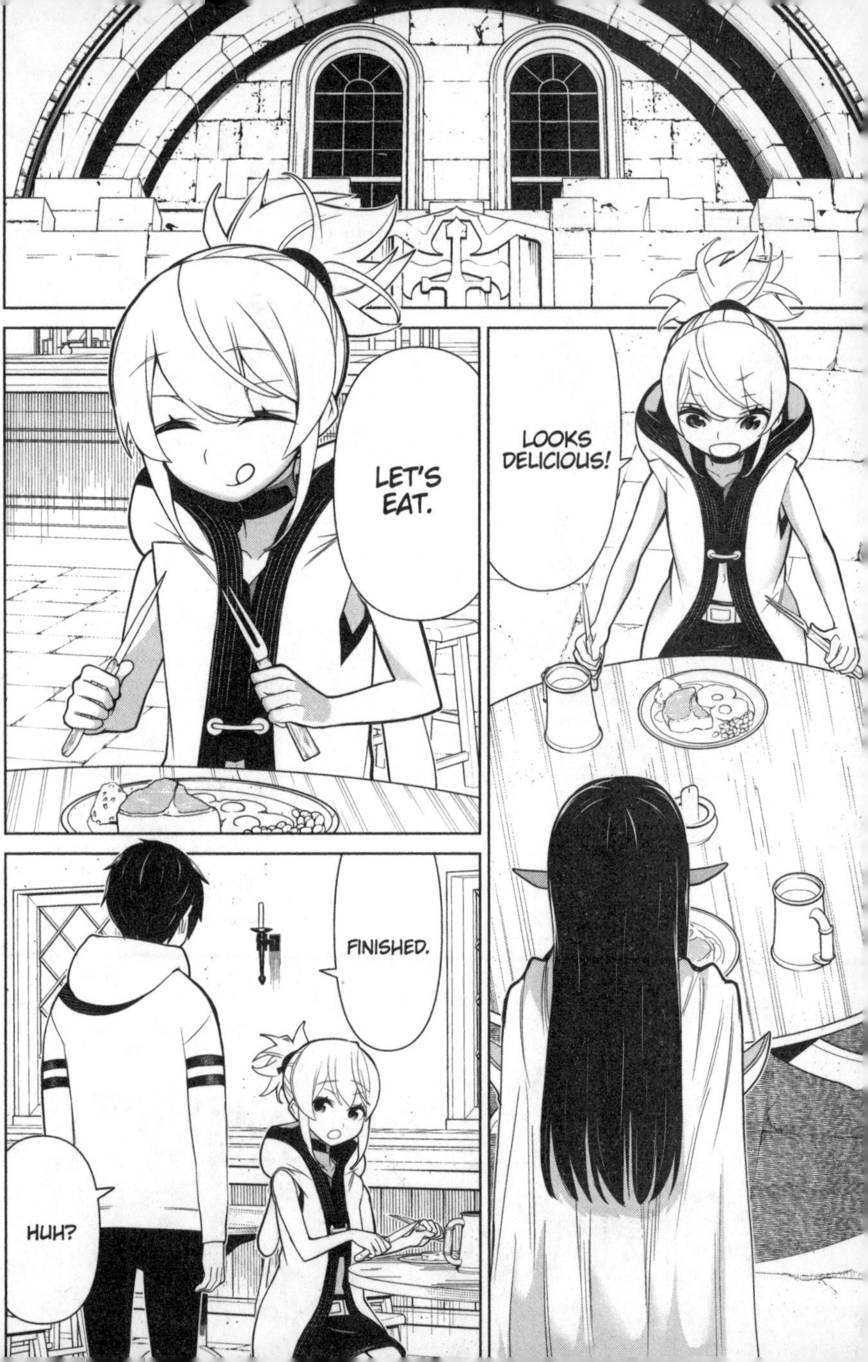
LOOKS DELICIOUS!
LET'S EAT.
FINISHED.
HUH?

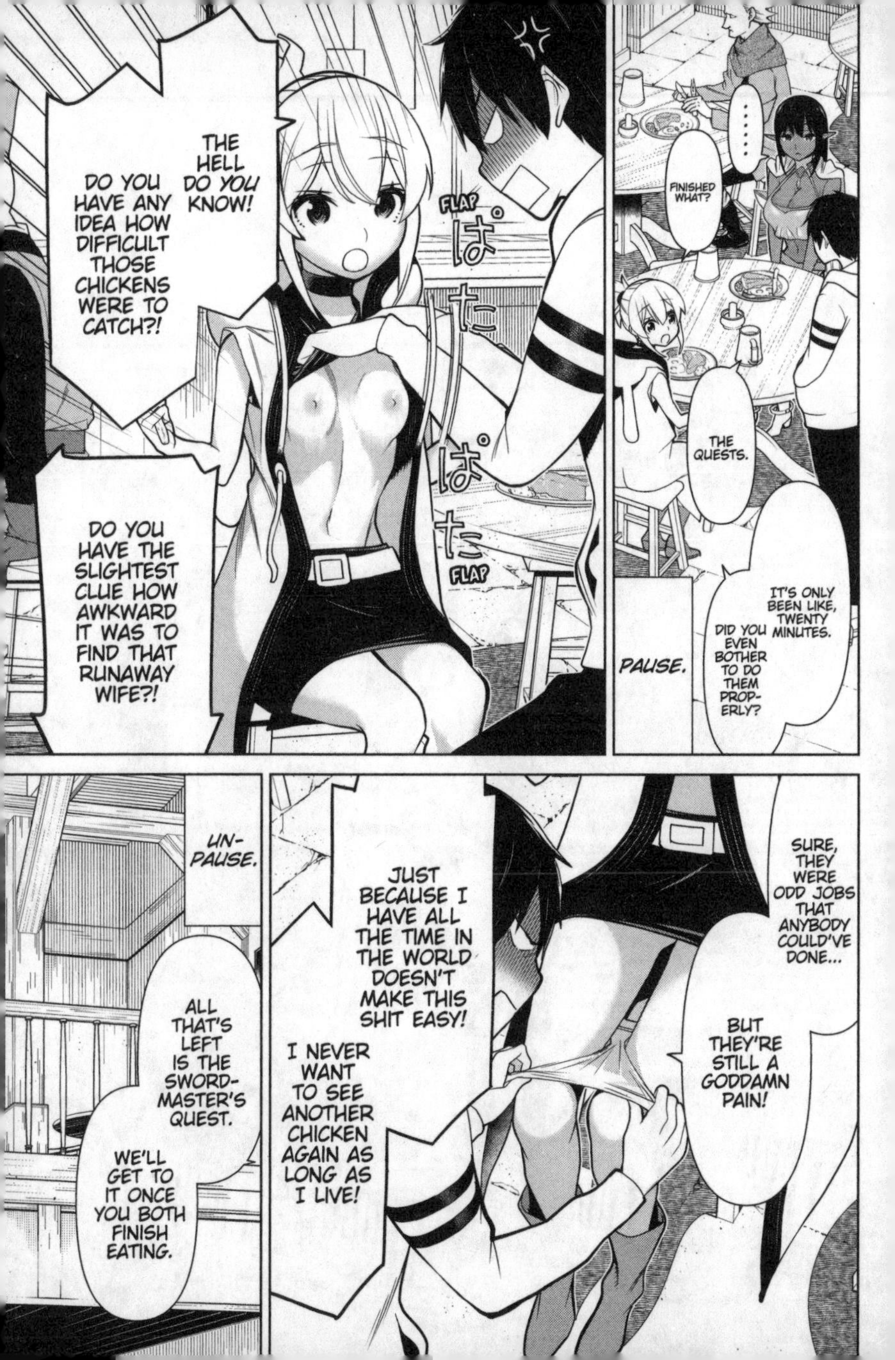
......
FINISHED WHAT?
THE QUESTS.
IT'S ONLY BEEN LIKE, TWENTY MINUTES.
DID YOU EVEN BOTHER TO DO THEM PROPERLY?
PAUSE.
FLAP ぱたぱた FLAP
THE HELL DO YOU KNOW!
DO YOU HAVE ANY IDEA HOW DIFFICULT THOSE CHICKENS WERE TO CATCH?!
DO YOU HAVE THE SLIGHTEST CLUE HOW AWKWARD IT WAS TO FIND THAT RUNAWAY WIFE?!
SURE, THEY WERE ODD JOBS THAT ANYBODY COULD'VE DONE...
BUT THEY'RE STILL A GODDAMN PAIN!
JUST BECAUSE I HAVE ALL THE TIME IN THE WORLD DOESN'T MAKE THIS SHIT EASY!
I NEVER WANT TO SEE ANOTHER CHICKEN AGAIN AS LONG AS I LIVE!
UN-PAUSE.
ALL THAT'S LEFT IS THE SWORD-MASTER'S QUEST.
WE'LL GET TO IT ONCE YOU BOTH FINISH EATING.

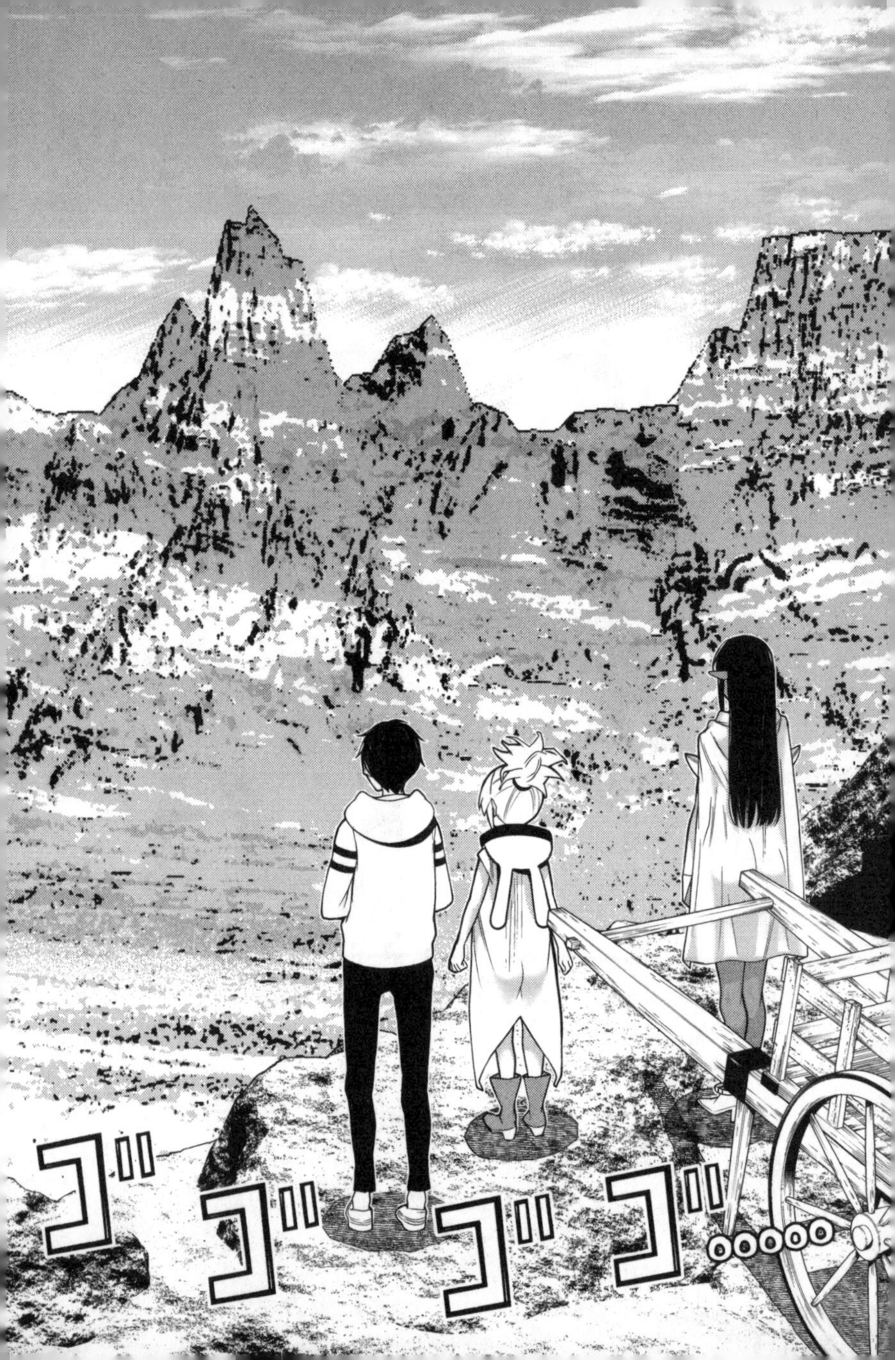
ゴゴゴゴ

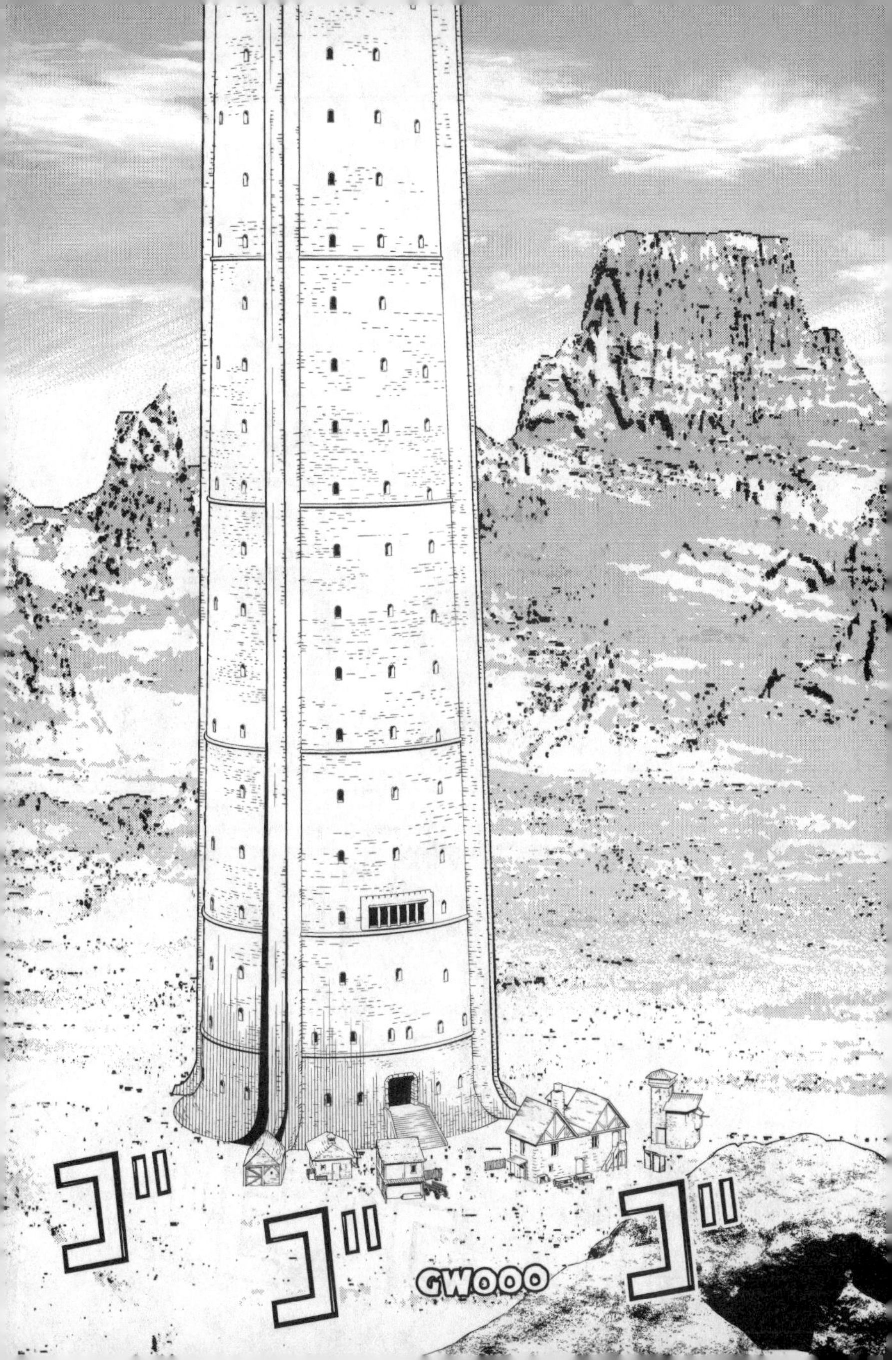
ゴ
ゴ
ゴ
GWOOO

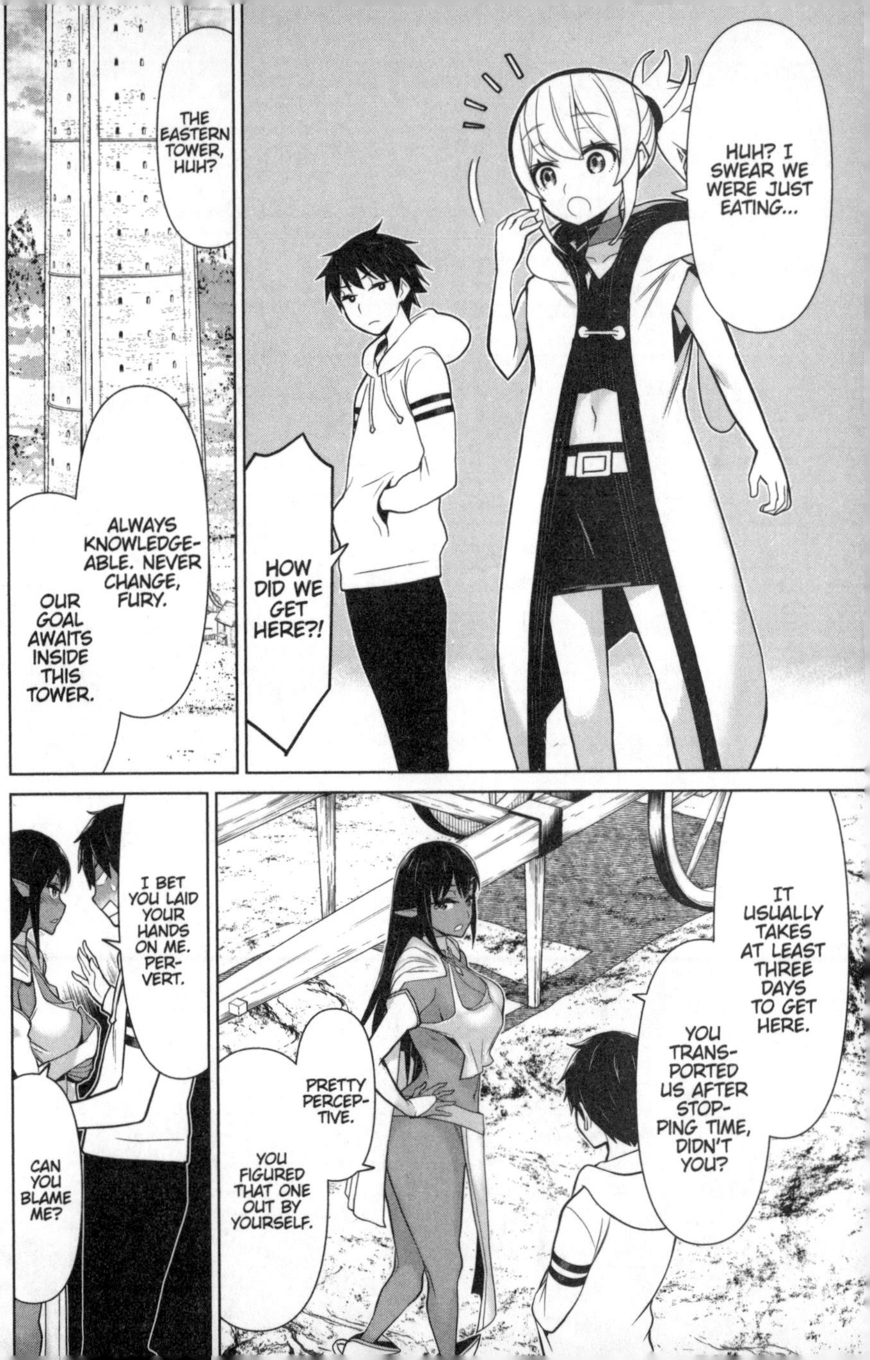
HUH? I SWEAR WE WERE JUST EATING...
HOW DID WE GET HERE?!
THE EASTERN TOWER, HUH?
ALWAYS KNOWLEDGE-ABLE. NEVER CHANGE, FURY.
OUR GOAL AWAITS INSIDE THIS TOWER.
IT USUALLY TAKES AT LEAST THREE DAYS TO GET HERE.
YOU TRANS-PORTED US AFTER STOP-PING TIME, DIDN'T YOU?
PRETTY PERCEP-TIVE.
YOU FIGURED THAT ONE OUT BY YOURSELF.
I BET YOU LAID YOUR HANDS ON ME. PER-VERT.
CAN YOU BLAME ME?

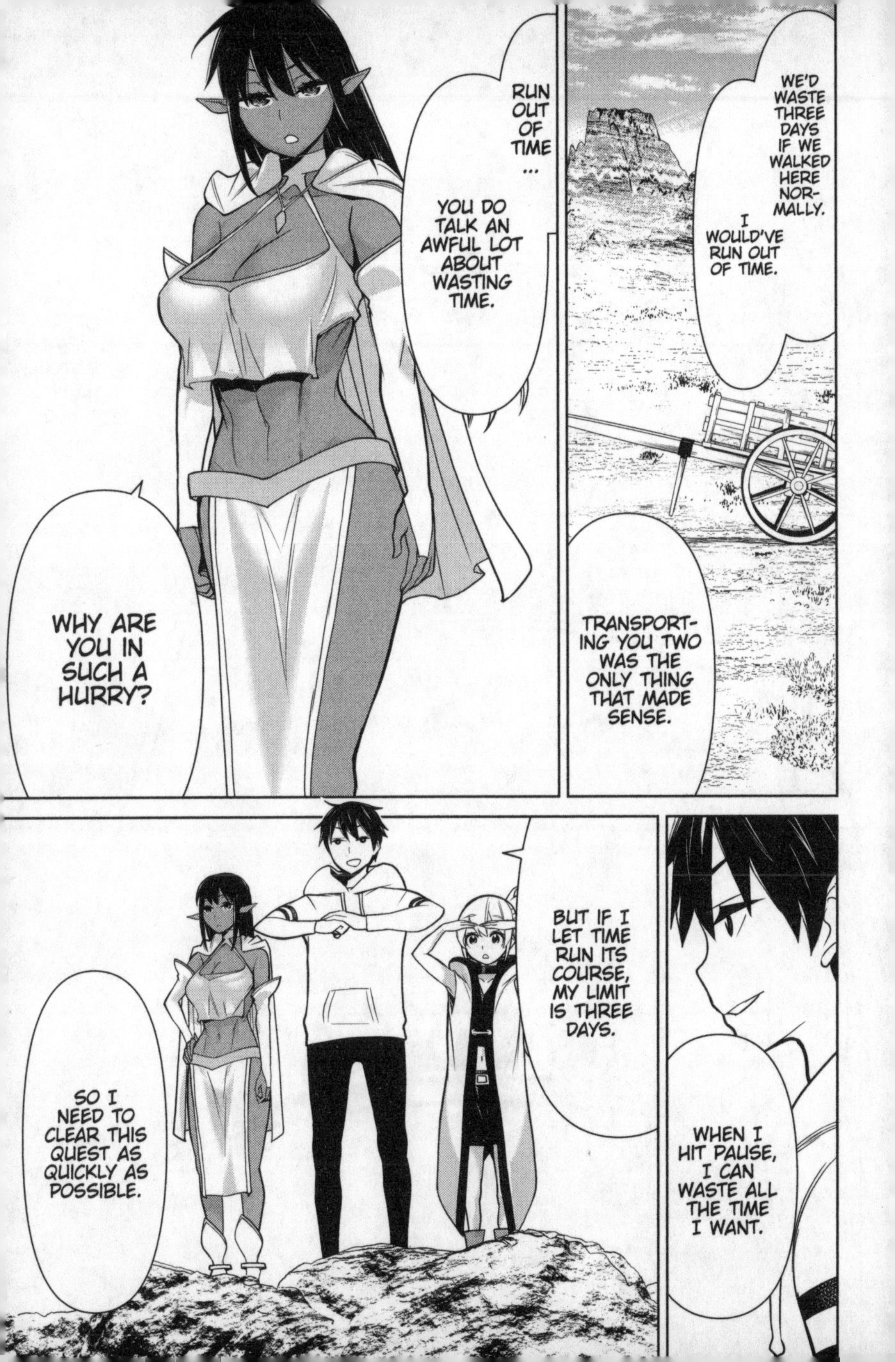
WE'D WASTE THREE DAYS IF WE WALKED HERE NORMALLY.
I WOULD'VE RUN OUT OF TIME.
TRANSPORTING YOU TWO WAS THE ONLY THING THAT MADE SENSE.
RUN OUT OF TIME...
YOU DO TALK AN AWFUL LOT ABOUT WASTING TIME.
WHY ARE YOU IN SUCH A HURRY?
WHEN I HIT PAUSE, I CAN WASTE ALL THE TIME I WANT.
BUT IF I LET TIME RUN ITS COURSE, MY LIMIT IS THREE DAYS.
SO I NEED TO CLEAR THIS QUEST AS QUICKLY AS POSSIBLE.

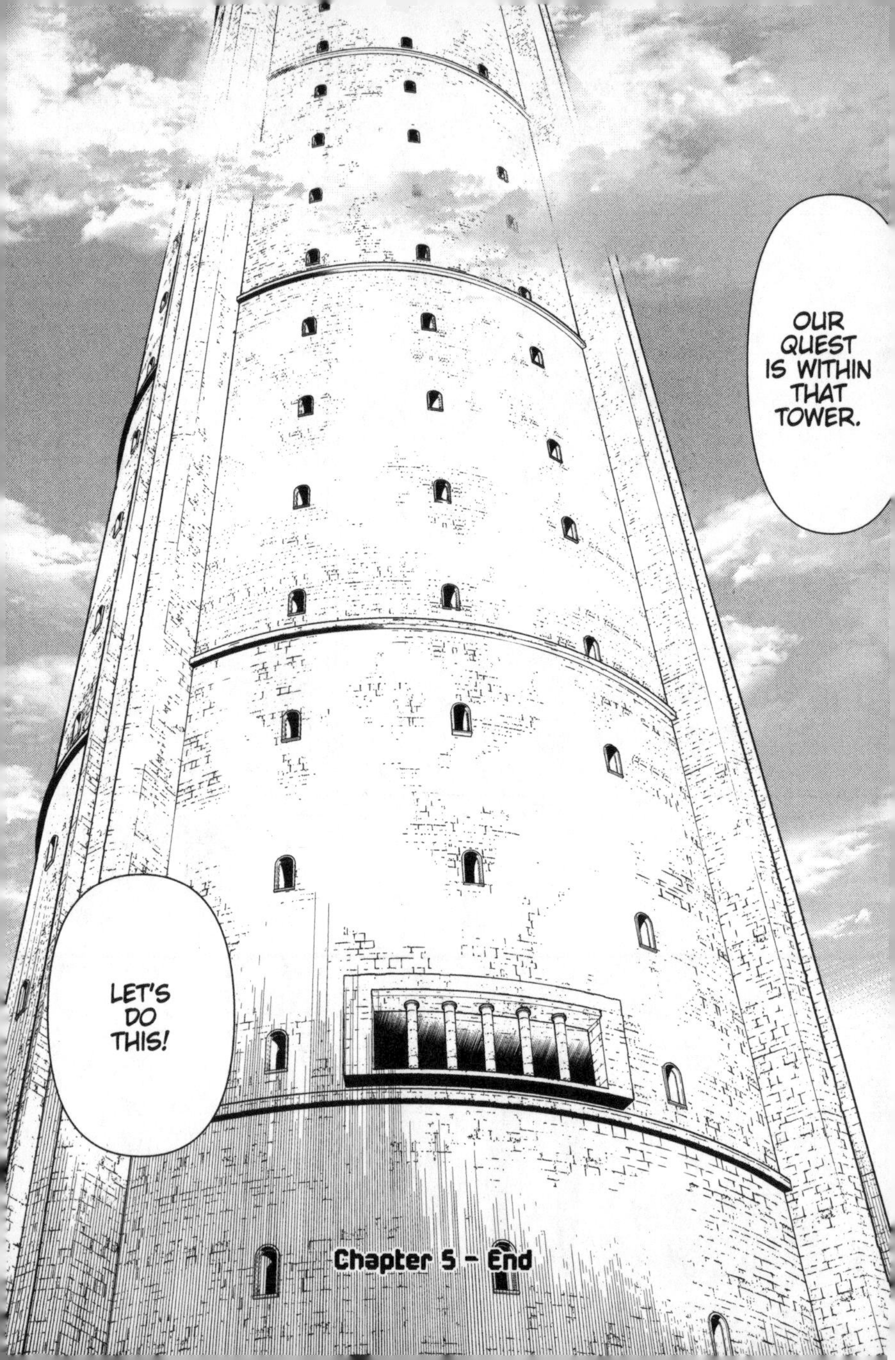
OUR QUEST IS WITHIN THAT TOWER.
LET'S DO THIS!
Chapter 5 - End

2 3 4 5 6 7 8

START
▶ PAUSE

▶ START
PAUSE

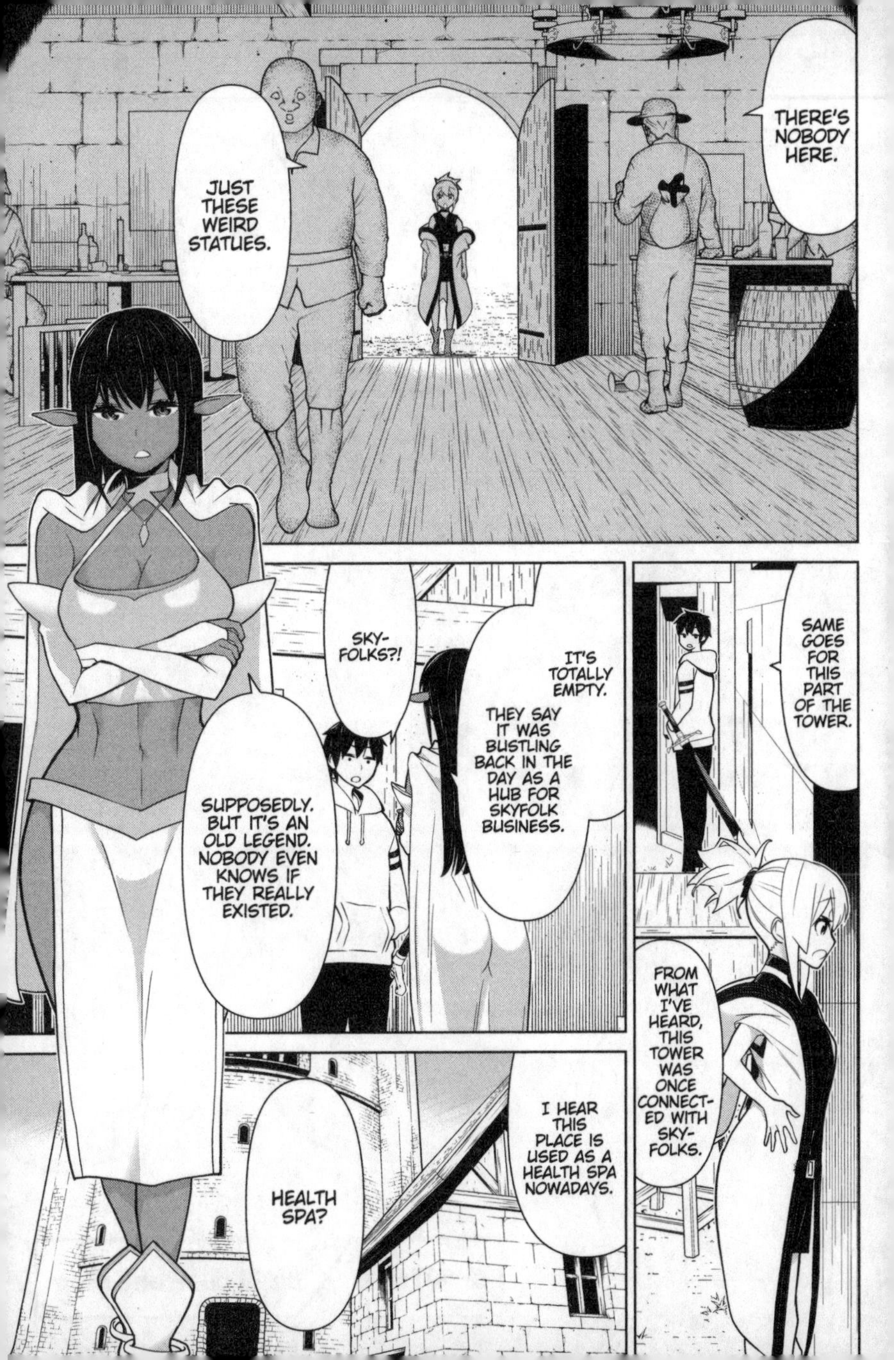

THERE'S NOBODY HERE.
JUST THESE WEIRD STATUES.
SAME GOES FOR THIS PART OF THE TOWER.
FROM WHAT I'VE HEARD, THIS TOWER WAS ONCE CONNECT-ED WITH SKY-FOLKS.
IT'S TOTALLY EMPTY.
THEY SAY IT WAS BUSTLING BACK IN THE DAY AS A HUB FOR SKYFOLK BUSINESS.
SKY-FOLKS?!
SUPPOSEDLY. BUT IT'S AN OLD LEGEND. NOBODY EVEN KNOWS IF THEY REALLY EXISTED.
I HEAR THIS PLACE IS USED AS A HEALTH SPA NOWADAYS.
HEALTH SPA?

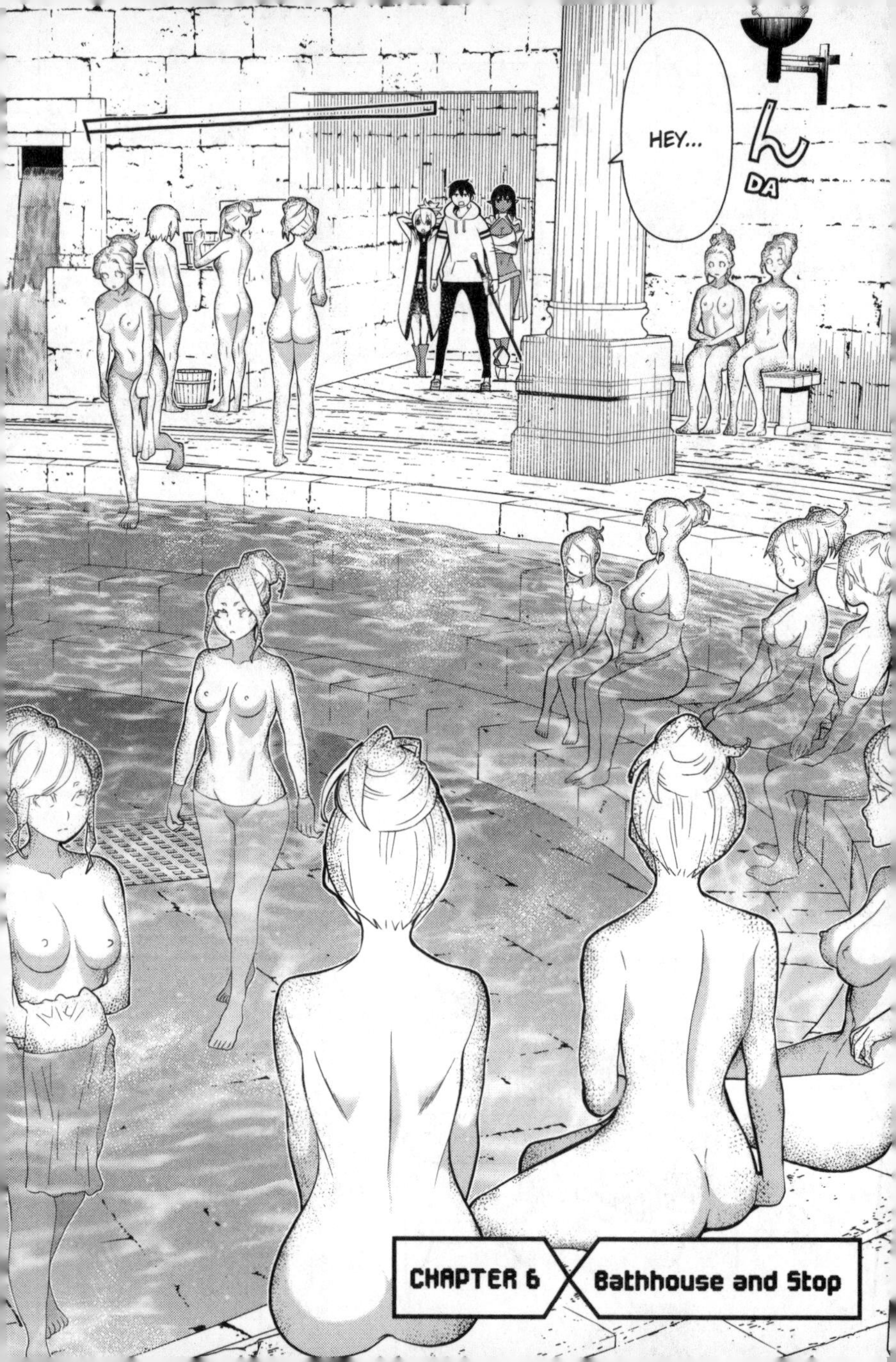
DA
HEY...
CHAPTER 6
Bathhouse and Stop

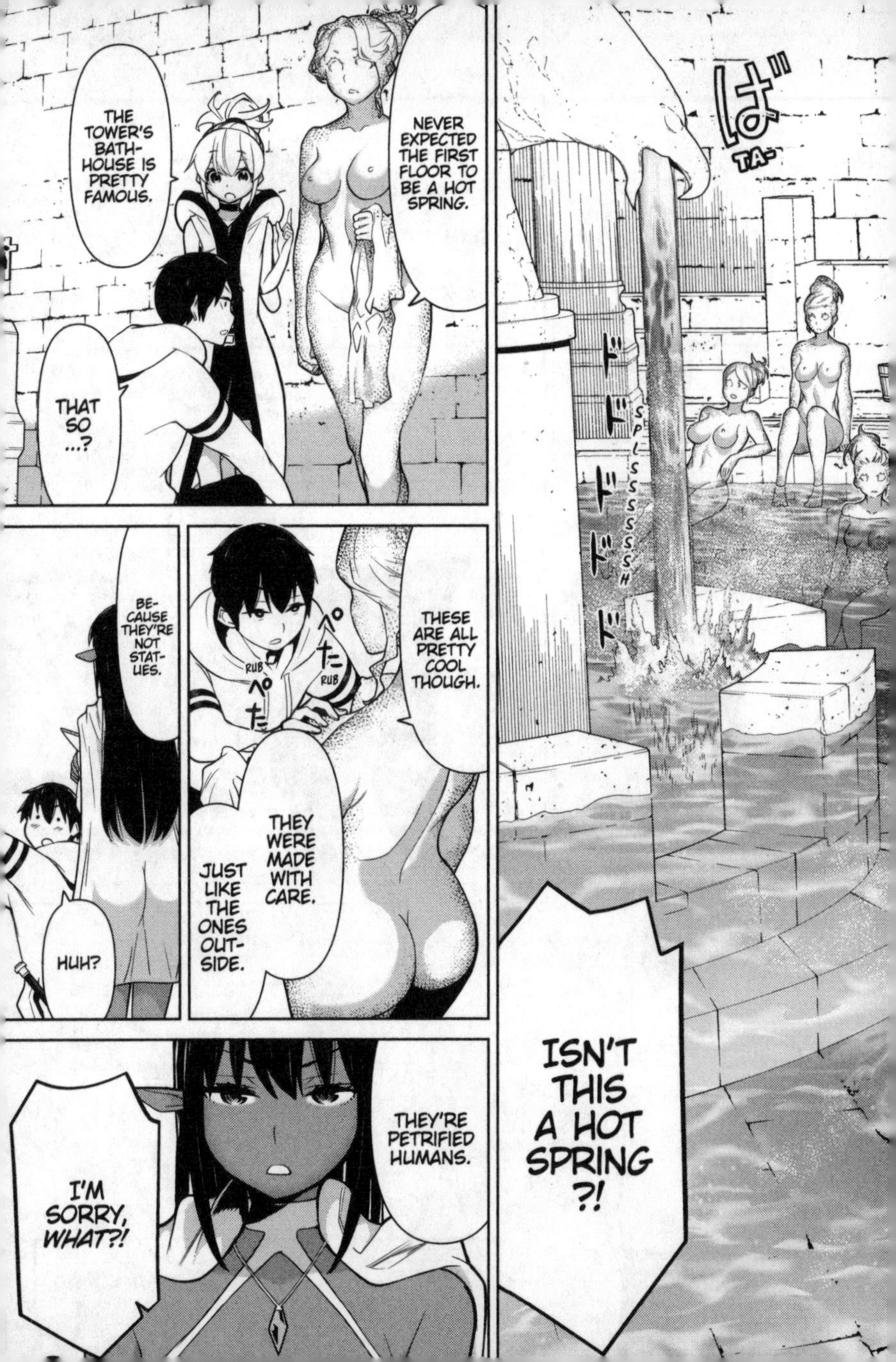
ば
TA-
ドドドドド
SPLSSSSSSSSH
ISN'T THIS A HOT SPRING ?!
NEVER EXPECTED THE FIRST FLOOR TO BE A HOT SPRING.
THE TOWER'S BATH-HOUSE IS PRETTY FAMOUS.
THAT SO ...?
THESE ARE ALL PRETTY COOL THOUGH.
ぺた
RUB
ぺた
RUB
THEY WERE MADE WITH CARE.
JUST LIKE THE ONES OUT-SIDE.
BE-CAUSE THEY'RE NOT STAT-UES.
HUH?
THEY'RE PETRIFIED HUMANS.
I'M SORRY, WHAT?!

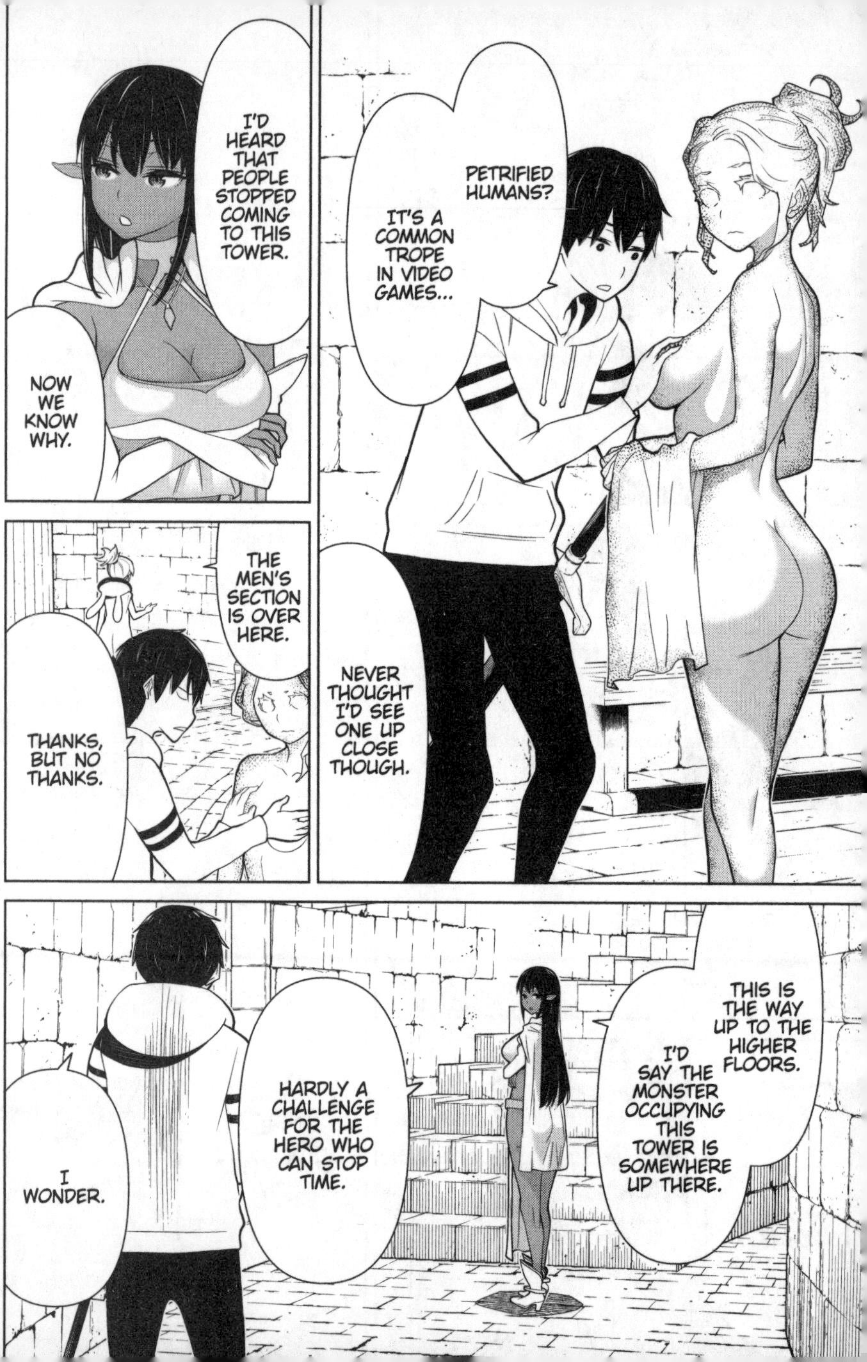

PETRIFIED HUMANS? IT'S A COMMON TROPE IN VIDEO GAMES...
NEVER THOUGHT I'D SEE ONE UP CLOSE THOUGH.
I'D HEARD THAT PEOPLE STOPPED COMING TO THIS TOWER.
NOW WE KNOW WHY.
THE MEN'S SECTION IS OVER HERE.
THANKS, BUT NO THANKS.
THIS IS THE WAY UP TO THE HIGHER FLOORS. I'D SAY THE MONSTER OCCUPYING THIS TOWER IS SOMEWHERE UP THERE.
HARDLY A CHALLENGE FOR THE HERO WHO CAN STOP TIME.
I WONDER.

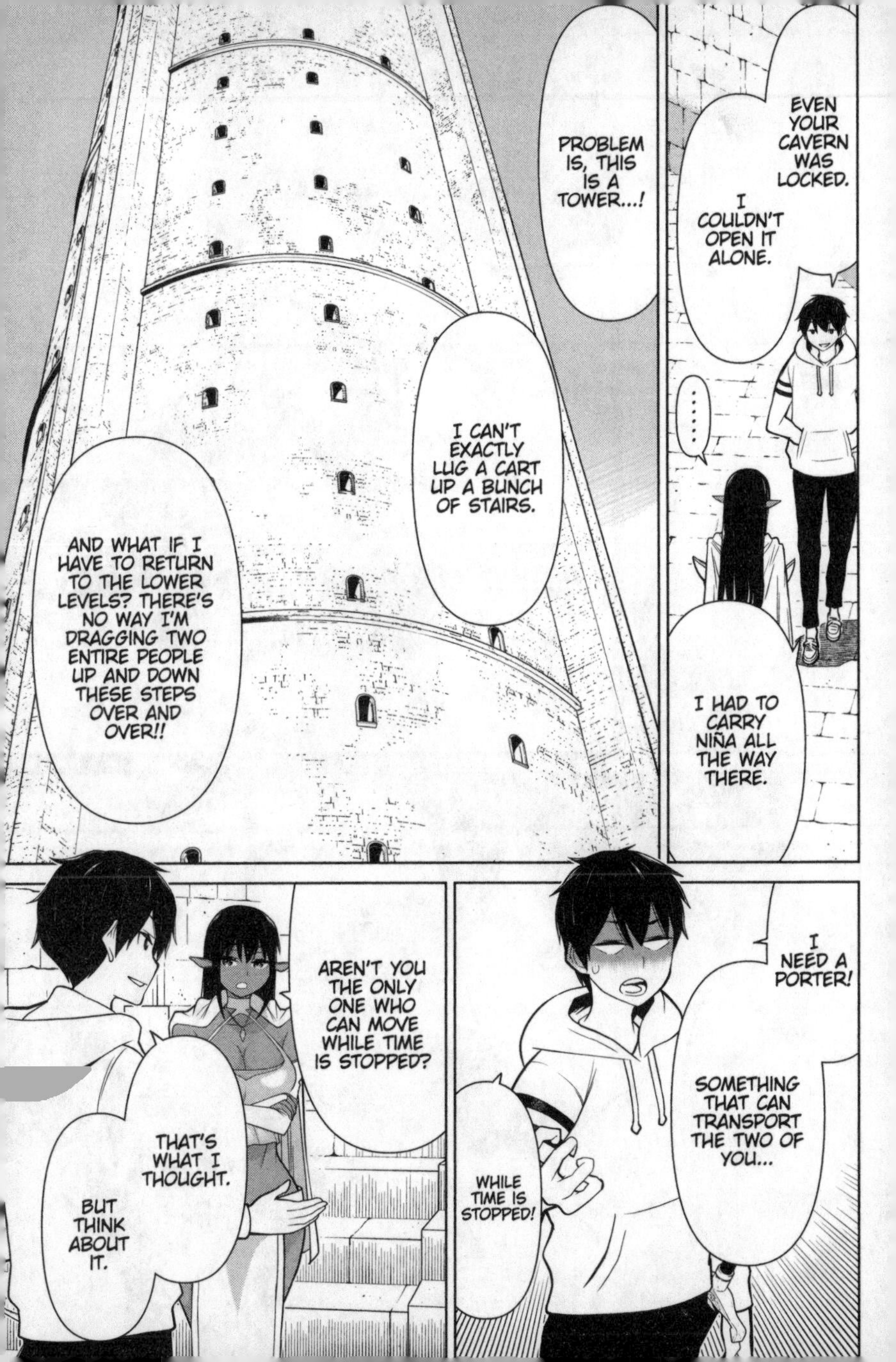

EVEN YOUR CAVERN WAS LOCKED.
I COULDN'T OPEN IT ALONE.
......
I HAD TO CARRY NIÑA ALL THE WAY THERE.
PROBLEM IS, THIS IS A TOWER...!
I CAN'T EXACTLY LUG A CART UP A BUNCH OF STAIRS.
AND WHAT IF I HAVE TO RETURN TO THE LOWER LEVELS? THERE'S NO WAY I'M DRAGGING TWO ENTIRE PEOPLE UP AND DOWN THESE STEPS OVER AND OVER!!
I NEED A PORTER!
SOMETHING THAT CAN TRANSPORT THE TWO OF YOU...
WHILE TIME IS STOPPED!
AREN'T YOU THE ONLY ONE WHO CAN MOVE WHILE TIME IS STOPPED?
THAT'S WHAT I THOUGHT.
BUT THINK ABOUT IT.

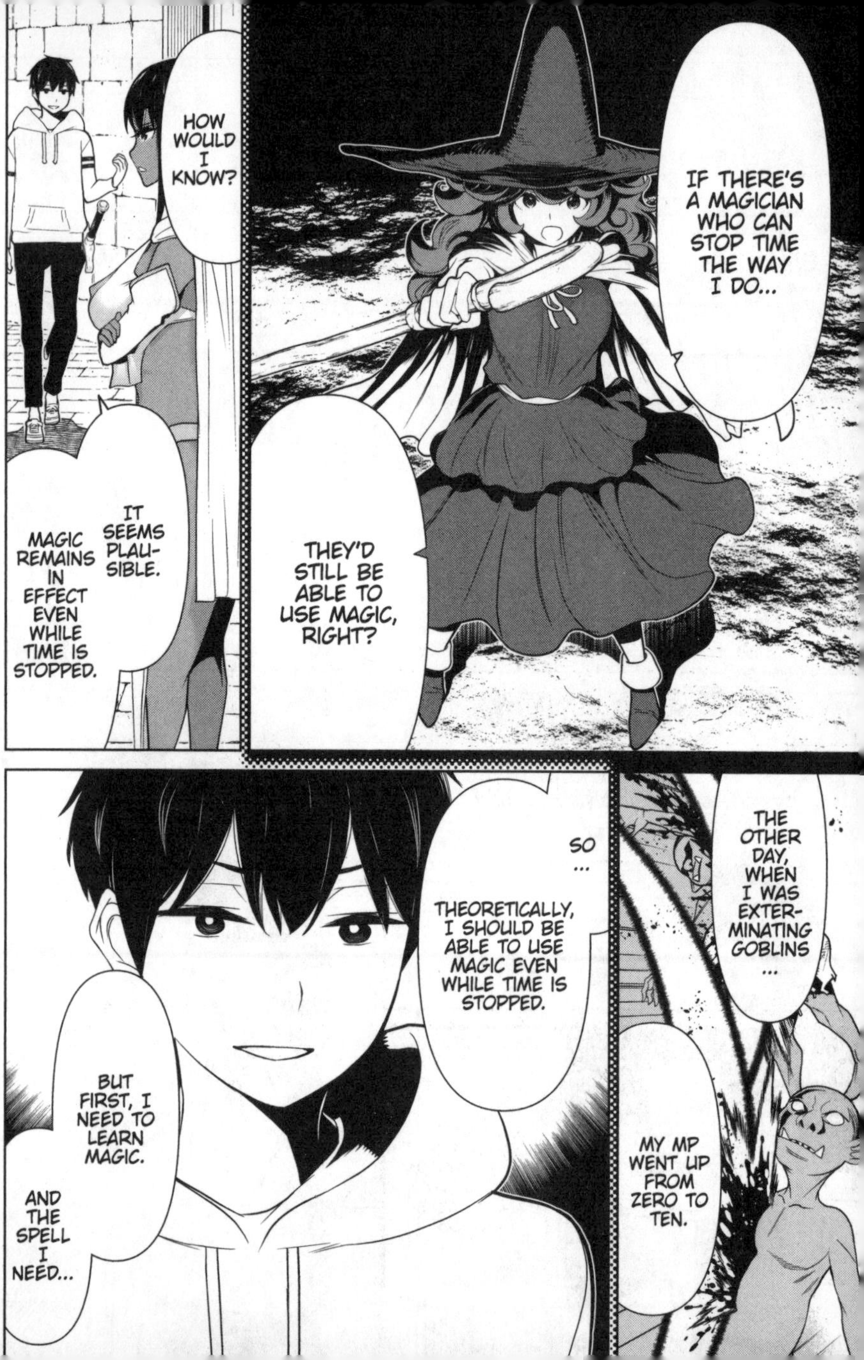
IF THERE'S A MAGICIAN WHO CAN STOP TIME THE WAY I DO...
THEY'D STILL BE ABLE TO USE MAGIC, RIGHT?
HOW WOULD I KNOW?
IT SEEMS PLAUSIBLE.
MAGIC REMAINS IN EFFECT EVEN WHILE TIME IS STOPPED.
THE OTHER DAY, WHEN I WAS EXTERMINATING GOBLINS...
MY MP WENT UP FROM ZERO TO TEN.
SO...
THEORETICALLY, I SHOULD BE ABLE TO USE MAGIC EVEN WHILE TIME IS STOPPED.
BUT FIRST, I NEED TO LEARN MAGIC.
AND THE SPELL I NEED...

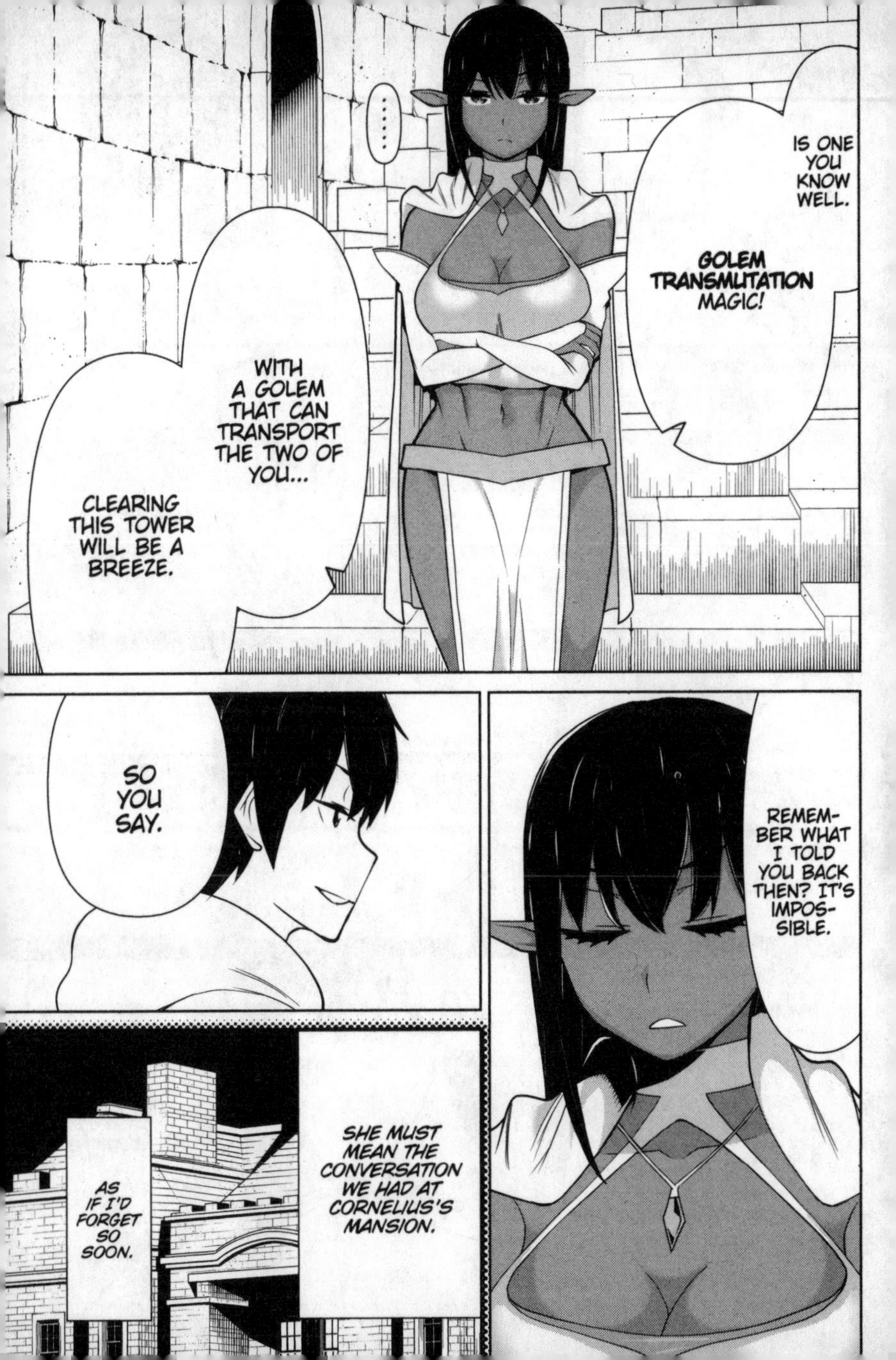
IS ONE YOU KNOW WELL.
GOLEM TRANSMUTATION MAGIC!
......
WITH A GOLEM THAT CAN TRANSPORT THE TWO OF YOU...
CLEARING THIS TOWER WILL BE A BREEZE.
REMEMBER WHAT I TOLD YOU BACK THEN? IT'S IMPOSSIBLE.
SO YOU SAY.
SHE MUST MEAN THE CONVERSATION WE HAD AT CORNELIUS'S MANSION.
AS IF I'D FORGET SO SOON.

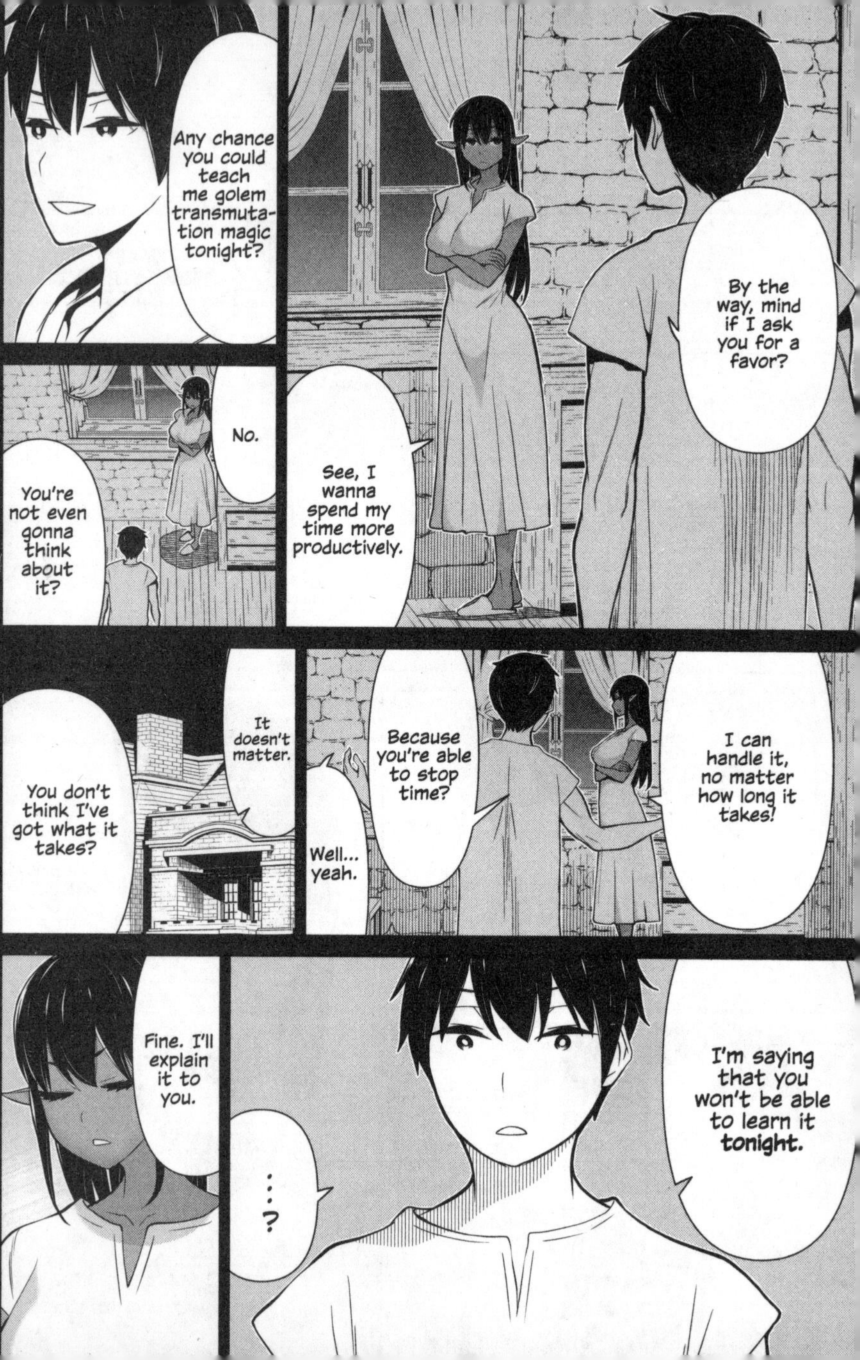

By the way, mind if I ask you for a favor?
See, I wanna spend my time more productively.
Any chance you could teach me golem transmutation magic tonight?
No.
You're not even gonna think about it?
I can handle it, no matter how long it takes!
Because you're able to stop time?
Well... yeah.
It doesn't matter.
You don't think I've got what it takes?
I'm saying that you won't be able to learn it **tonight.**
...?
Fine. I'll explain it to you.

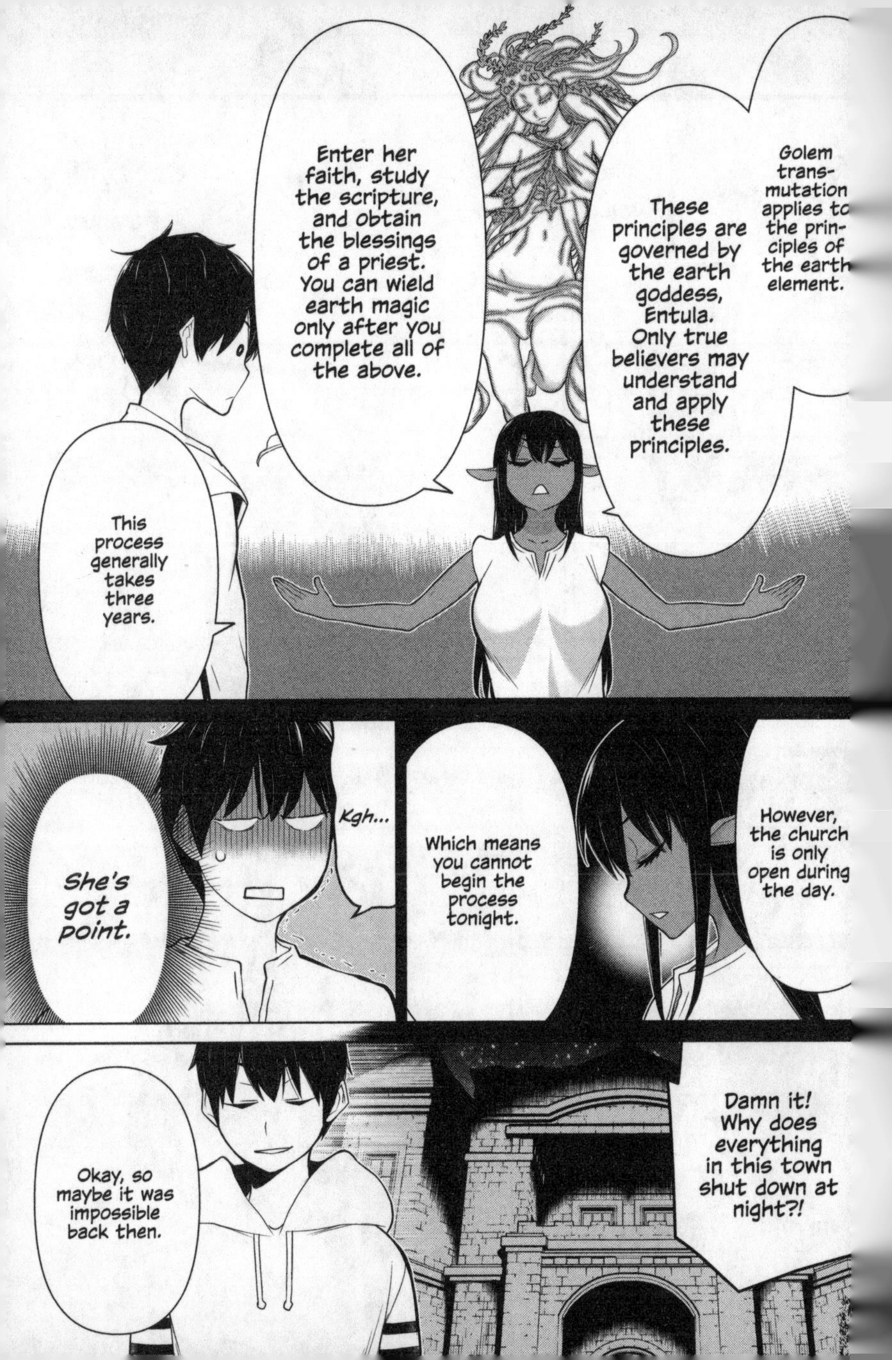
Golem transmutation applies to the principles of the earth element.
These principles are governed by the earth goddess, Entula. Only true believers may understand and apply these principles.
Enter her faith, study the scripture, and obtain the blessings of a priest. You can wield earth magic only after you complete all of the above.
This process generally takes three years.
However, the church is only open during the day.
Which means you cannot begin the process tonight.
Kgh...
She's got a point.
Damn it! Why does everything in this town shut down at night?!
Okay, so maybe it was impossible back then.

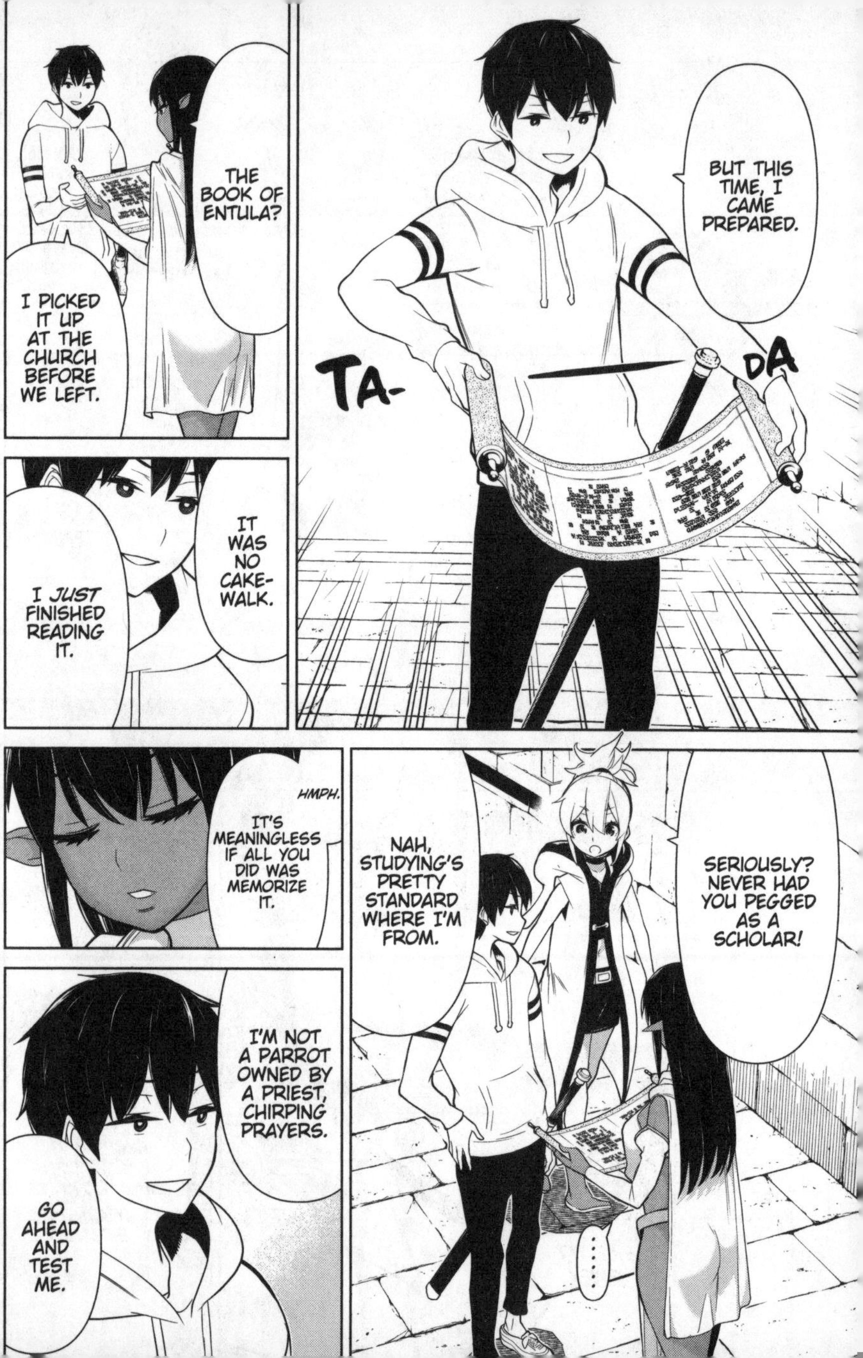
BUT THIS TIME, I CAME PREPARED.
TA-DA
THE BOOK OF ENTULA?
I PICKED IT UP AT THE CHURCH BEFORE WE LEFT.
IT WAS NO CAKE-WALK.
I *JUST* FINISHED READING IT.
SERIOUSLY? NEVER HAD YOU PEGGED AS A SCHOLAR!
NAH, STUDYING'S PRETTY STANDARD WHERE I'M FROM.
......
HMPH.
IT'S MEANINGLESS IF ALL YOU DID WAS MEMORIZE IT.
I'M NOT A PARROT OWNED BY A PRIEST, CHIRPING PRAYERS.
GO AHEAD AND TEST ME.

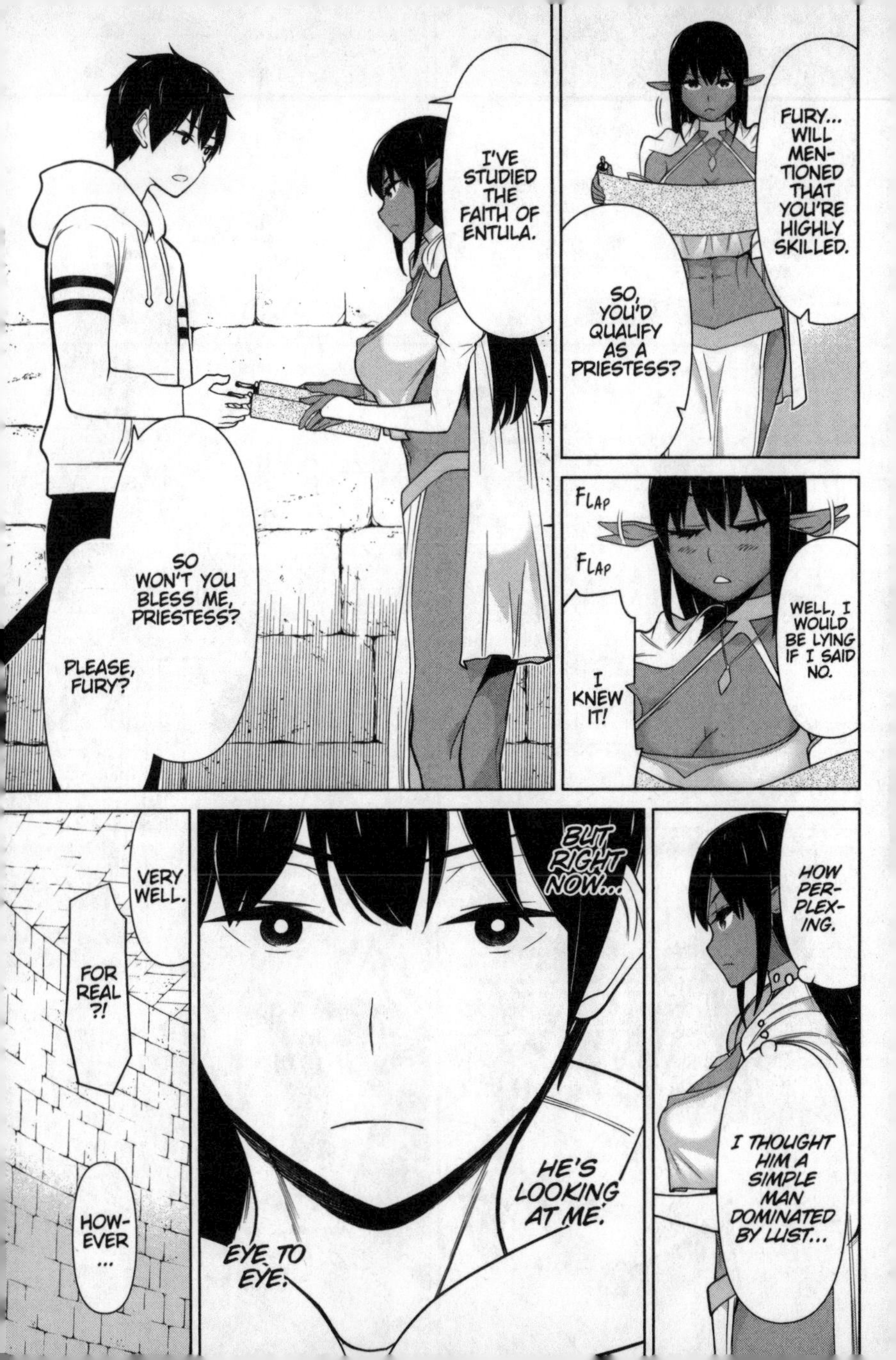
FURY... WILL MENTIONED THAT YOU'RE HIGHLY SKILLED.
SO, YOU'D QUALIFY AS A PRIESTESS?
FLAP
FLAP
WELL, I WOULD BE LYING IF I SAID NO.
I KNEW IT!
I'VE STUDIED THE FAITH OF ENTULA.
SO WON'T YOU BLESS ME, PRIESTESS?
PLEASE, FURY?
HOW PERPLEXING.
I THOUGHT HIM A SIMPLE MAN DOMINATED BY LUST...
BUT RIGHT NOW...
HE'S LOOKING AT ME.
EYE TO EYE.
VERY WELL.
FOR REAL?!
HOWEVER ...

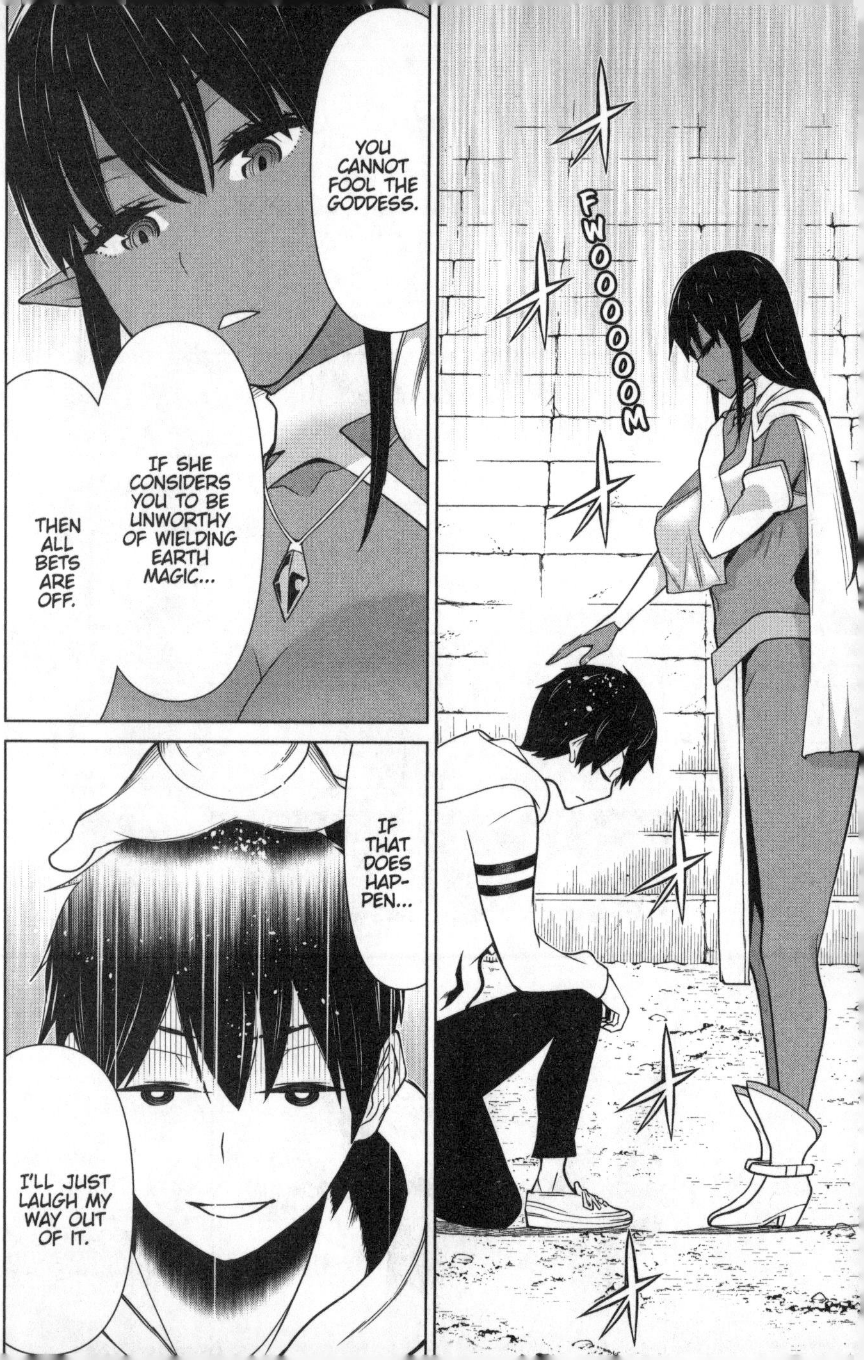
FWOOOOOOM
YOU CANNOT FOOL THE GODDESS.
IF SHE CONSIDERS YOU TO BE UNWORTHY OF WIELDING EARTH MAGIC...
THEN ALL BETS ARE OFF.
IF THAT DOES HAP-PEN...
I'LL JUST LAUGH MY WAY OUT OF IT.

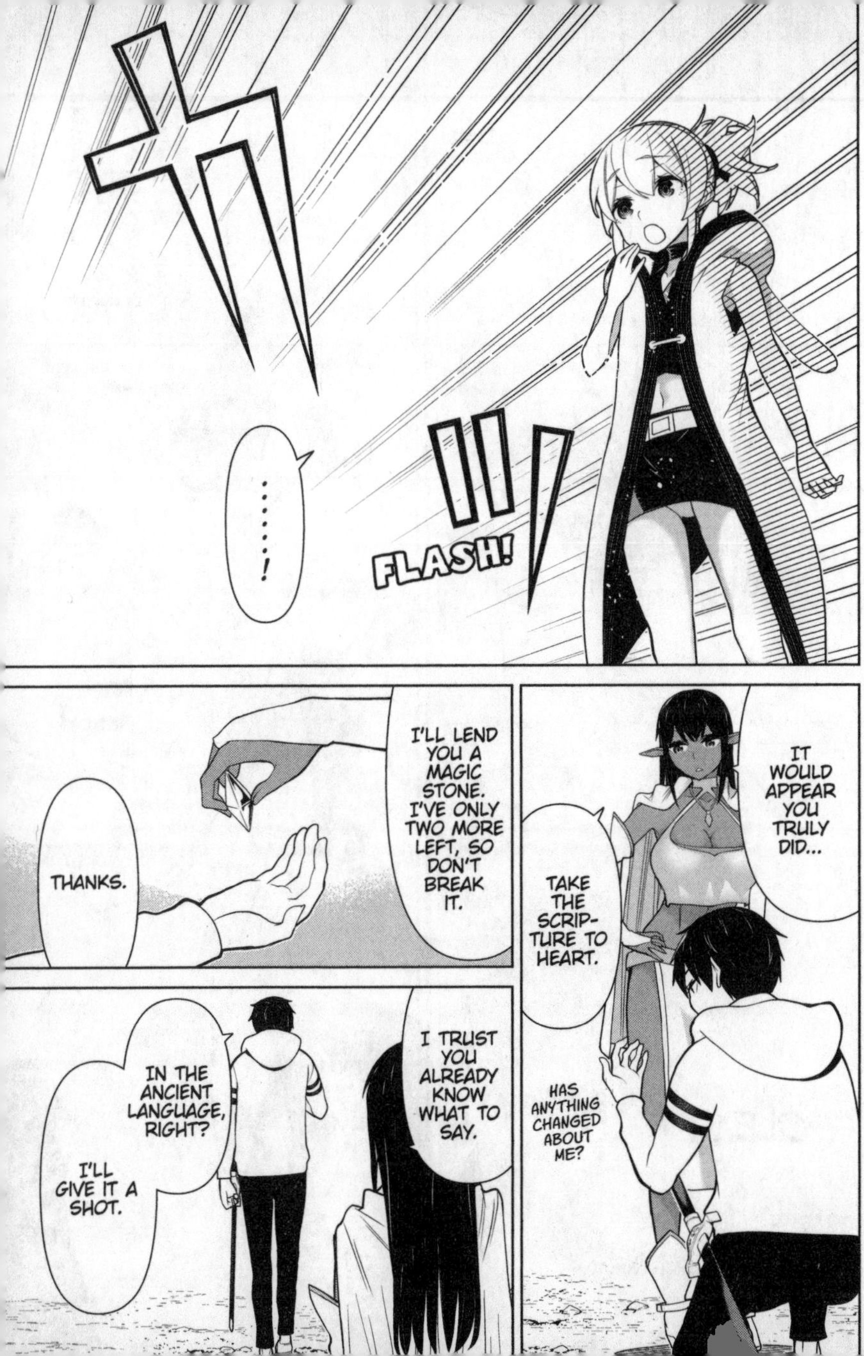
FLASH!
......!
IT WOULD APPEAR YOU TRULY DID...
TAKE THE SCRIPTURE TO HEART.
HAS ANYTHING CHANGED ABOUT ME?
I'LL LEND YOU A MAGIC STONE. I'VE ONLY TWO MORE LEFT, SO DON'T BREAK IT.
THANKS.
I TRUST YOU ALREADY KNOW WHAT TO SAY.
IN THE ANCIENT LANGUAGE, RIGHT?
I'LL GIVE IT A SHOT.

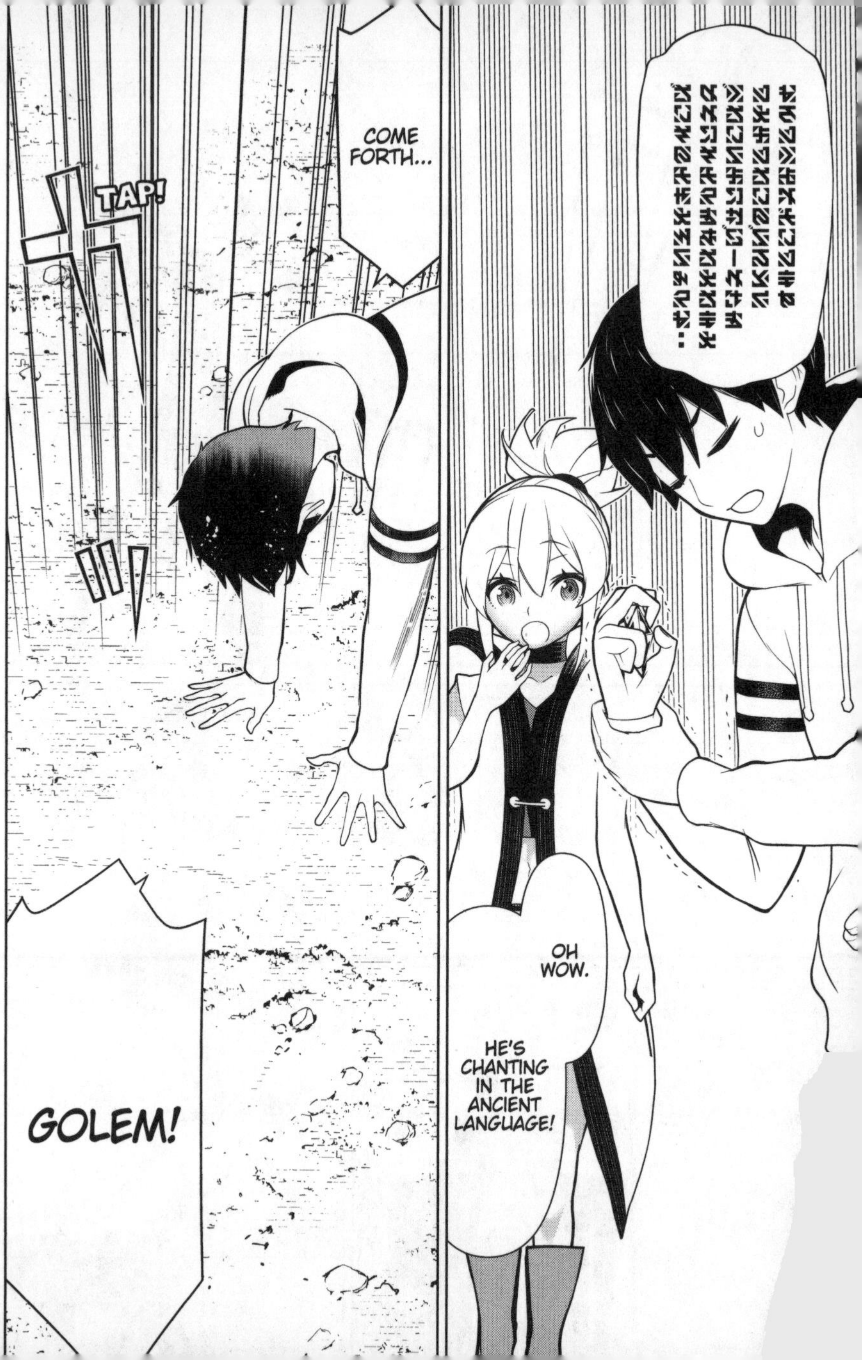
OH WOW.
HE'S CHANTING IN THE ANCIENT LANGUAGE!
COME FORTH...
TAP!
GOLEM!

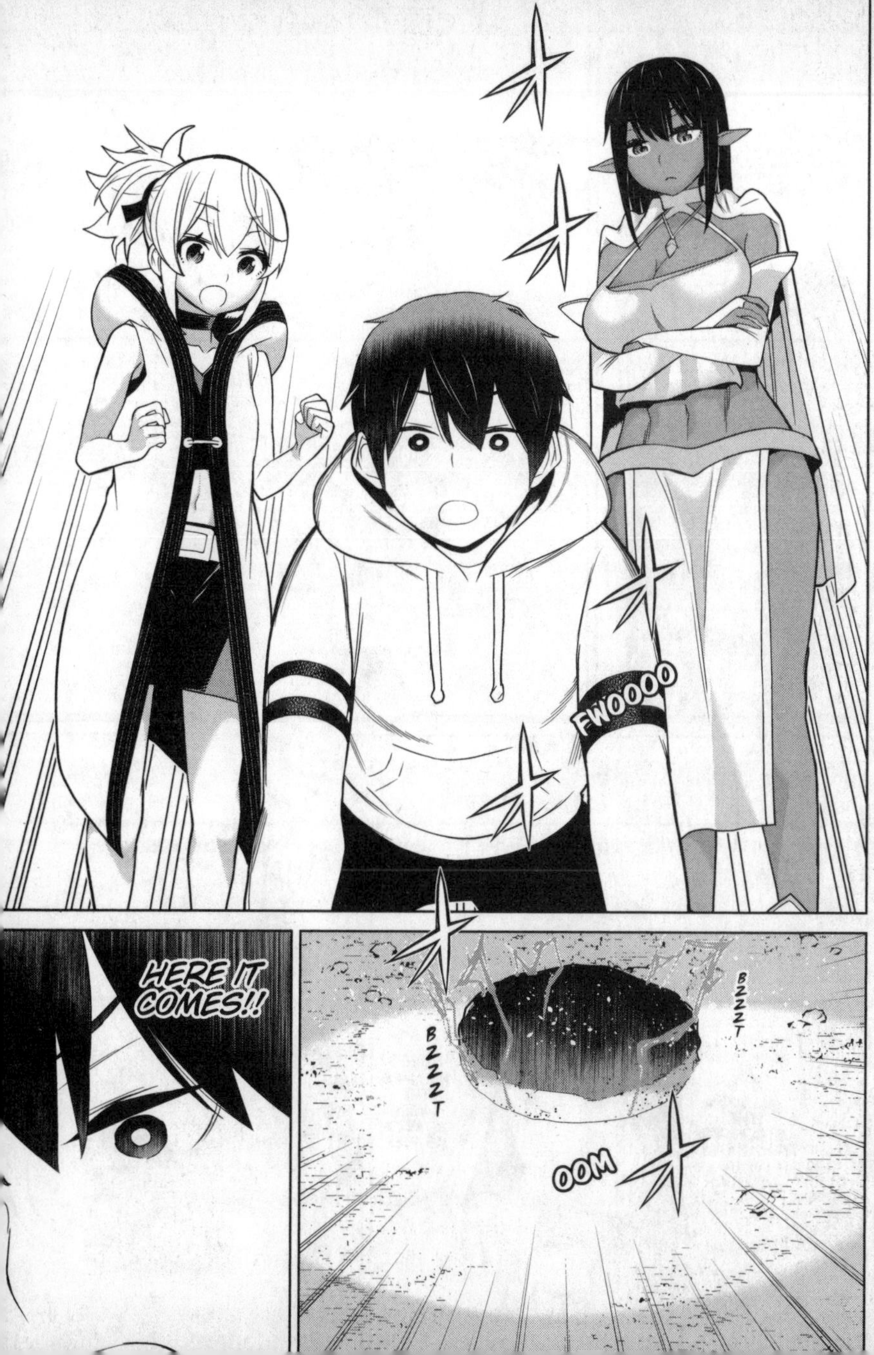
FWOOOO
BZZZT
BZZZT
OOM
HERE IT COMES!!

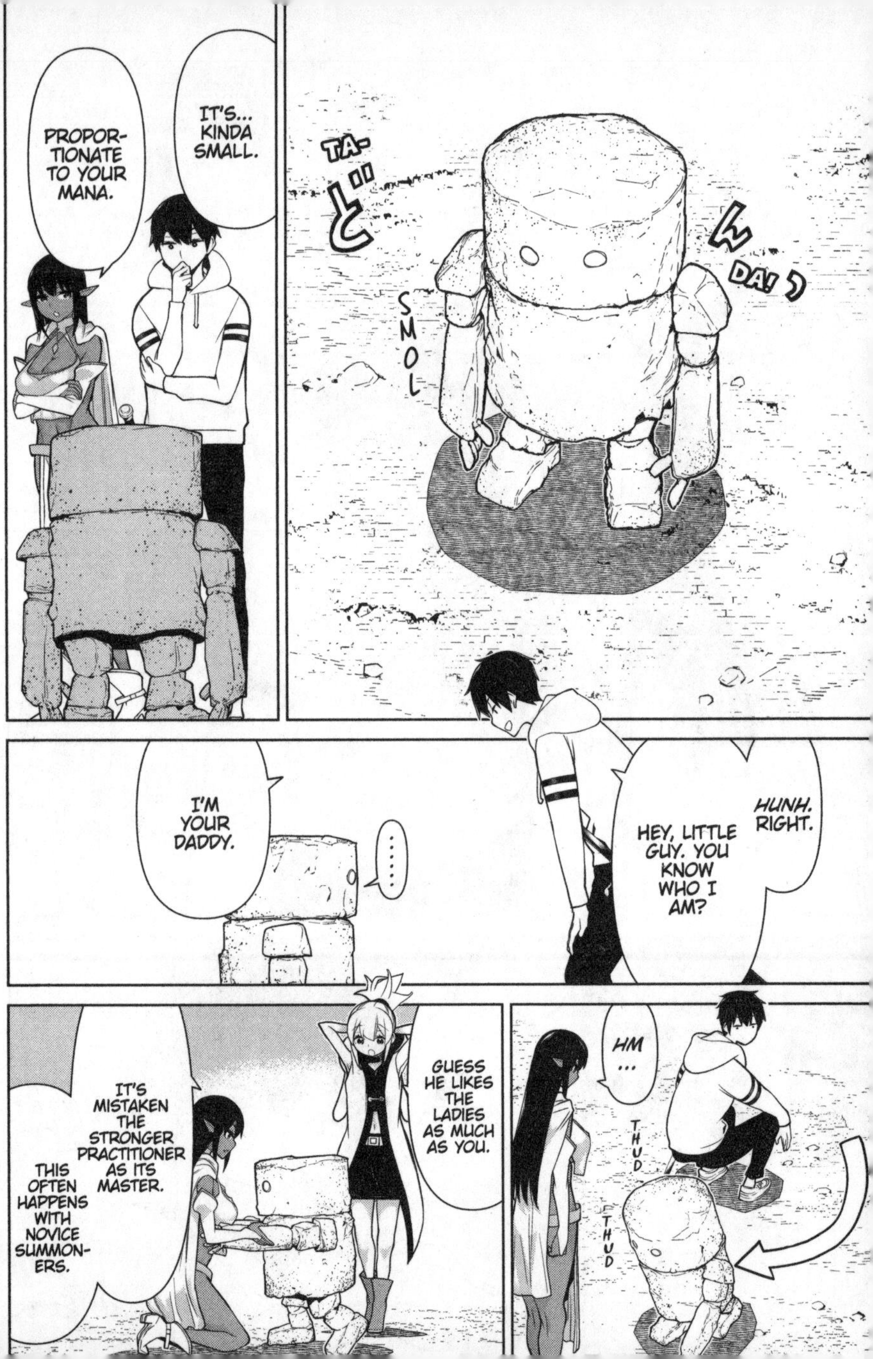
TA-
と
ん
DA!
SMOL
IT'S... KINDA SMALL.
PROPORTIONATE TO YOUR MANA.
HUNH. RIGHT.
HEY, LITTLE GUY. YOU KNOW WHO I AM?
I'M YOUR DADDY.
......
HM ...
THUD
THUD
GUESS HE LIKES THE LADIES AS MUCH AS YOU.
IT'S MISTAKEN THE STRONGER PRACTITIONER AS ITS MASTER.
THIS OFTEN HAPPENS WITH NOVICE SUMMONERS.

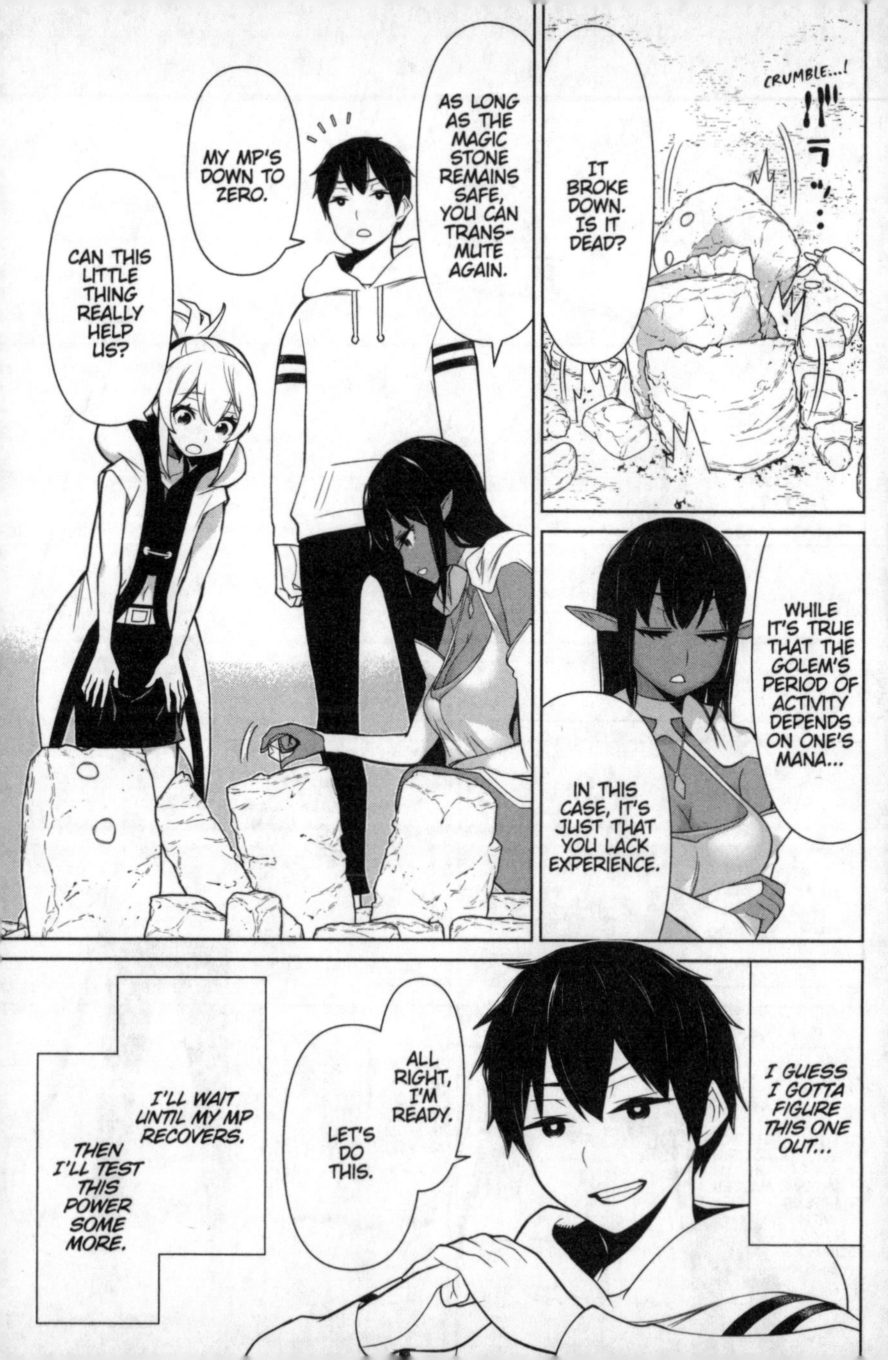
CRUMBLE...!
IT BROKE DOWN. IS IT DEAD?
WHILE IT'S TRUE THAT THE GOLEM'S PERIOD OF ACTIVITY DEPENDS ON ONE'S MANA...
IN THIS CASE, IT'S JUST THAT YOU LACK EXPERIENCE.
AS LONG AS THE MAGIC STONE REMAINS SAFE, YOU CAN TRANSMUTE AGAIN.
MY MP'S DOWN TO ZERO.
CAN THIS LITTLE THING REALLY HELP US?
I GUESS I GOTTA FIGURE THIS ONE OUT...
ALL RIGHT, I'M READY.
LET'S DO THIS.
I'LL WAIT UNTIL MY MP RECOVERS.
THEN I'LL TEST THIS POWER SOME MORE.

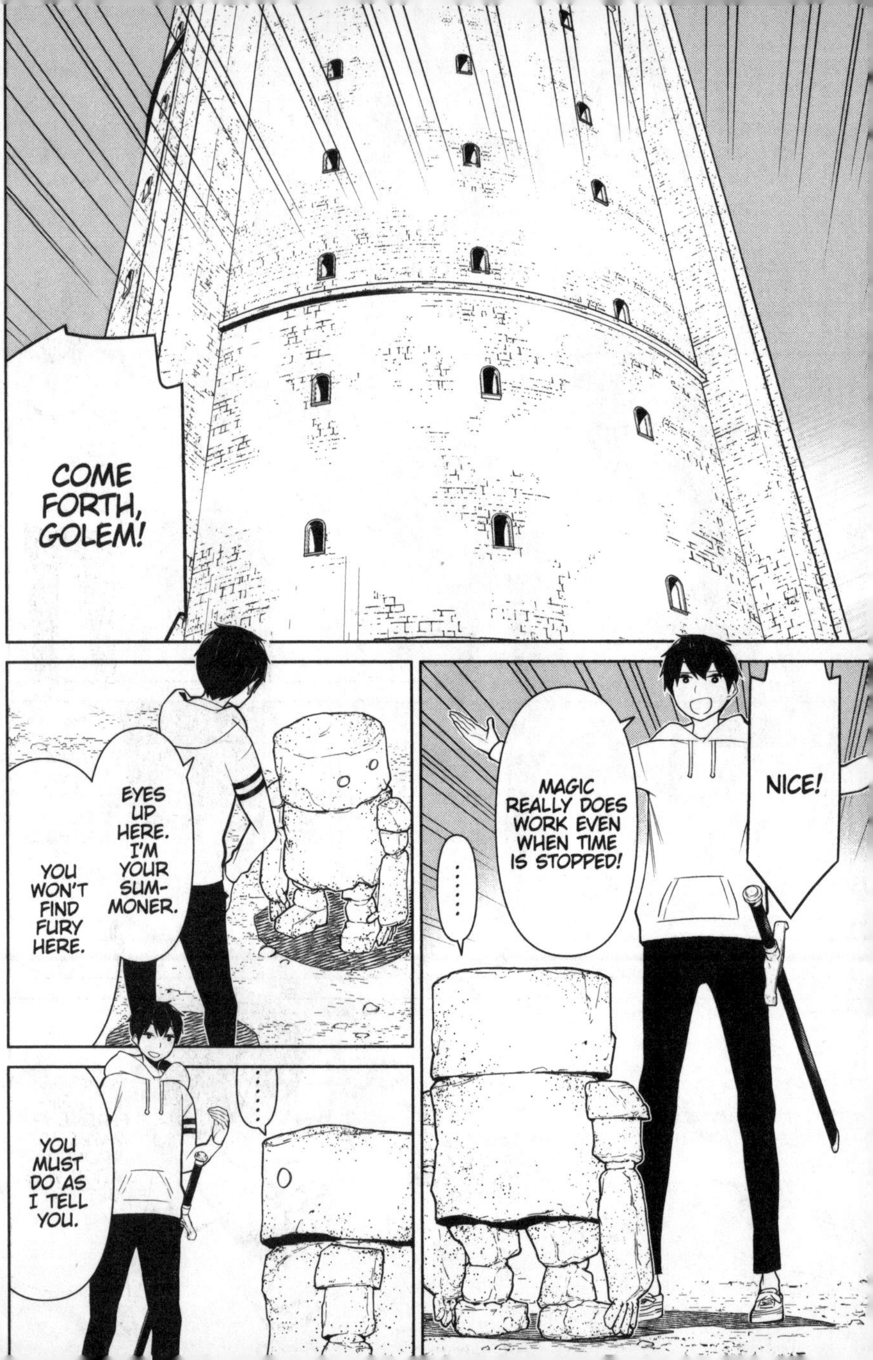
COME FORTH, GOLEM!
NICE!
MAGIC REALLY DOES WORK EVEN WHEN TIME IS STOPPED!
......
EYES UP HERE. I'M YOUR SUMMONER.
YOU WON'T FIND FURY HERE.
......
YOU MUST DO AS I TELL YOU.

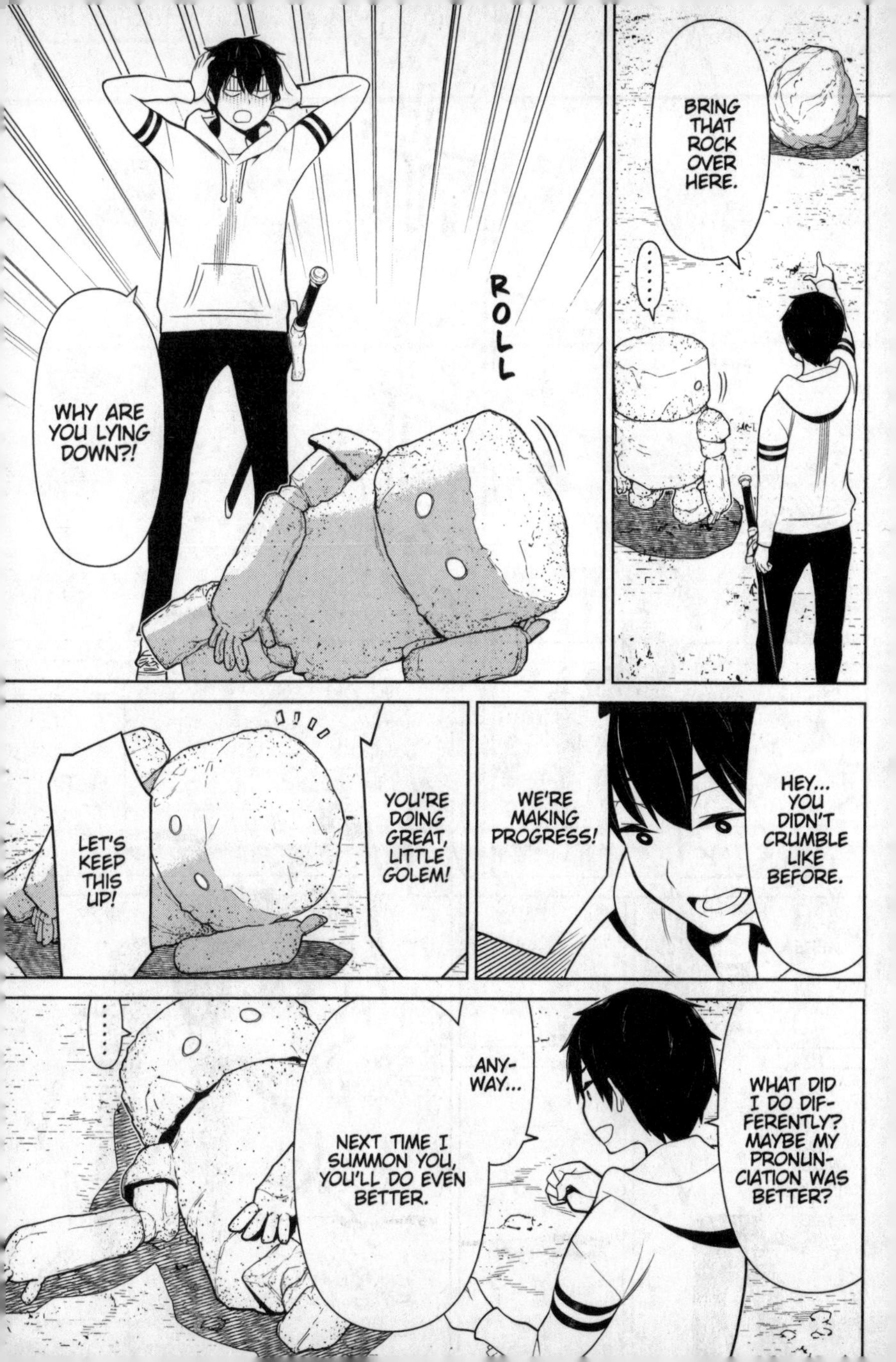

BRING THAT ROCK OVER HERE.
......
ROLL
WHY ARE YOU LYING DOWN?!
HEY... YOU DIDN'T CRUMBLE LIKE BEFORE.
WE'RE MAKING PROGRESS!
YOU'RE DOING GREAT, LITTLE GOLEM!
LET'S KEEP THIS UP!
WHAT DID I DO DIF-FERENTLY? MAYBE MY PRONUN-CIATION WAS BETTER?
ANY-WAY...
NEXT TIME I SUMMON YOU, YOU'LL DO EVEN BETTER.
......

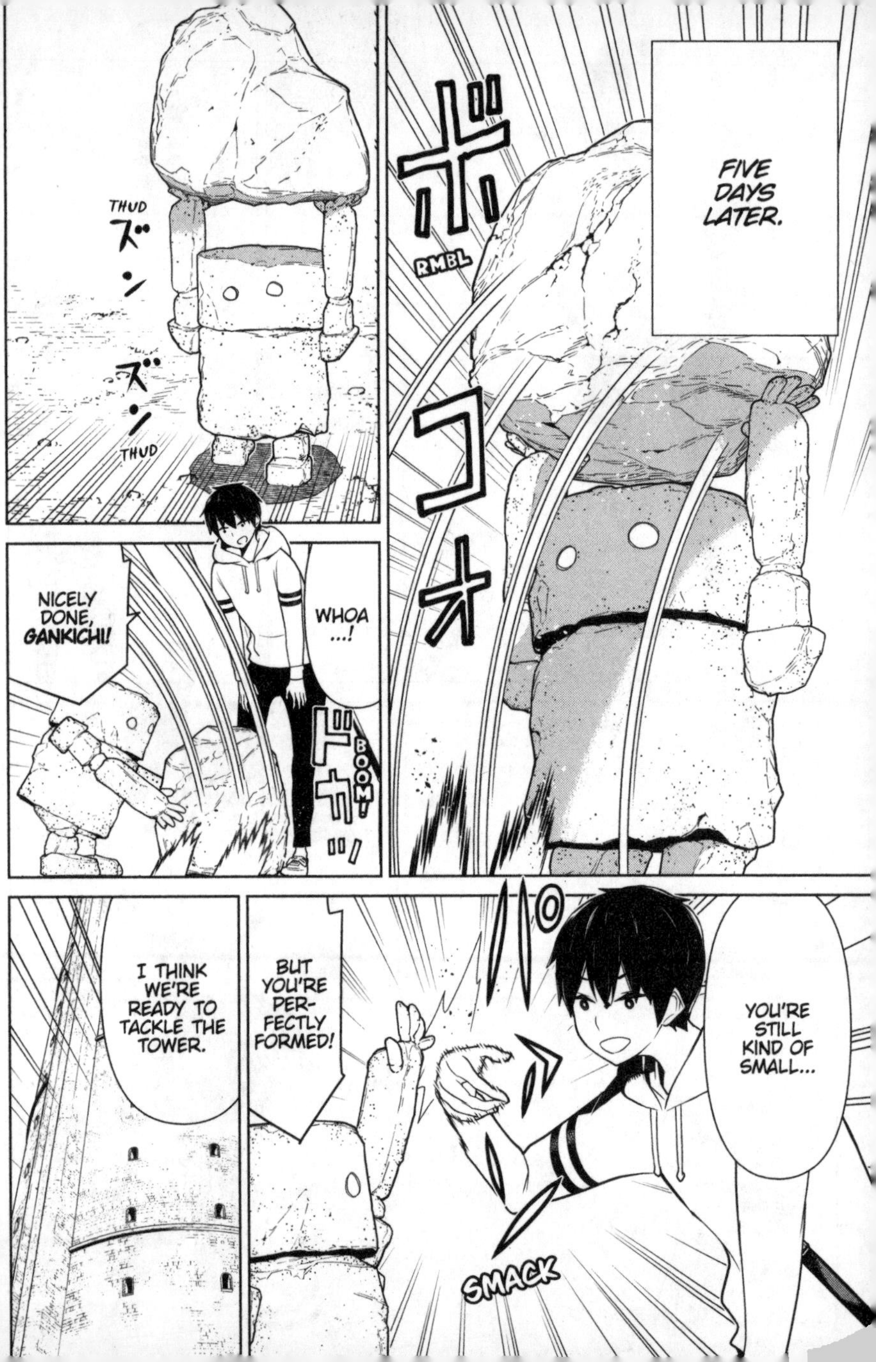
FIVE DAYS LATER.
RMBL
THUD
THUD
WHOA ...!
BOOM!
NICELY DONE, GANKICHI!
YOU'RE STILL KIND OF SMALL...
SMACK
BUT YOU'RE PER-FECTLY FORMED!
I THINK WE'RE READY TO TACKLE THE TOWER.

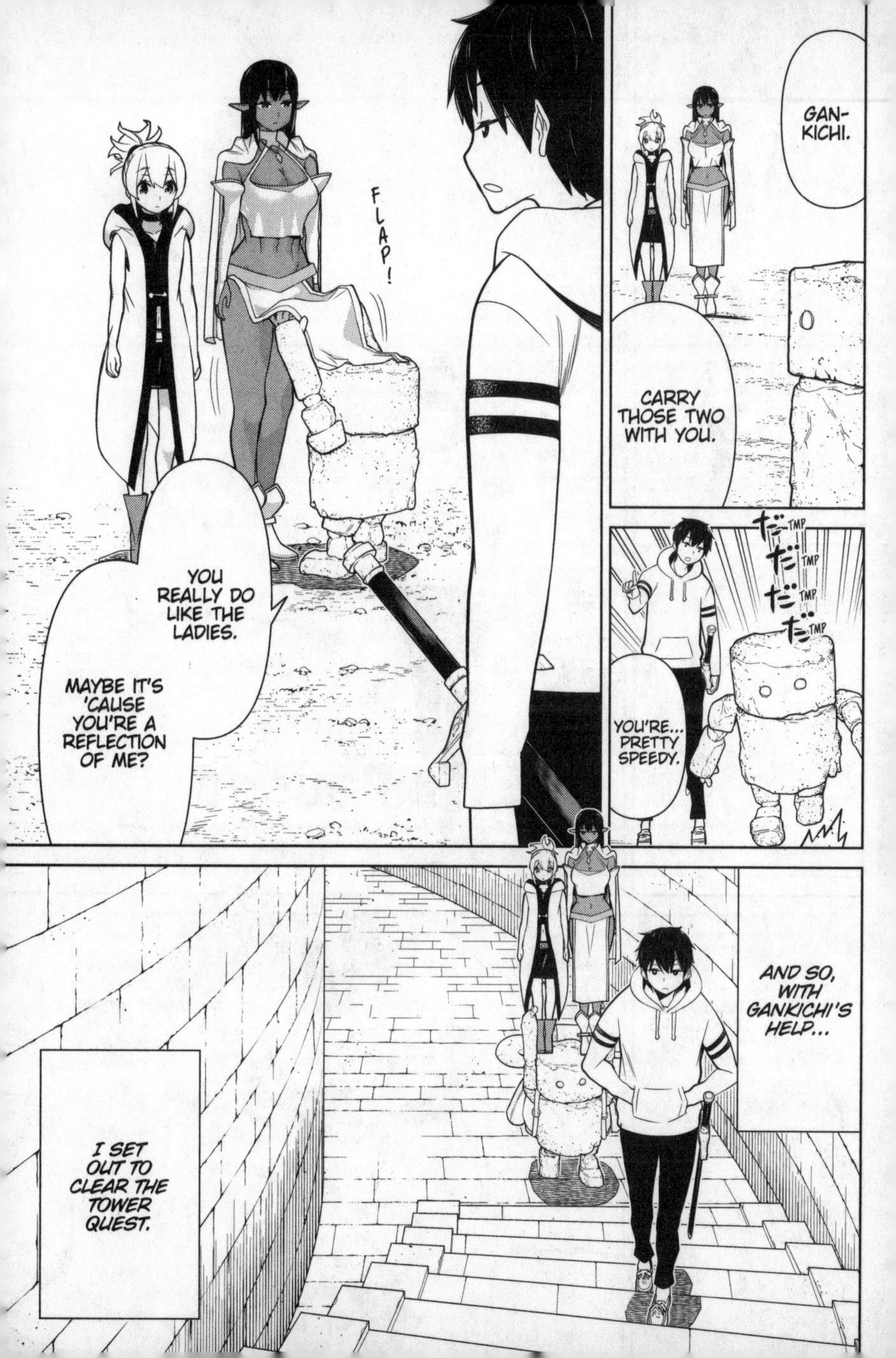
GAN-KICHI.
CARRY THOSE TWO WITH YOU.
だ TMP
だ TMP
だ TMP
だ TMP
YOU'RE... PRETTY SPEEDY.
FLAP!
YOU REALLY DO LIKE THE LADIES.
MAYBE IT'S 'CAUSE YOU'RE A REFLECTION OF ME?
AND SO, WITH GANKICHI'S HELP...
I SET OUT TO CLEAR THE TOWER QUEST.

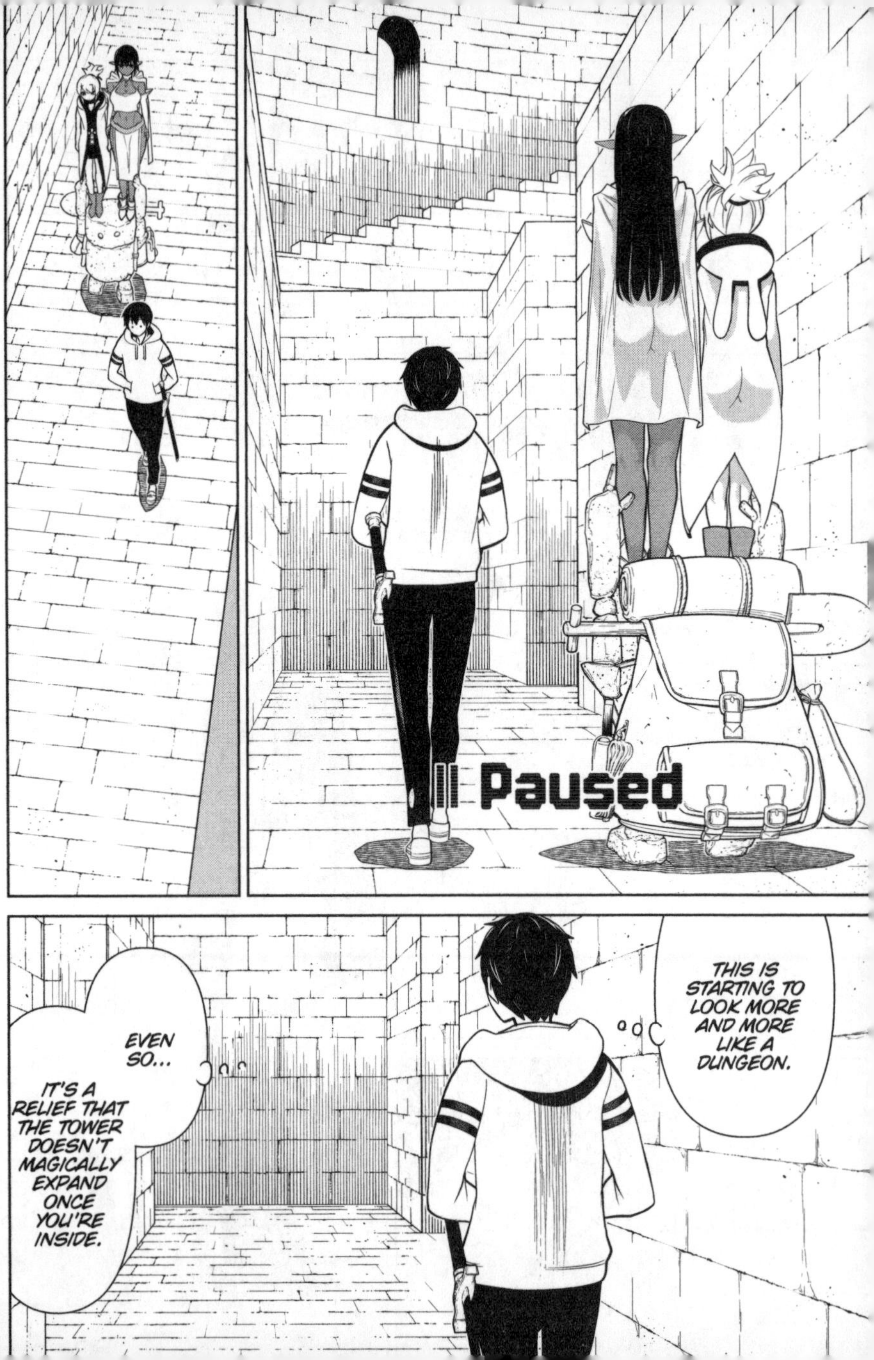
Paused
THIS IS STARTING TO LOOK MORE AND MORE LIKE A DUNGEON.
EVEN SO...
IT'S A RELIEF THAT THE TOWER DOESN'T MAGICALLY EXPAND ONCE YOU'RE INSIDE.

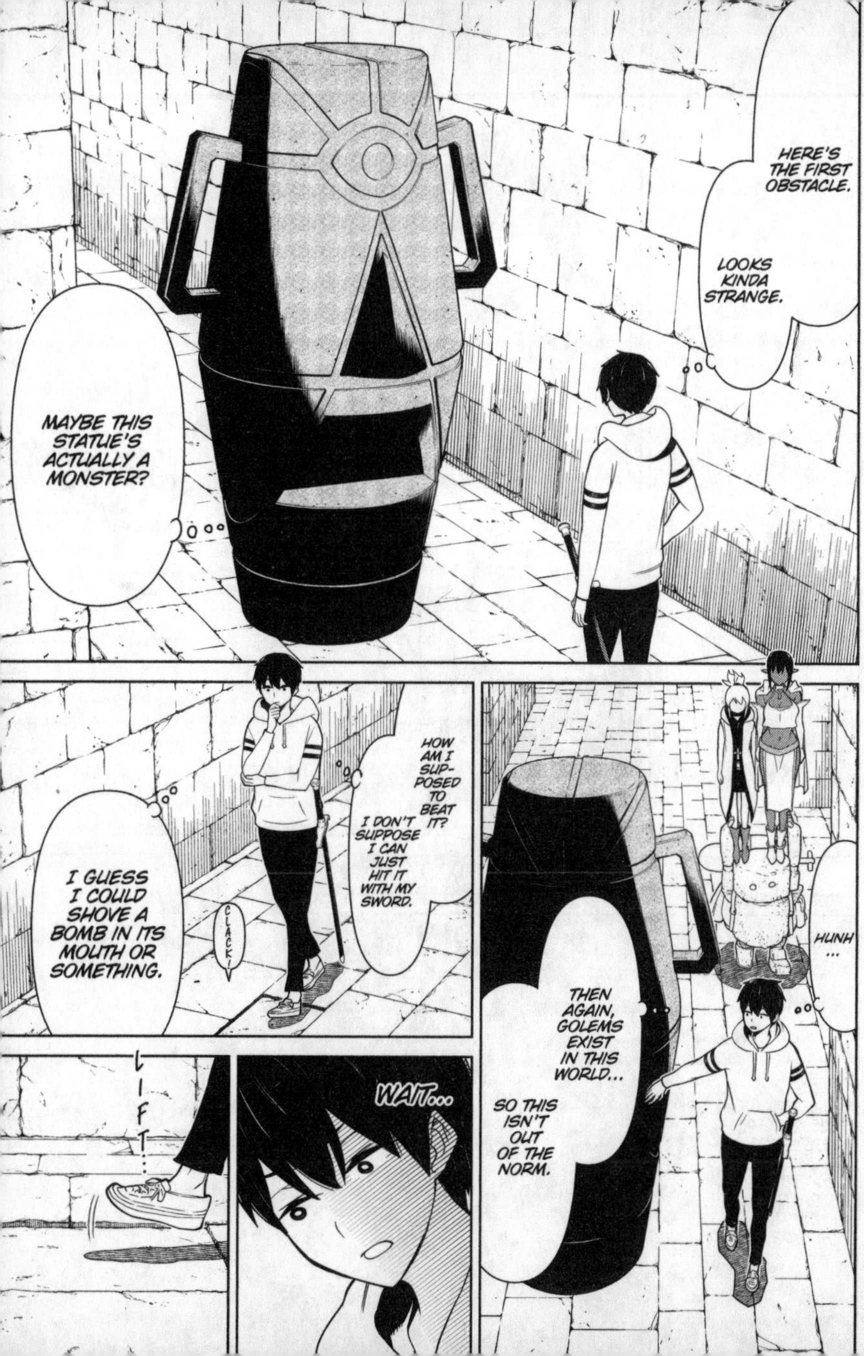
HERE'S THE FIRST OBSTACLE.
LOOKS KINDA STRANGE.
MAYBE THIS STATUE'S ACTUALLY A MONSTER?
HUNH ...
THEN AGAIN, GOLEMS EXIST IN THIS WORLD...
SO THIS ISN'T OUT OF THE NORM.
HOW AM I SUP-POSED TO BEAT IT?
I DON'T SUPPOSE I CAN JUST HIT IT WITH MY SWORD.
CLACK!
I GUESS I COULD SHOVE A BOMB IN ITS MOUTH OR SOMETHING.
WAIT...
LIFT...

CAREFUL, THE FLOOR'S RIGG--

GAN-KICHI?!

BWOOOOOSSHH!

RMBL

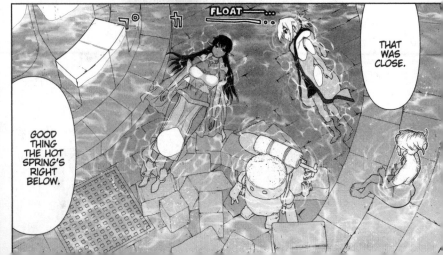

THAT WAS CLOSE.

FLOAT

GOOD THING THE HOT SPRING'S RIGHT BELOW.

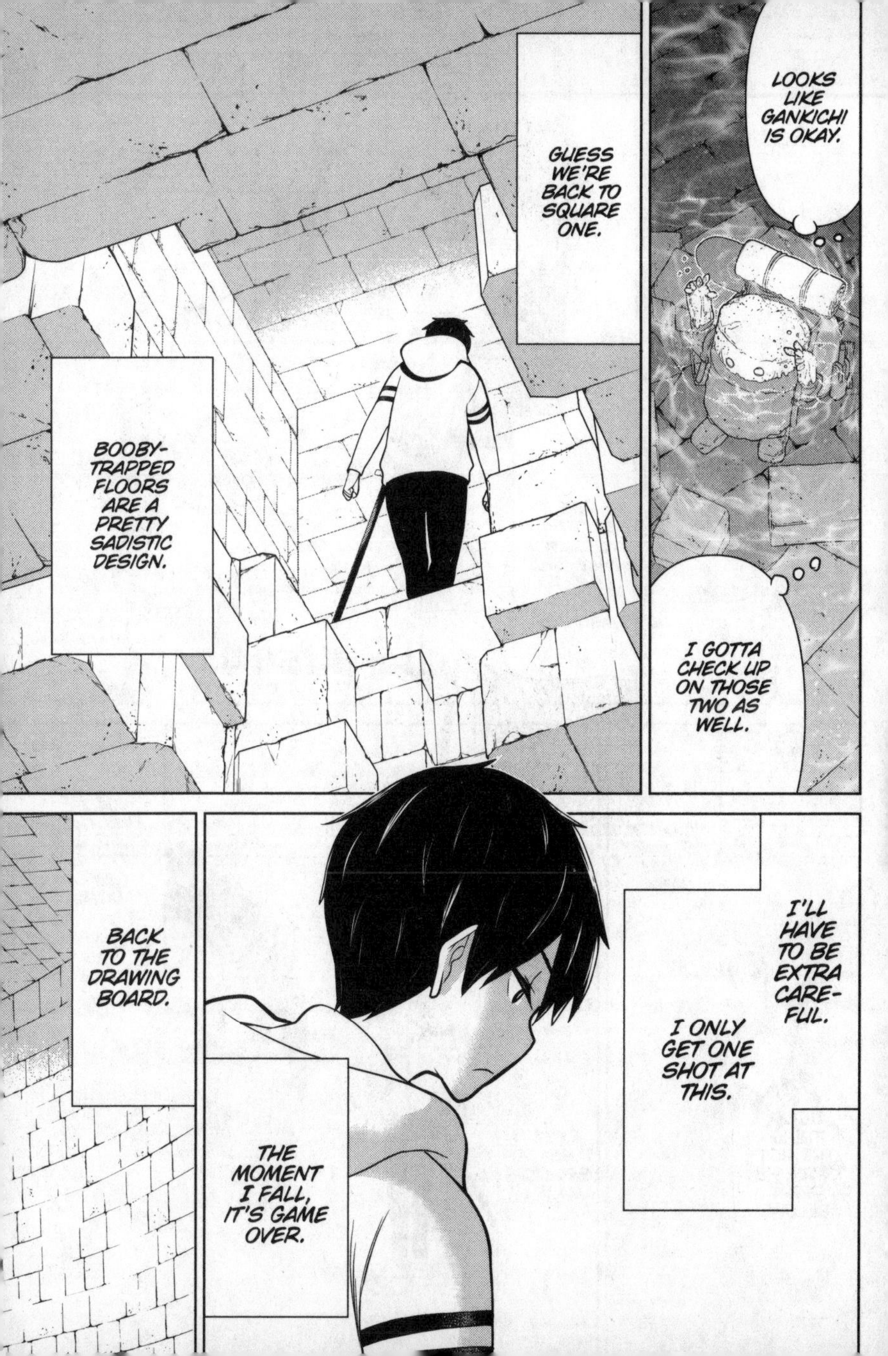
LOOKS LIKE GANKICHI IS OKAY.
I GOTTA CHECK UP ON THOSE TWO AS WELL.
GUESS WE'RE BACK TO SQUARE ONE.
BOOBY-TRAPPED FLOORS ARE A PRETTY SADISTIC DESIGN.
I'LL HAVE TO BE EXTRA CARE-FUL.
I ONLY GET ONE SHOT AT THIS.
THE MOMENT I FALL, IT'S GAME OVER.
BACK TO THE DRAWING BOARD.

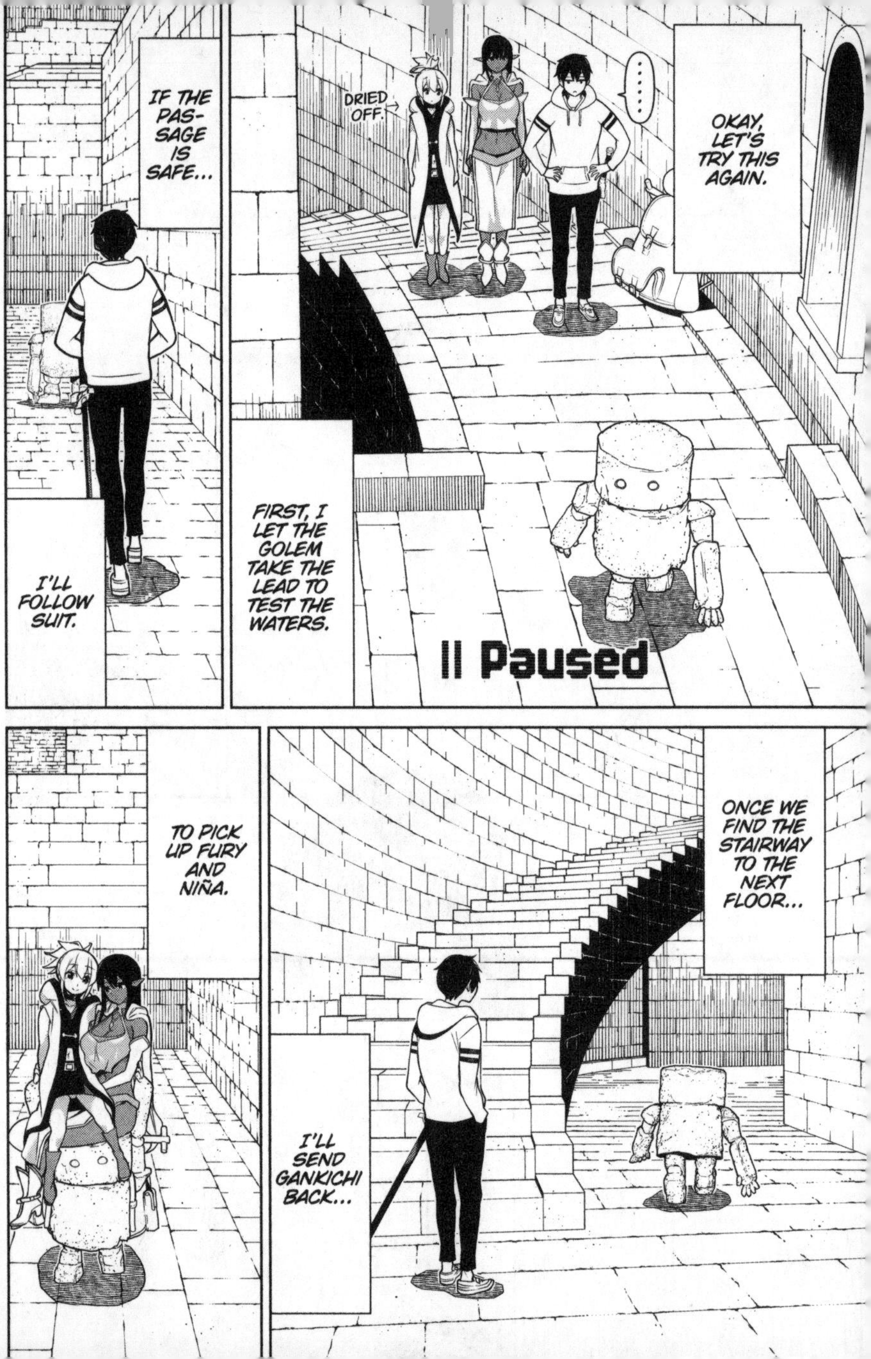
OKAY, LET'S TRY THIS AGAIN.
......
DRIED OFF.
FIRST, I LET THE GOLEM TAKE THE LEAD TO TEST THE WATERS.
II Paused
IF THE PAS-SAGE IS SAFE...
I'LL FOLLOW SUIT.
ONCE WE FIND THE STAIRWAY TO THE NEXT FLOOR...
I'LL SEND GANKICHI BACK...
TO PICK UP FURY AND NIÑA.

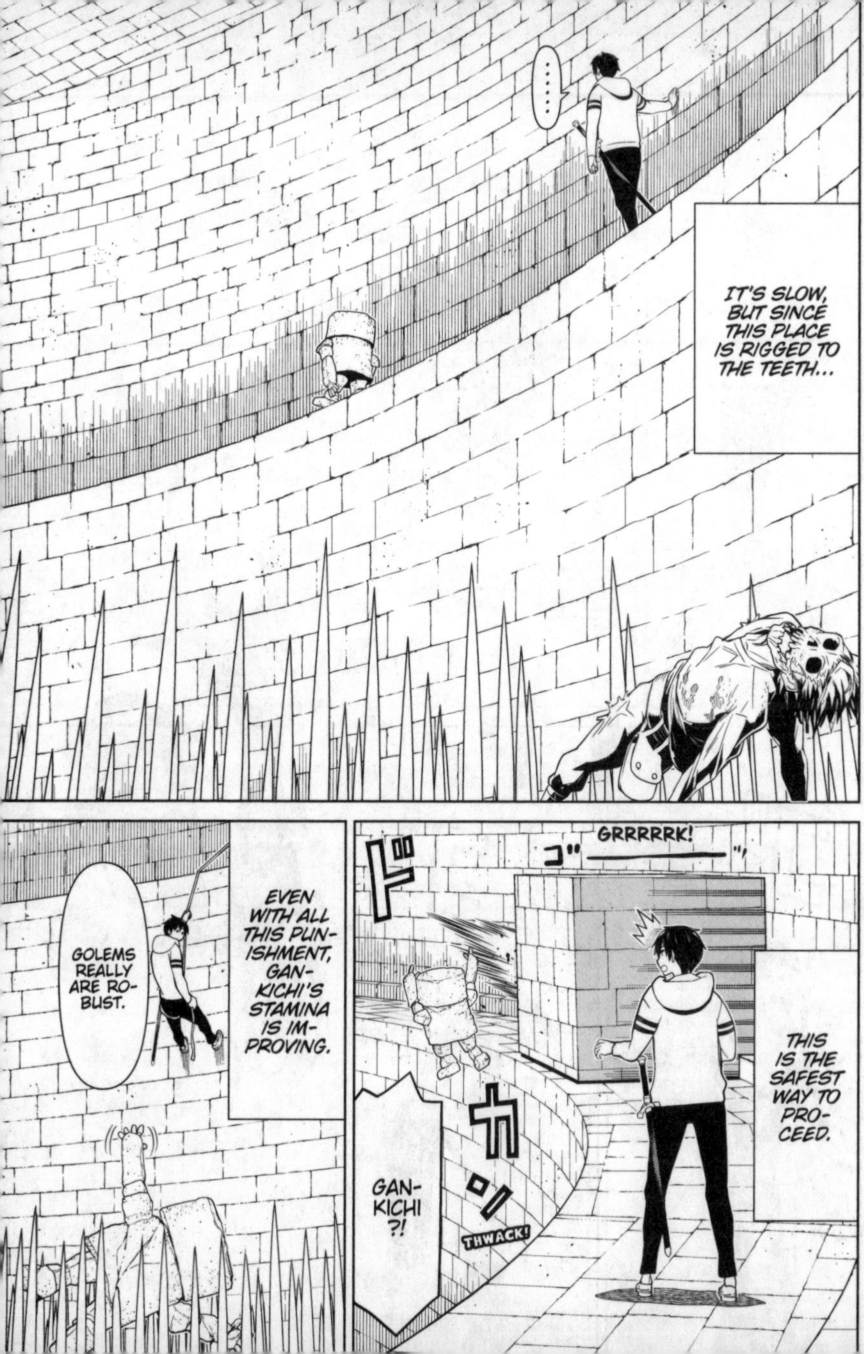
......
IT'S SLOW, BUT SINCE THIS PLACE IS RIGGED TO THE TEETH...
GRRRRK!
THIS IS THE SAFEST WAY TO PROCEED.
GANKICHI?!
THWACK!
EVEN WITH ALL THIS PUNISHMENT, GANKICHI'S STAMINA IS IMPROVING.
GOLEMS REALLY ARE ROBUST.

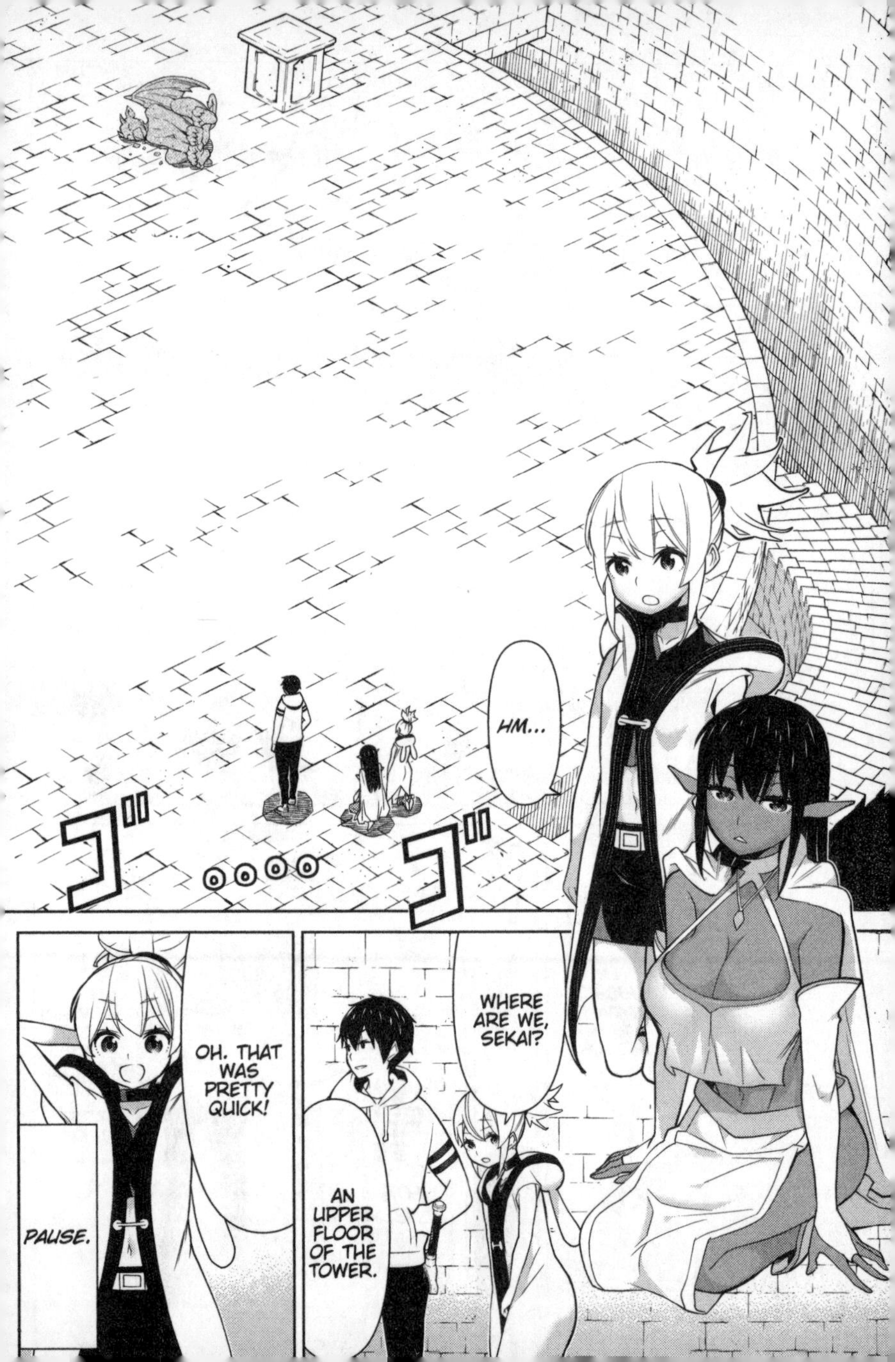

ゴ
ゴ
HM...
WHERE ARE WE, SEKAI?
AN UPPER FLOOR OF THE TOWER.
OH. THAT WAS PRETTY QUICK!
PAUSE.

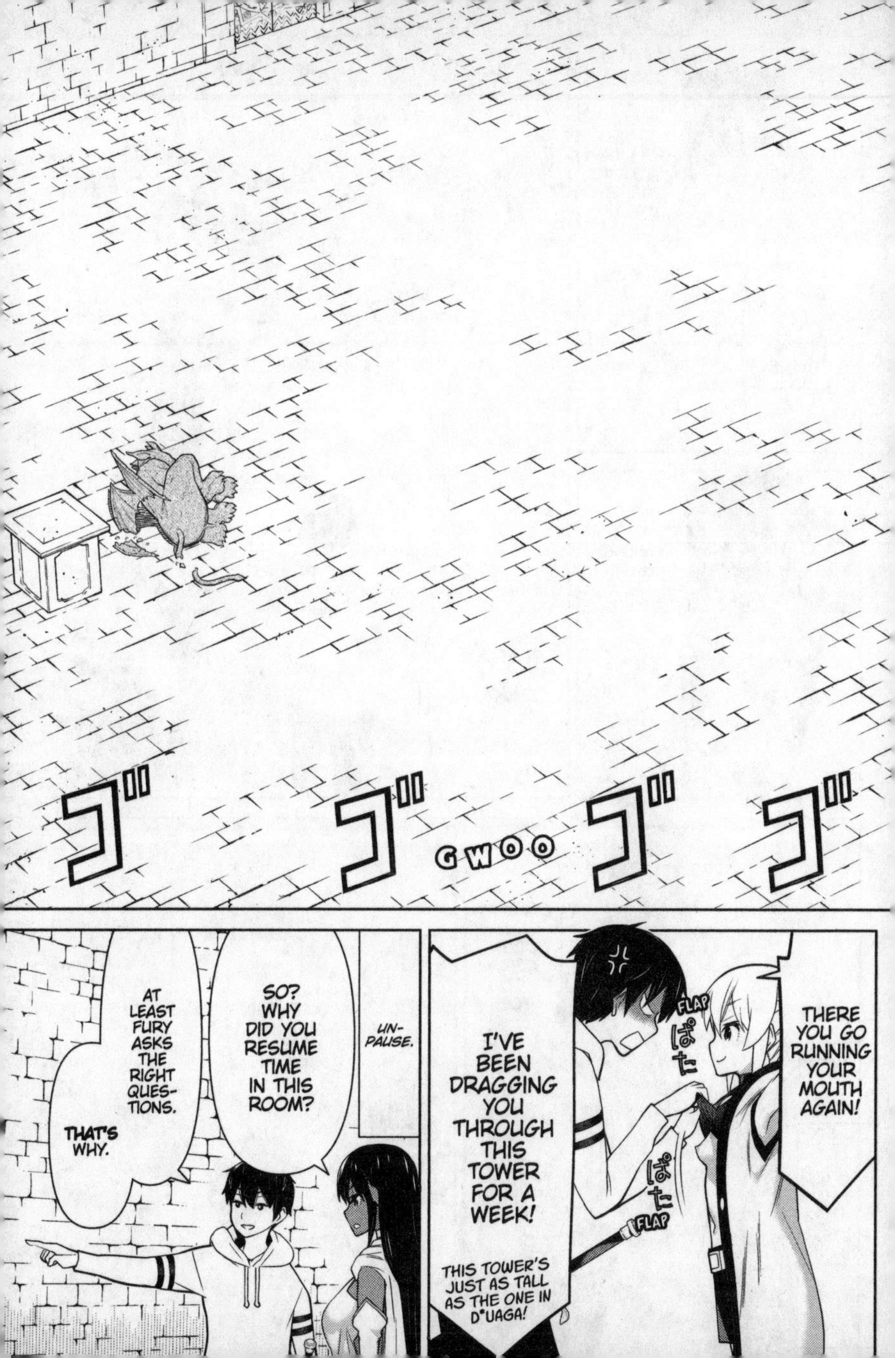
ゴ
ゴ
GWOO
ゴ
ゴ
THERE YOU GO RUNNING YOUR MOUTH AGAIN!
FLAP
ぱた
I'VE BEEN DRAGGING YOU THROUGH THIS TOWER FOR A WEEK!
ぱた
FLAP
THIS TOWER'S JUST AS TALL AS THE ONE IN D*UAGA!
UN-PAUSE.
SO? WHY DID YOU RESUME TIME IN THIS ROOM?
AT LEAST FURY ASKS THE RIGHT QUES-TIONS.
THAT'S WHY.

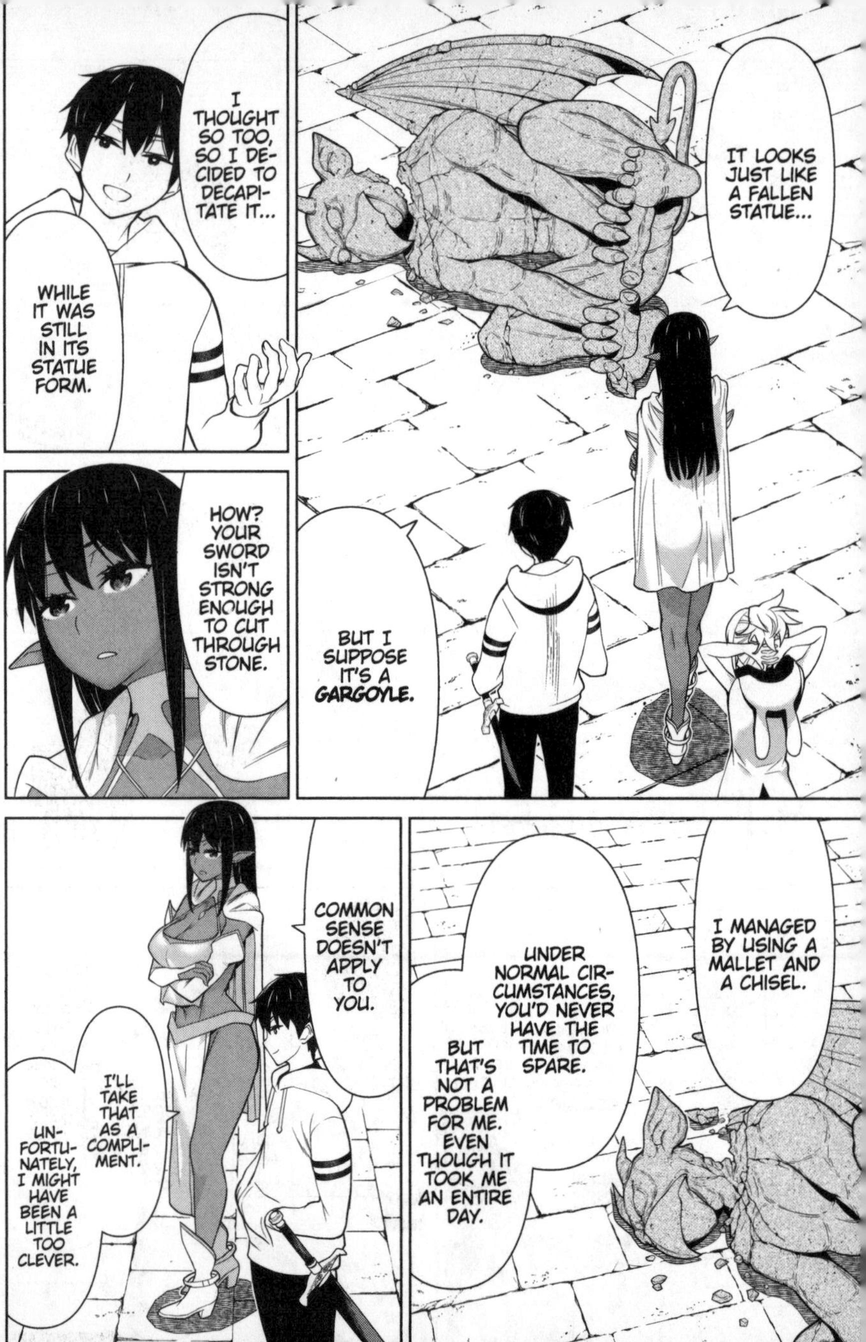
IT LOOKS JUST LIKE A FALLEN STATUE...
BUT I SUPPOSE IT'S A **GARGOYLE.**
I THOUGHT SO TOO, SO I DECIDED TO DECAPITATE IT...
WHILE IT WAS STILL IN ITS STATUE FORM.
HOW? YOUR SWORD ISN'T STRONG ENOUGH TO CUT THROUGH STONE.
I MANAGED BY USING A MALLET AND A CHISEL.
UNDER NORMAL CIRCUMSTANCES, YOU'D NEVER HAVE THE TIME TO SPARE.
BUT THAT'S NOT A PROBLEM FOR ME. EVEN THOUGH IT TOOK ME AN ENTIRE DAY.
COMMON SENSE DOESN'T APPLY TO YOU.
I'LL TAKE THAT AS A COMPLIMENT.
UNFORTUNATELY, I MIGHT HAVE BEEN A LITTLE TOO CLEVER.

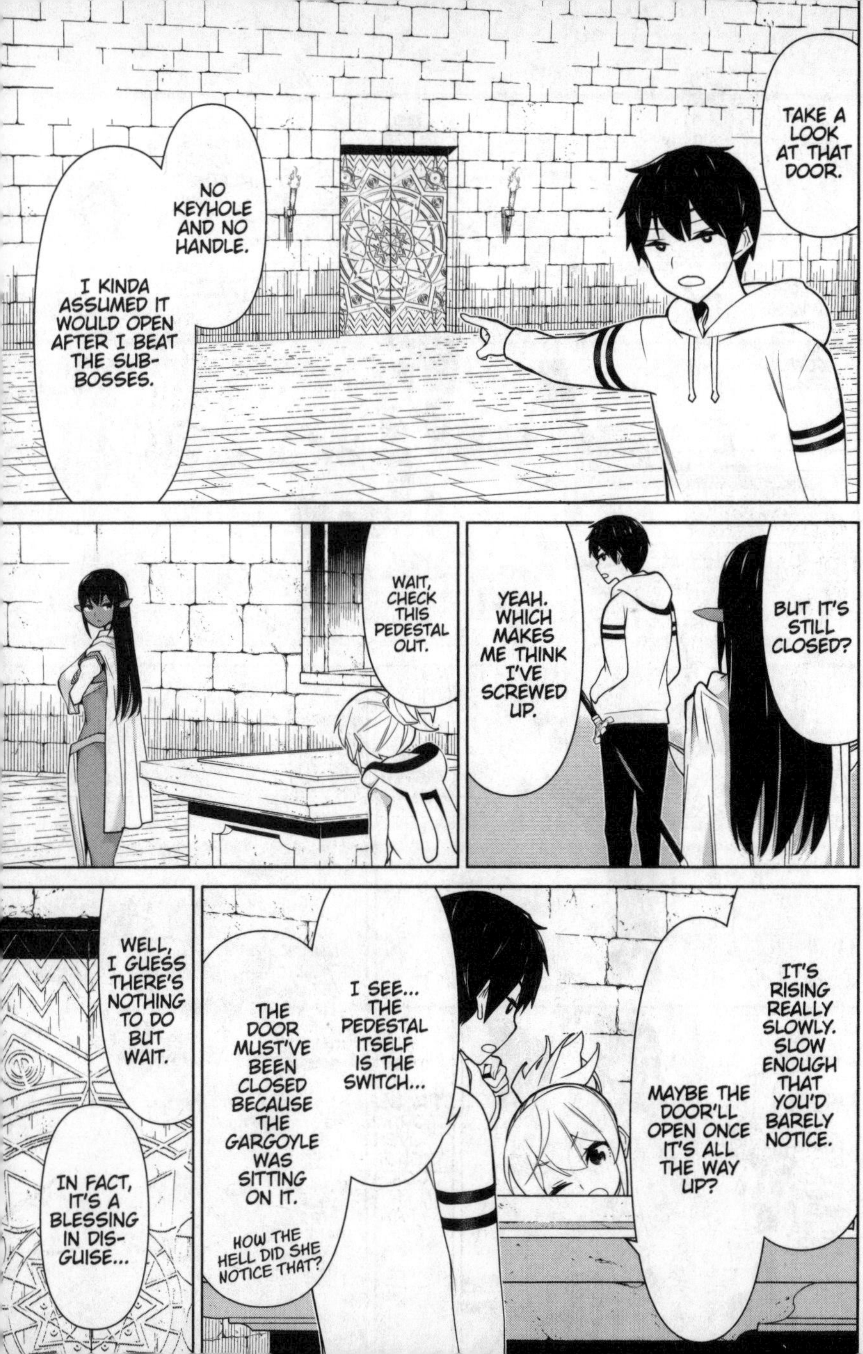
TAKE A LOOK AT THAT DOOR.
NO KEYHOLE AND NO HANDLE.
I KINDA ASSUMED IT WOULD OPEN AFTER I BEAT THE SUB-BOSSES.
BUT IT'S STILL CLOSED?
YEAH. WHICH MAKES ME THINK I'VE SCREWED UP.
WAIT, CHECK THIS PEDESTAL OUT.
IT'S RISING REALLY SLOWLY. SLOW ENOUGH THAT YOU'D BARELY NOTICE.
MAYBE THE DOOR'LL OPEN ONCE IT'S ALL THE WAY UP?
I SEE... THE PEDESTAL ITSELF IS THE SWITCH...
THE DOOR MUST'VE BEEN CLOSED BECAUSE THE GARGOYLE WAS SITTING ON IT.
HOW THE HELL DID SHE NOTICE THAT?
WELL, I GUESS THERE'S NOTHING TO DO BUT WAIT.
IN FACT, IT'S A BLESSING IN DISGUISE...

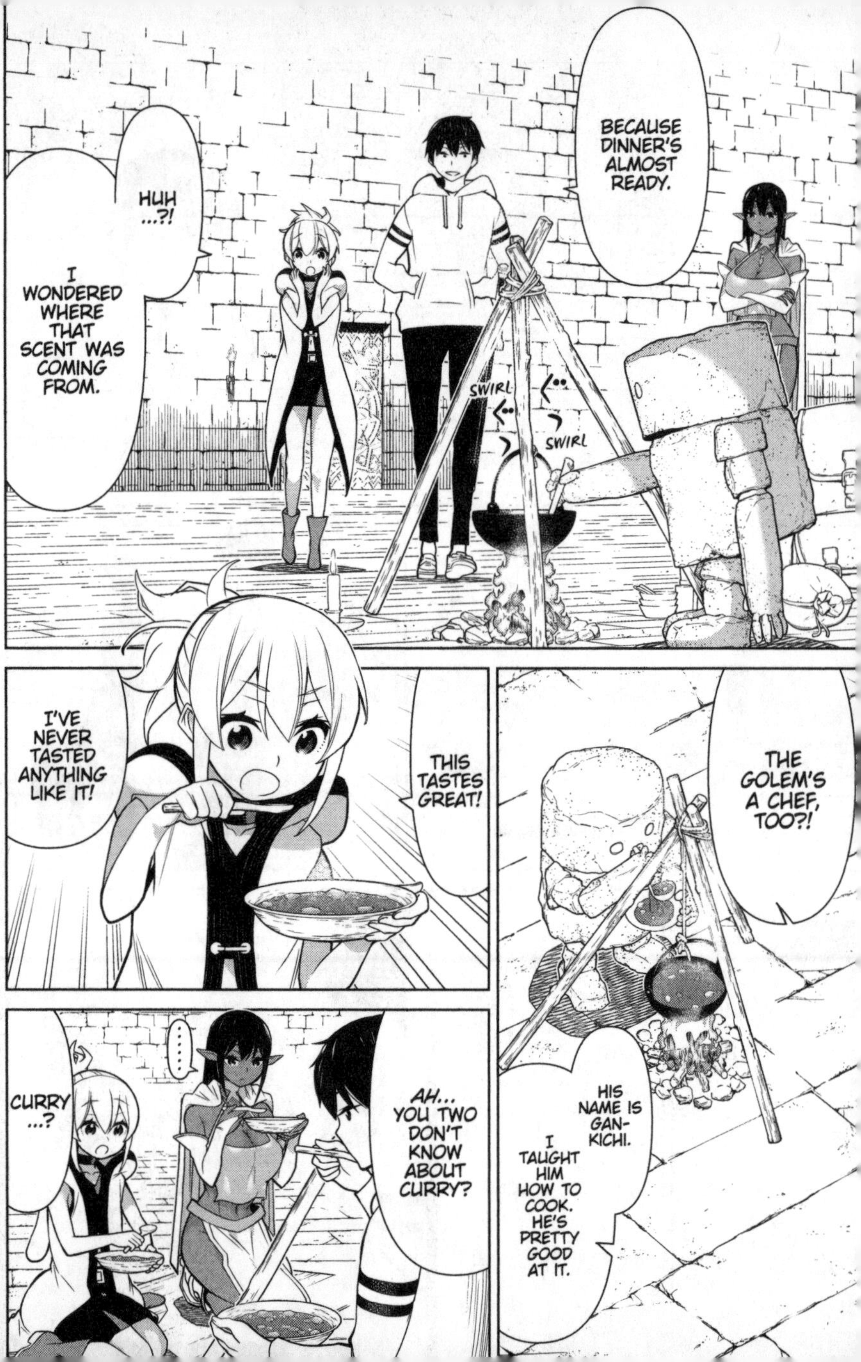
BECAUSE DINNER'S ALMOST READY.
SWIRL
SWIRL
HUH ...?!
I WONDERED WHERE THAT SCENT WAS COMING FROM.
THE GOLEM'S A CHEF, TOO?!
HIS NAME IS GAN-KICHI.
I TAUGHT HIM HOW TO COOK. HE'S PRETTY GOOD AT IT.
THIS TASTES GREAT!
I'VE NEVER TASTED ANYTHING LIKE IT!
AH... YOU TWO DON'T KNOW ABOUT CURRY?
......
CURRY ...?

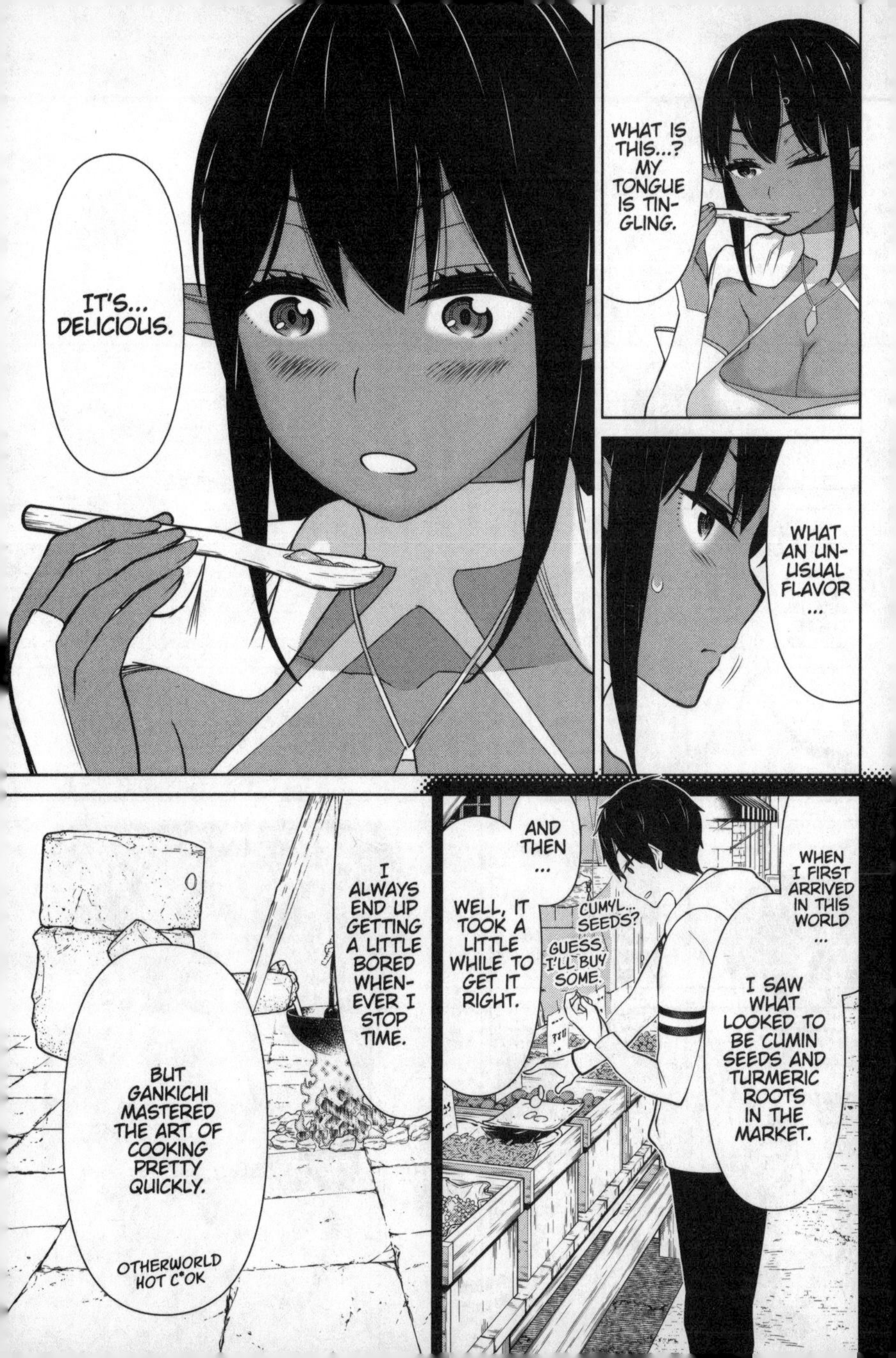
WHAT IS THIS...? MY TONGUE IS TINGLING.
WHAT AN UNUSUAL FLAVOR...
IT'S... DELICIOUS.
WHEN I FIRST ARRIVED IN THIS WORLD...
I SAW WHAT LOOKED TO BE CUMIN SEEDS AND TURMERIC ROOTS IN THE MARKET.
CUMYL... SEEDS?
GUESS I'LL BUY SOME.
AND THEN...
WELL, IT TOOK A LITTLE WHILE TO GET IT RIGHT.
I ALWAYS END UP GETTING A LITTLE BORED WHENEVER I STOP TIME.
BUT GANKICHI MASTERED THE ART OF COOKING PRETTY QUICKLY.
OTHERWORLD HOT C°OK

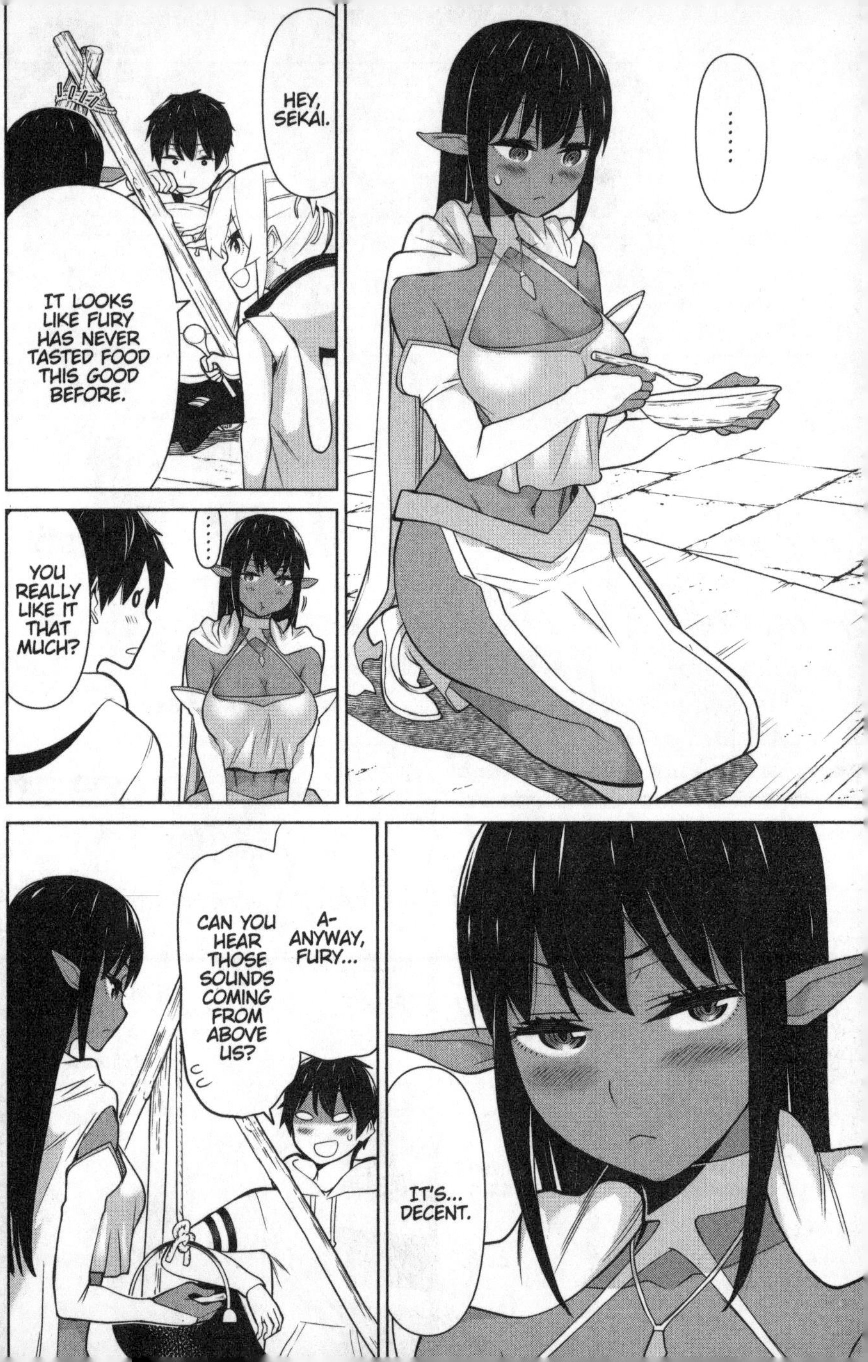
……
HEY, SEKAI.
IT LOOKS LIKE FURY HAS NEVER TASTED FOOD THIS GOOD BEFORE.
……
YOU REALLY LIKE IT THAT MUCH?
IT'S... DECENT.
A- ANYWAY, FURY...
CAN YOU HEAR THOSE SOUNDS COMING FROM ABOVE US?

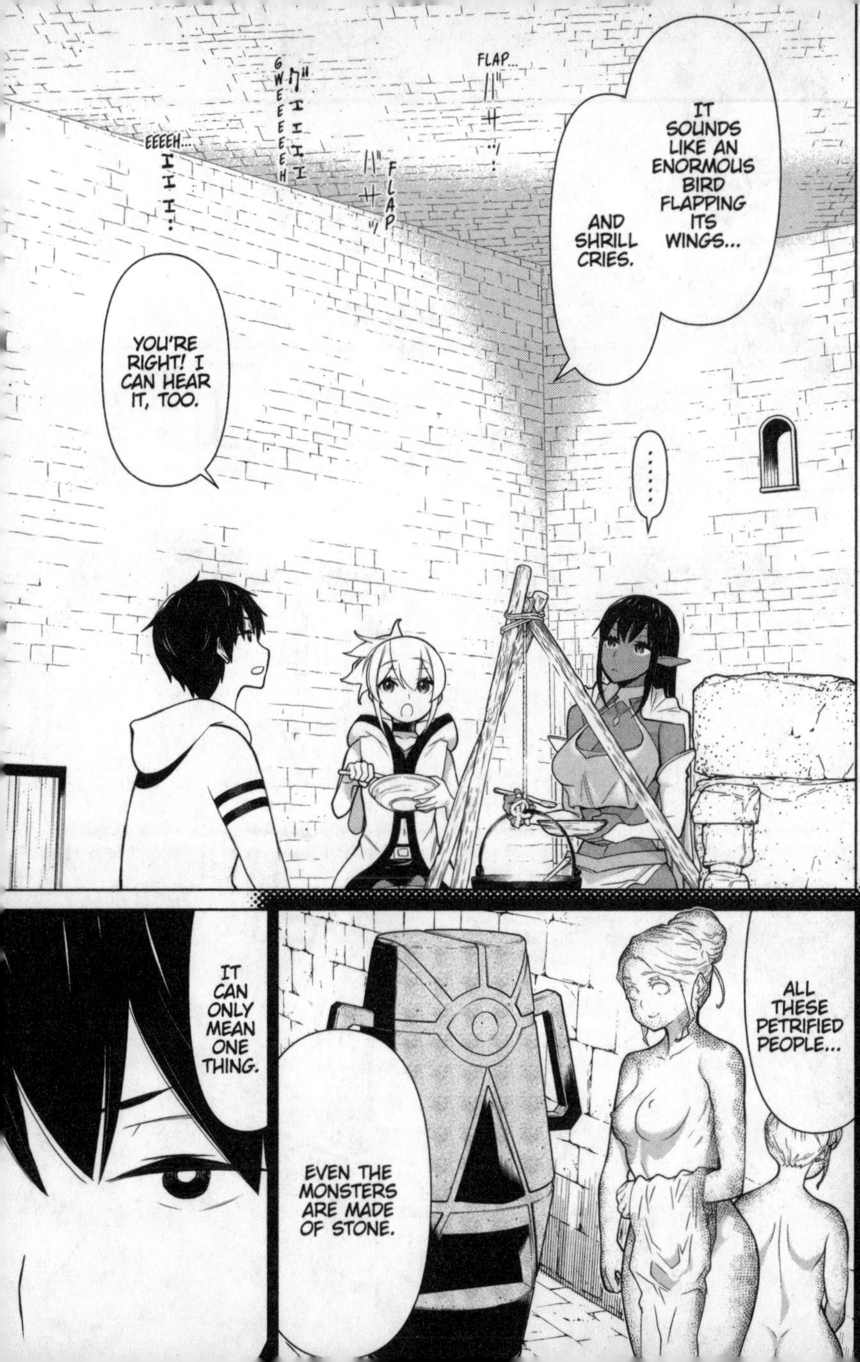
IT SOUNDS LIKE AN ENORMOUS BIRD FLAPPING ITS WINGS...
AND SHRILL CRIES.
FLAP...
FLAP
GWEEEEEEH
EEEEEH...
......
YOU'RE RIGHT! I CAN HEAR IT, TOO.
ALL THESE PETRIFIED PEOPLE...
EVEN THE MONSTERS ARE MADE OF STONE.
IT CAN ONLY MEAN ONE THING.

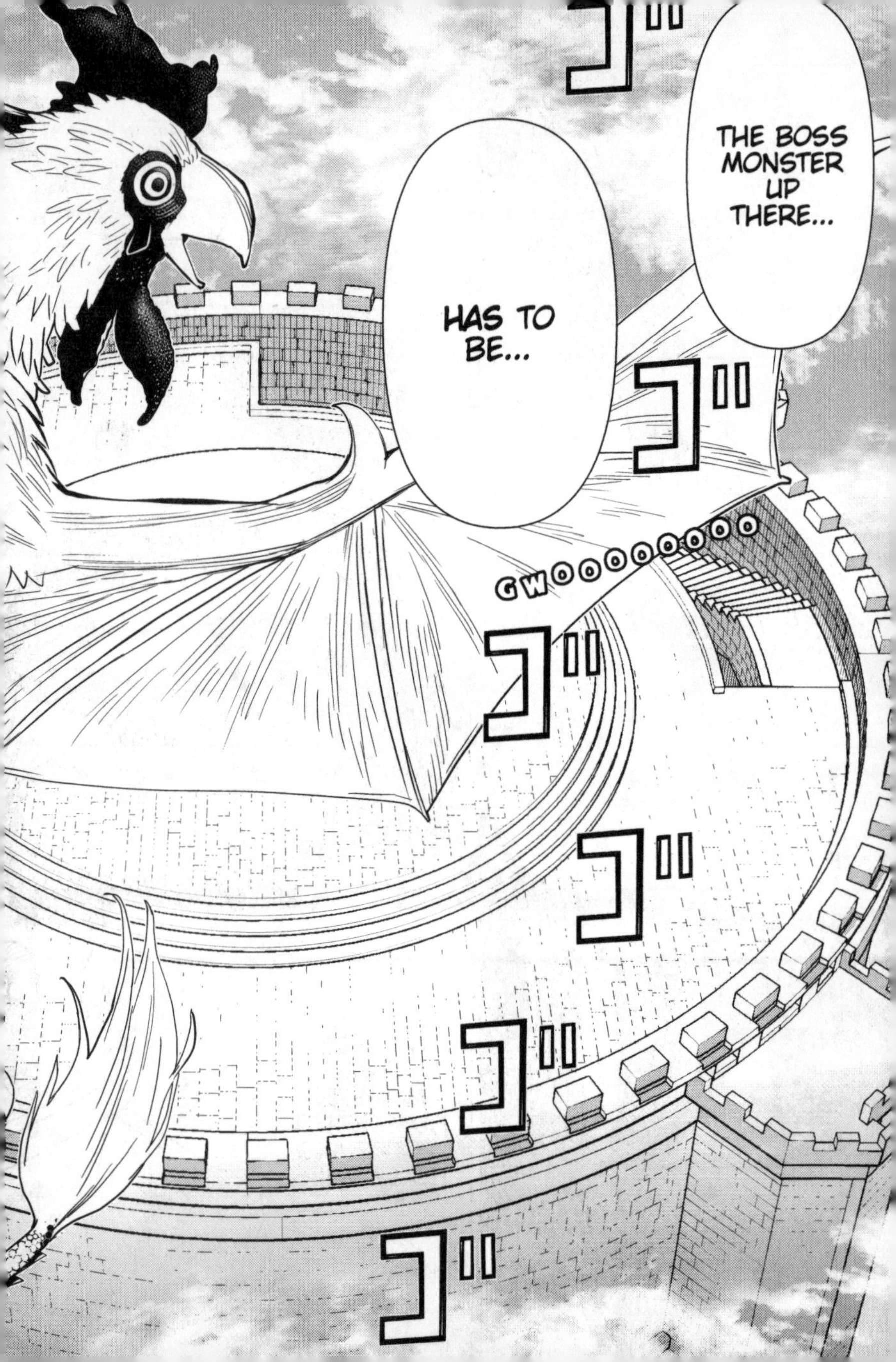
THE BOSS MONSTER UP THERE...
HAS TO BE...
GWOOOOOOOOOO

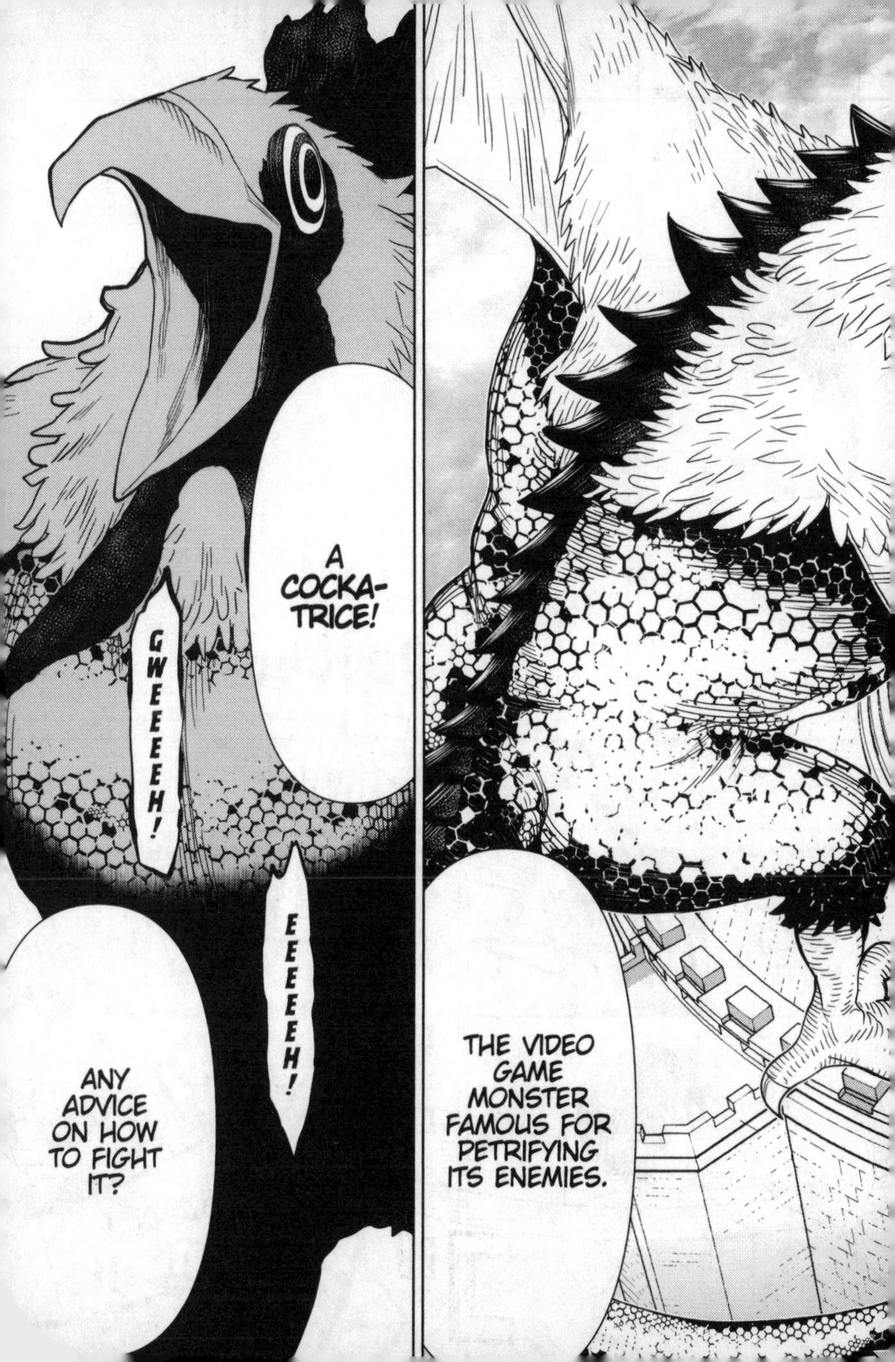
THE VIDEO GAME MONSTER FAMOUS FOR PETRIFYING ITS ENEMIES.
A COCKA-TRICE!
GWEEEEEH!
EEEEEEH!
ANY ADVICE ON HOW TO FIGHT IT?

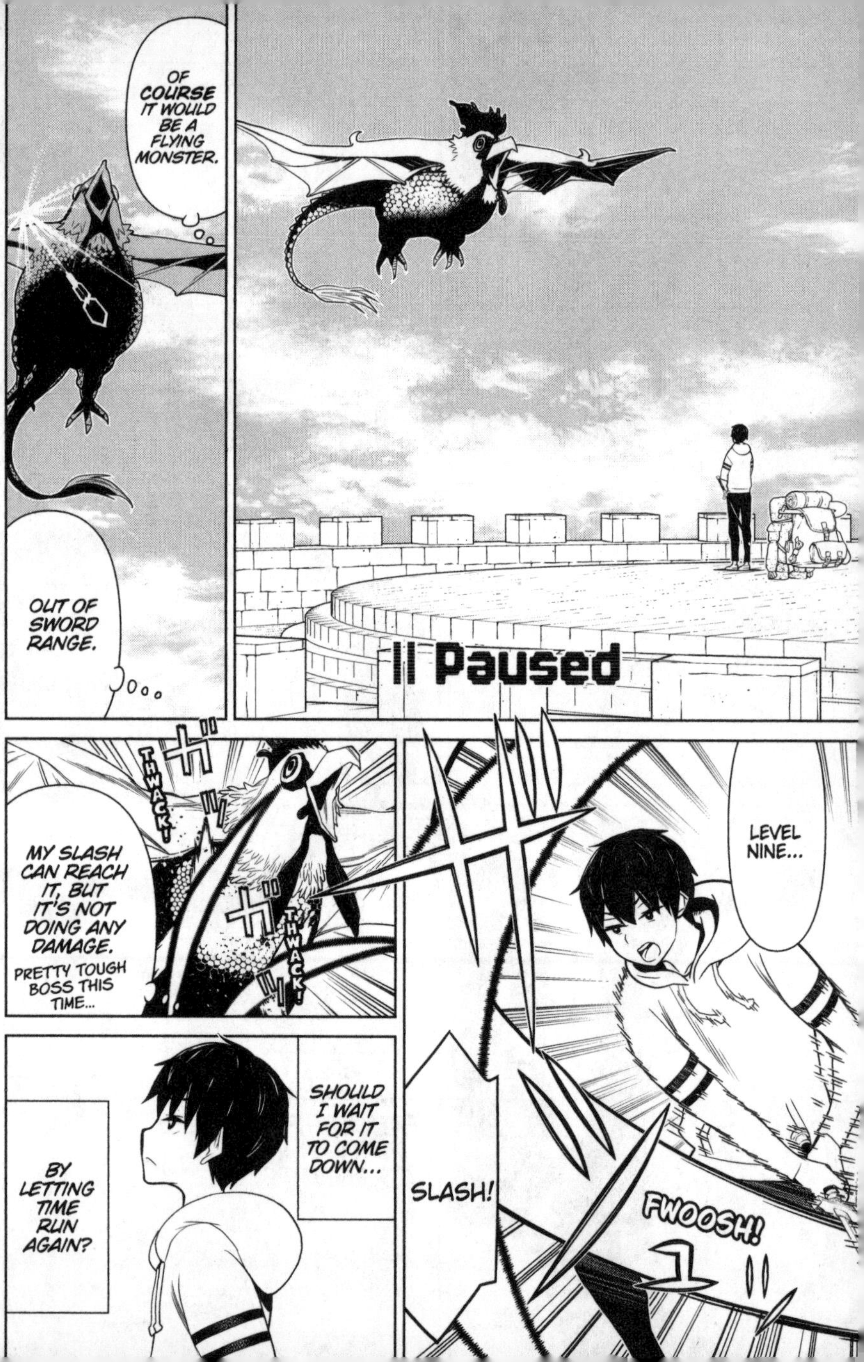
Paused
OF COURSE IT WOULD BE A FLYING MONSTER.
OUT OF SWORD RANGE.
LEVEL NINE...
SLASH!
FWOOSH!
THWACK!
THWACK!
MY SLASH CAN REACH IT, BUT IT'S NOT DOING ANY DAMAGE.
PRETTY TOUGH BOSS THIS TIME...
SHOULD I WAIT FOR IT TO COME DOWN...
BY LETTING TIME RUN AGAIN?

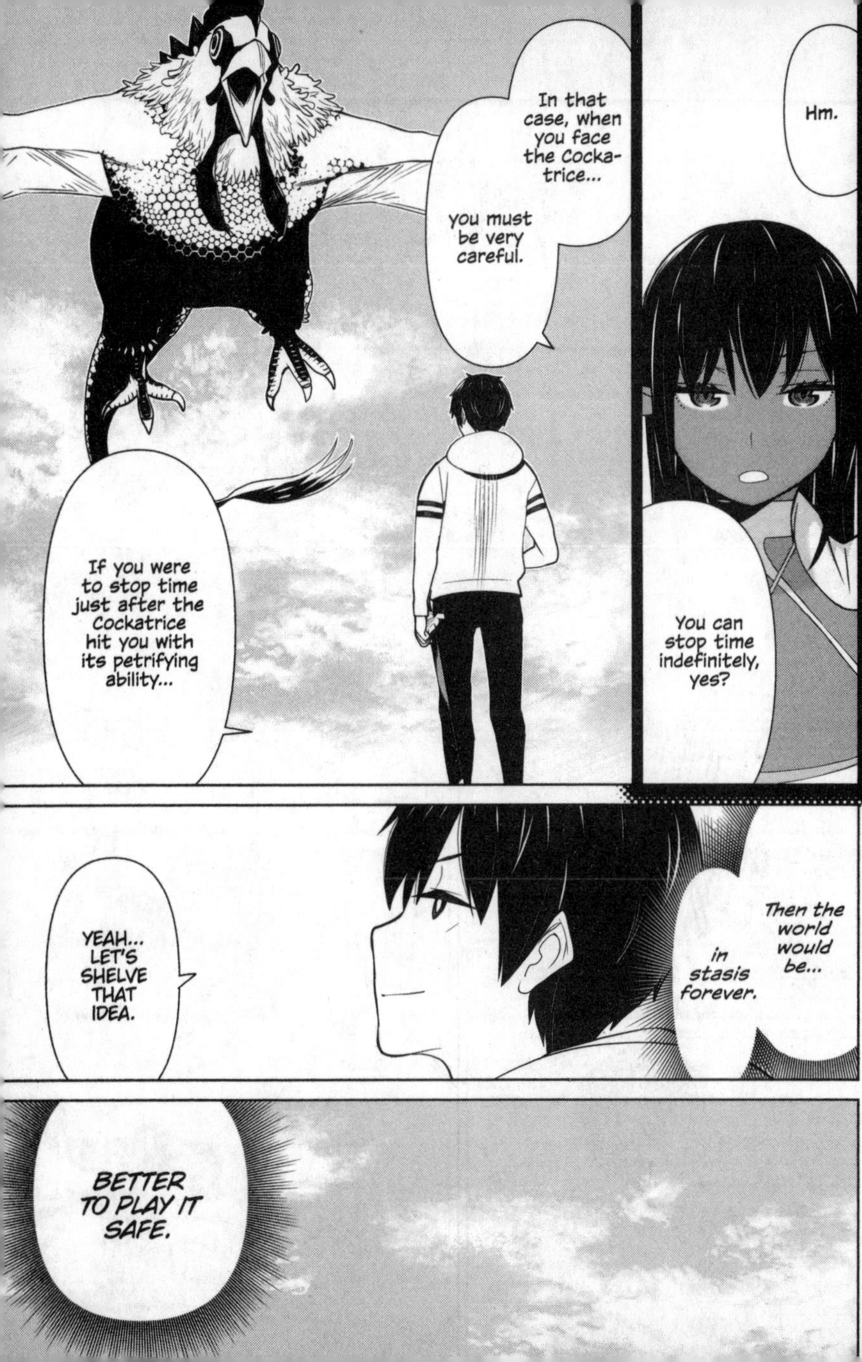
Hm.
You can stop time indefinitely, yes?
In that case, when you face the Cockatrice...
you must be very careful.
If you were to stop time just after the Cockatrice hit you with its petrifying ability...
Then the world would be...
in stasis forever.
YEAH... LET'S SHELVE THAT IDEA.
BETTER TO PLAY IT SAFE.

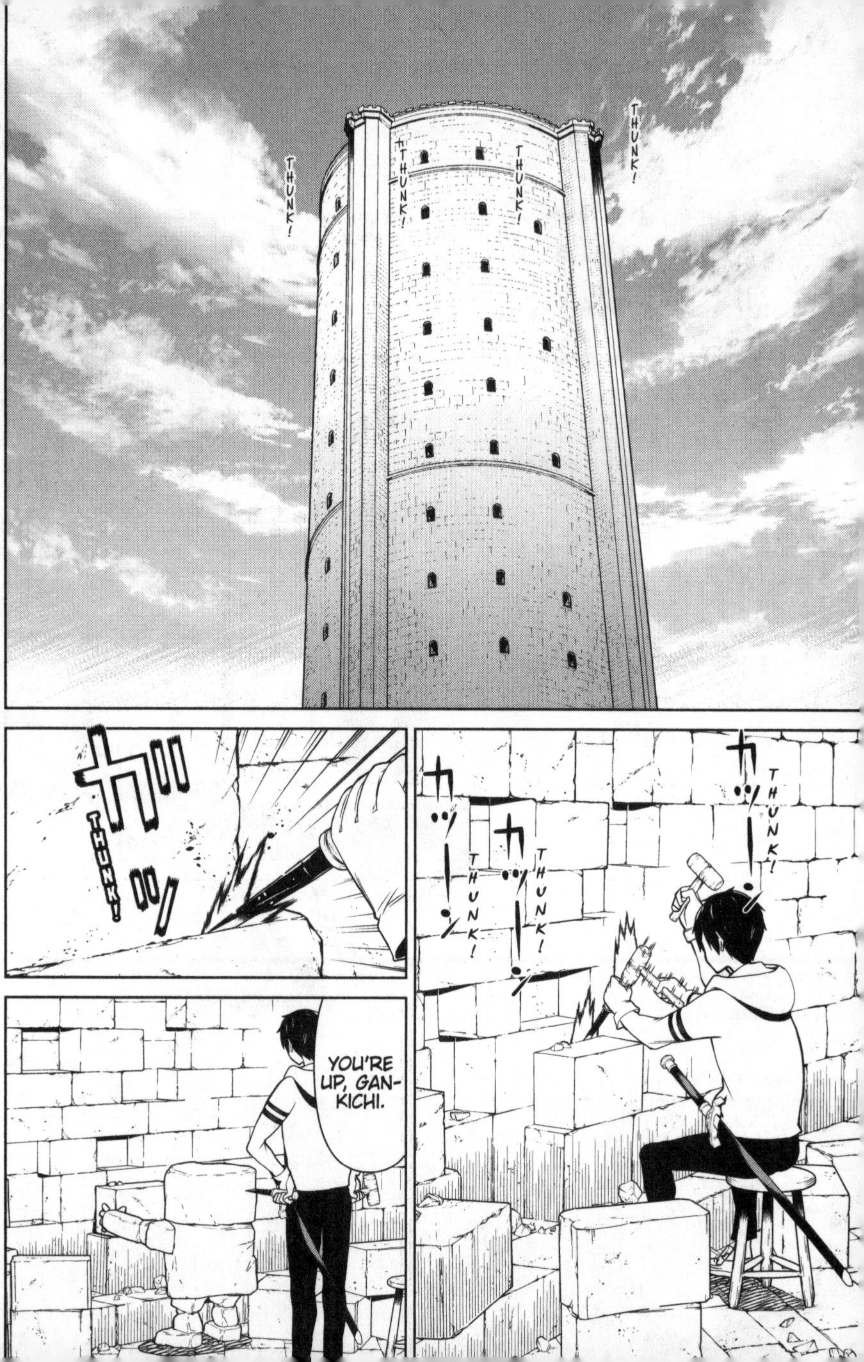
THUNK!
THUNK!
THUNK!
THUNK!
THUNK!
THUNK!
THUNK!
THUNK!
YOU'RE UP, GAN-KICHI.

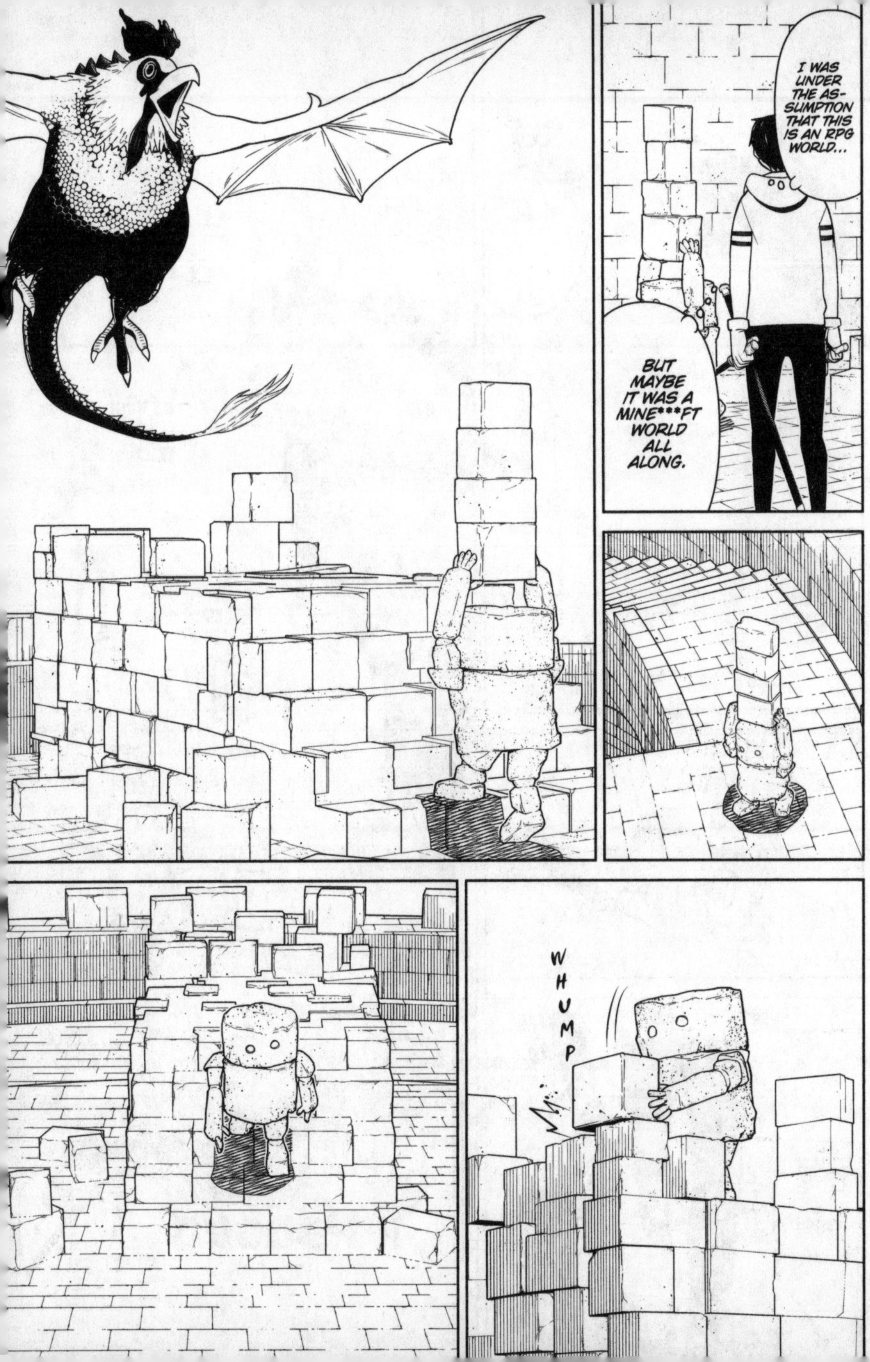
I WAS UNDER THE AS-SUMPTION THAT THIS IS AN RPG WORLD...
BUT MAYBE IT WAS A MINE***FT WORLD ALL ALONG.
WHUMP

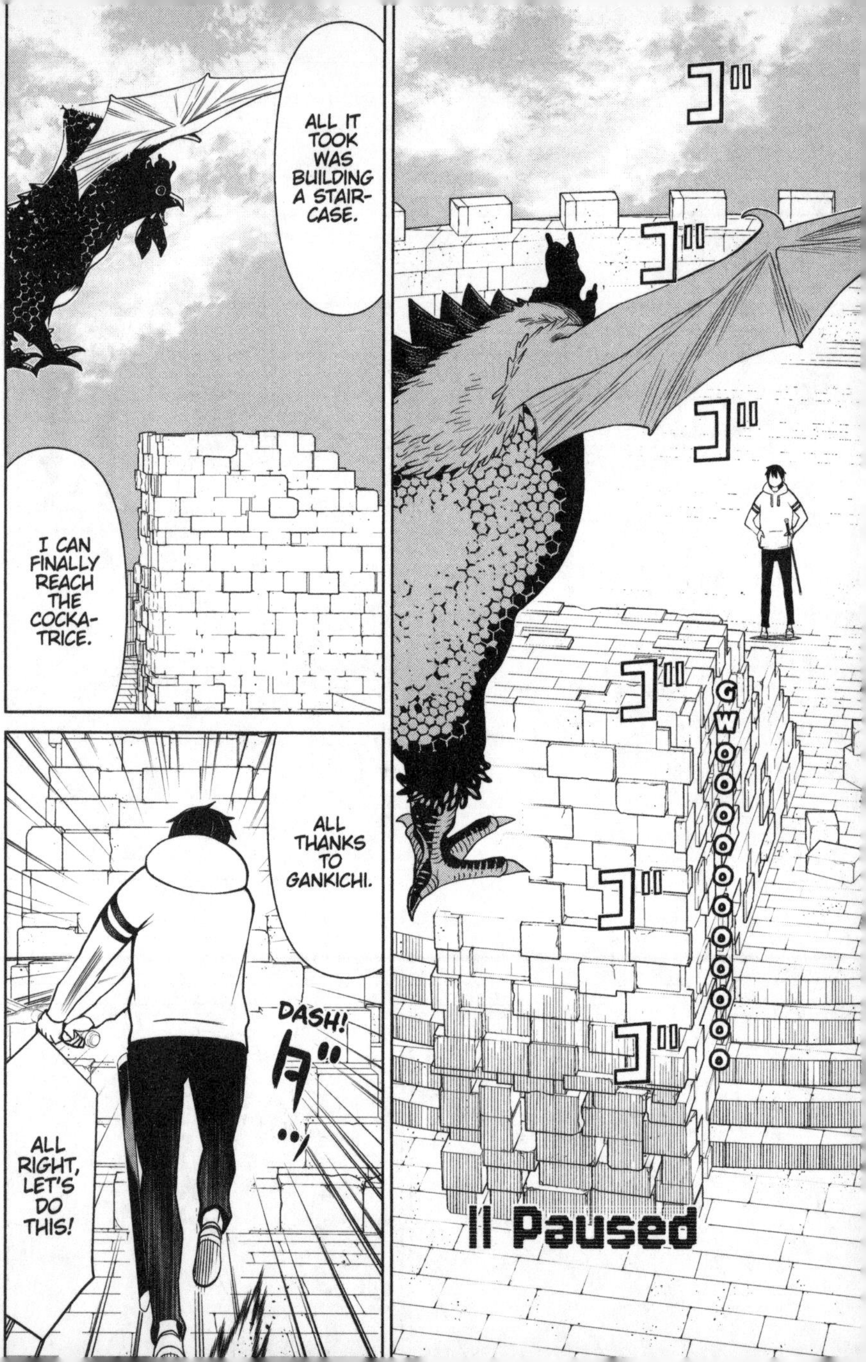

GWOOOOOOOOOOO
Paused
ALL IT TOOK WAS BUILDING A STAIRCASE.
I CAN FINALLY REACH THE COCKATRICE.
ALL THANKS TO GANKICHI.
DASH!
ALL RIGHT, LET'S DO THIS!

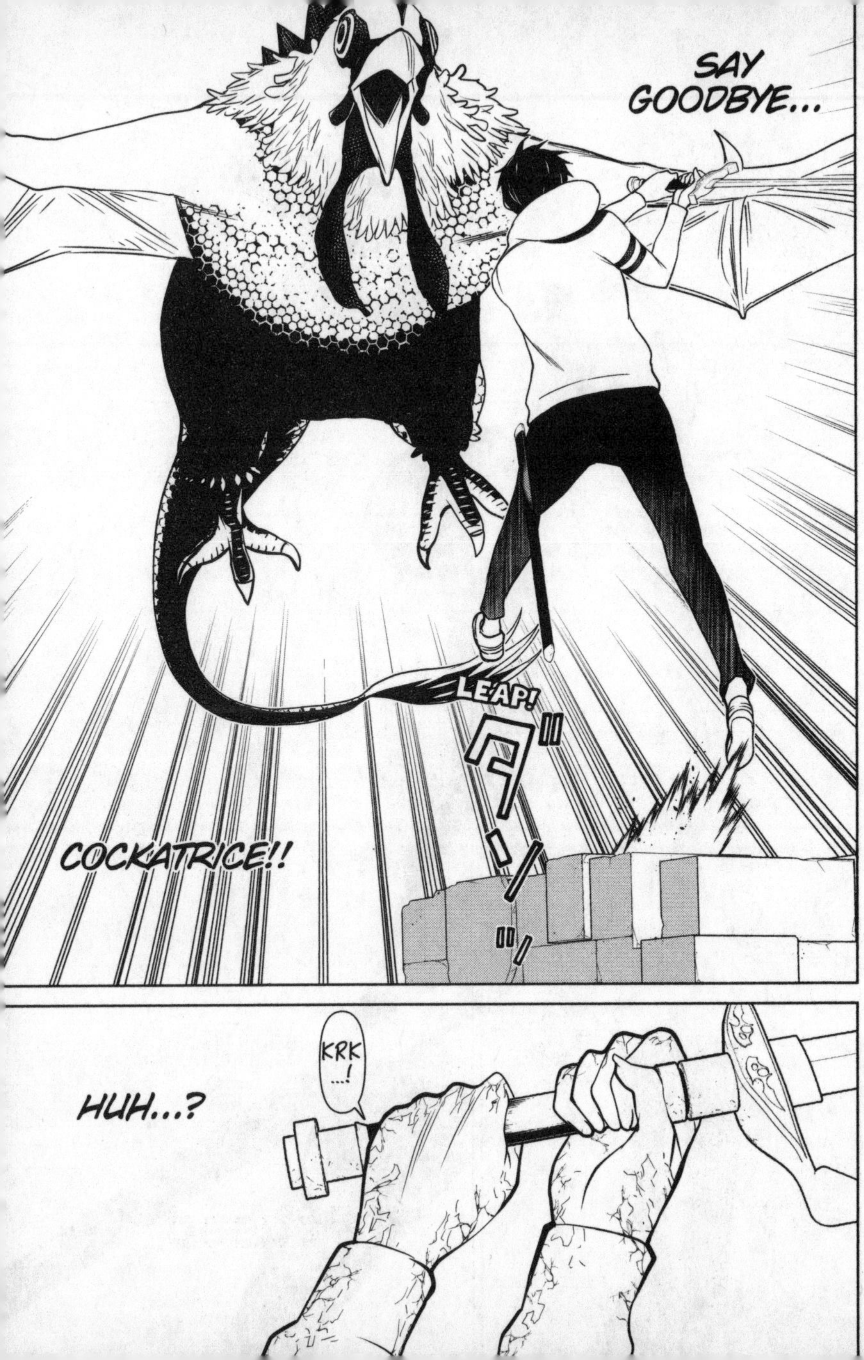
SAY GOODBYE...
LEAP!
COCKATRICE!!
KRK ...!
HUH...?

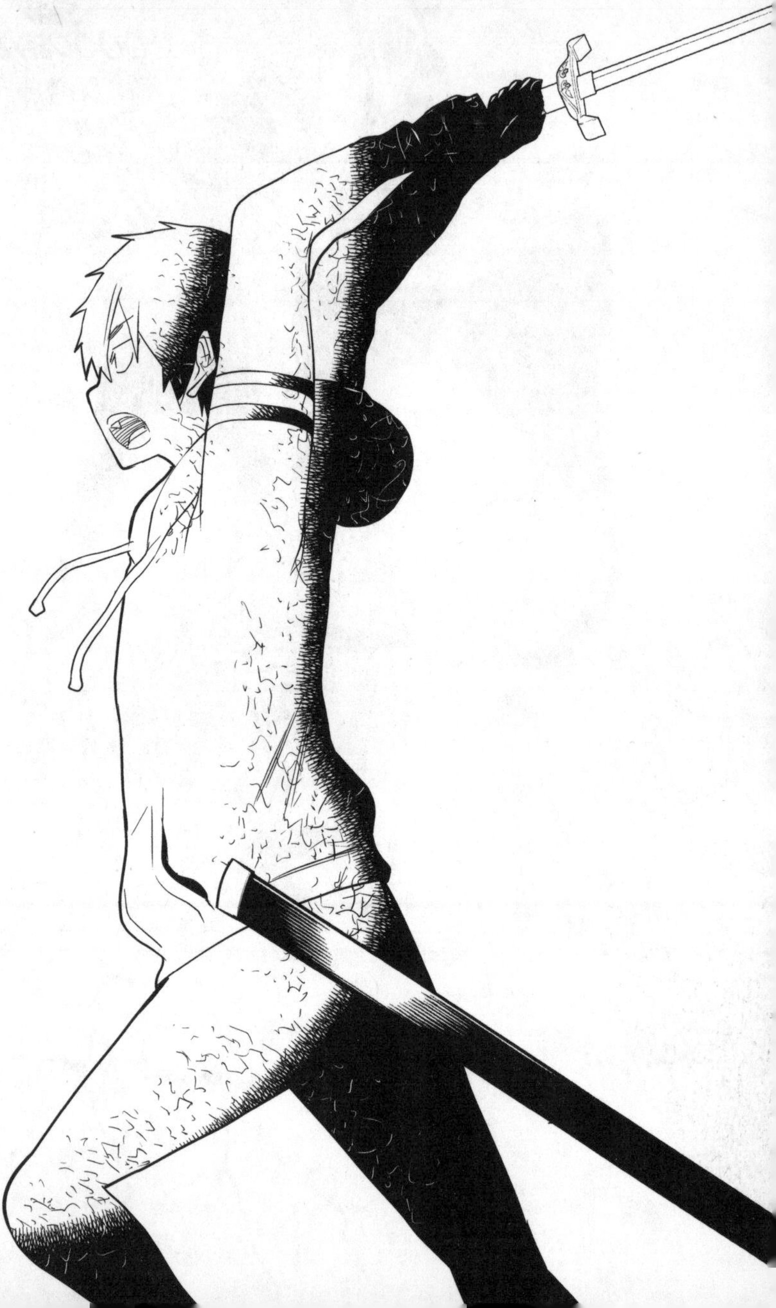

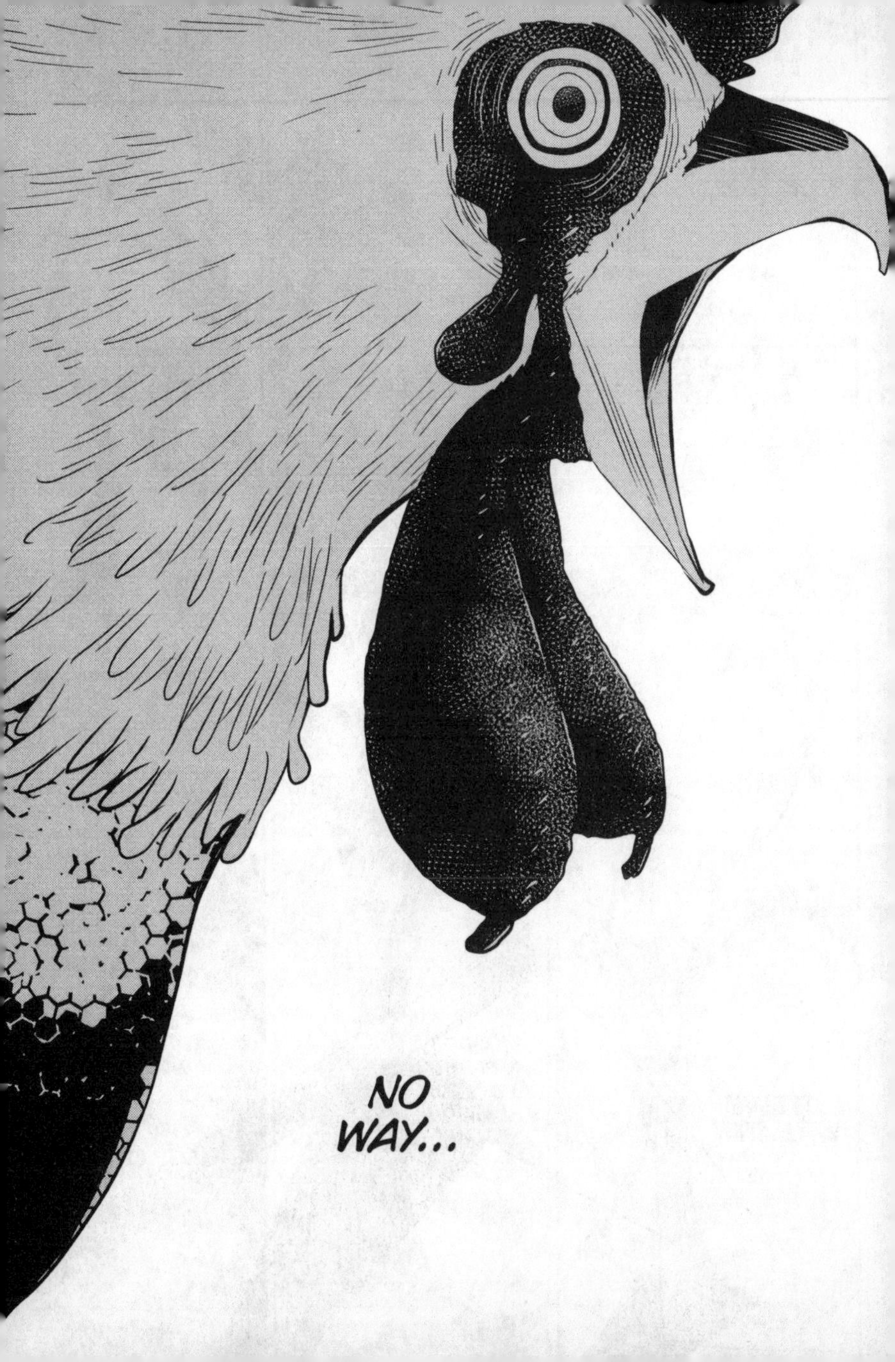
NO WAY...

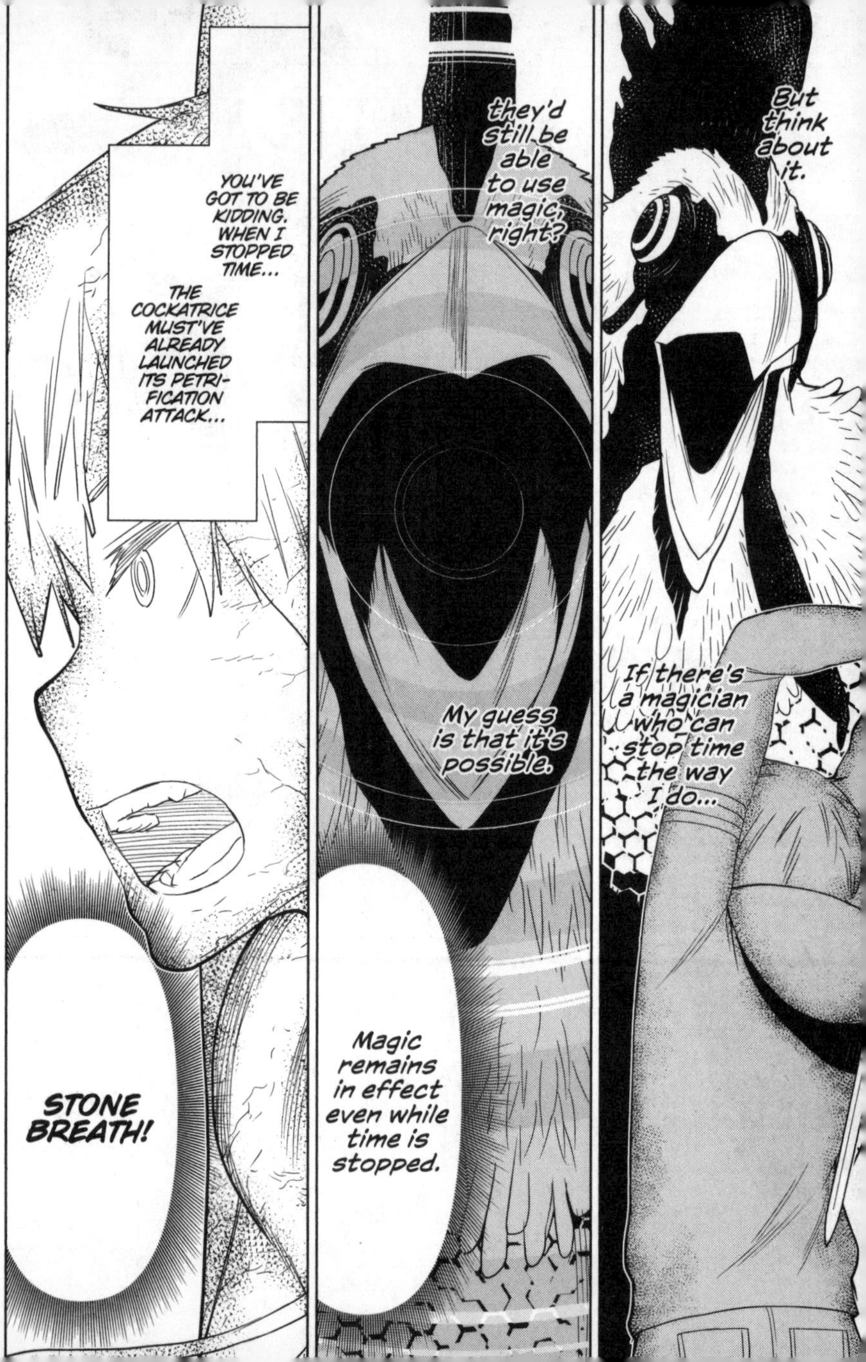
But think about it.
If there's a magician who can stop time the way I do...
they'd still be able to use magic, right?
My guess is that it's possible.
Magic remains in effect even while time is stopped.
YOU'VE GOT TO BE KIDDING. WHEN I STOPPED TIME...
THE COCKATRICE MUST'VE ALREADY LAUNCHED ITS PETRIFICATION ATTACK...
STONE BREATH!

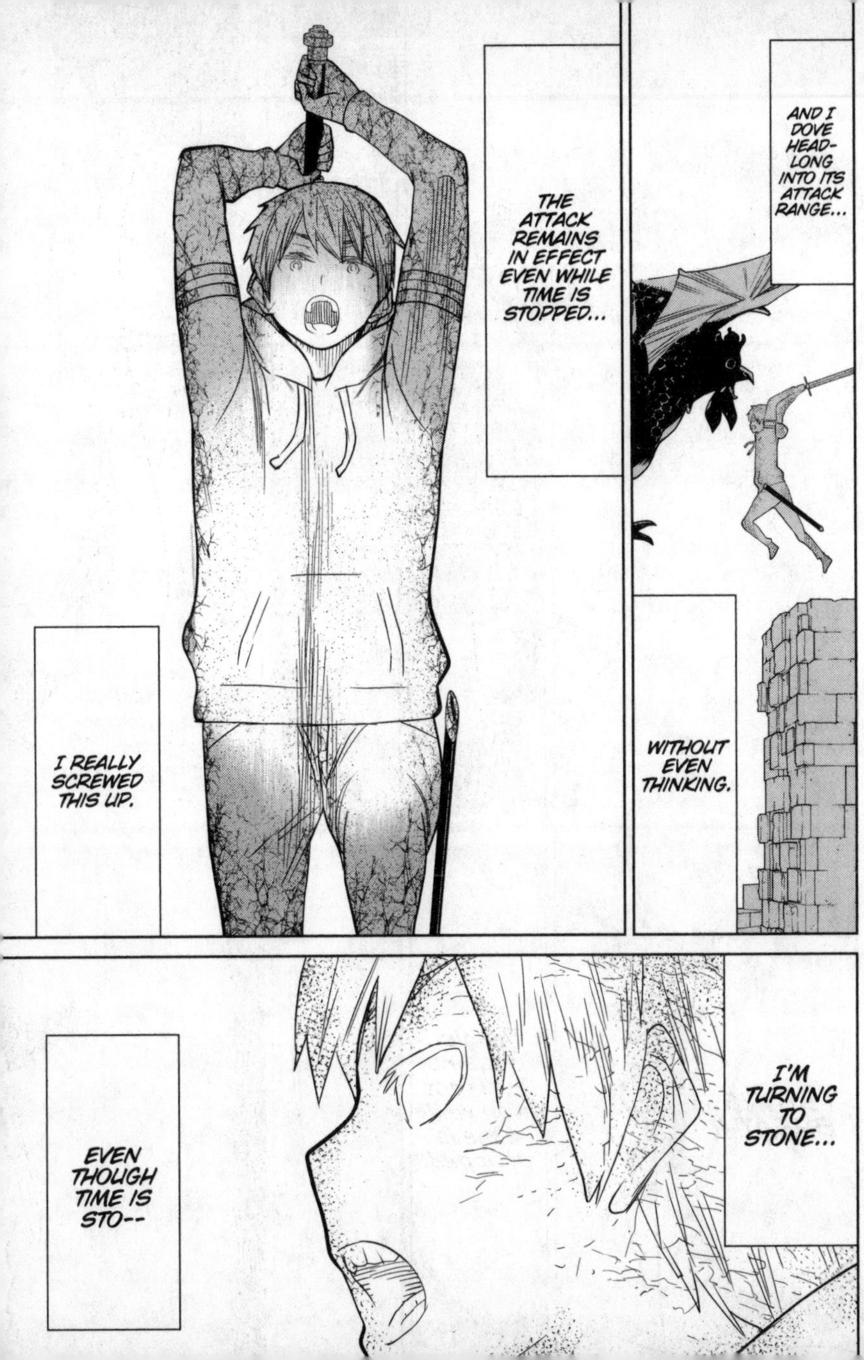
AND I DOVE HEAD-LONG INTO ITS ATTACK RANGE...
WITHOUT EVEN THINKING.
THE ATTACK REMAINS IN EFFECT EVEN WHILE TIME IS STOPPED...
I REALLY SCREWED THIS UP.
I'M TURNING TO STONE...
EVEN THOUGH TIME IS STO--

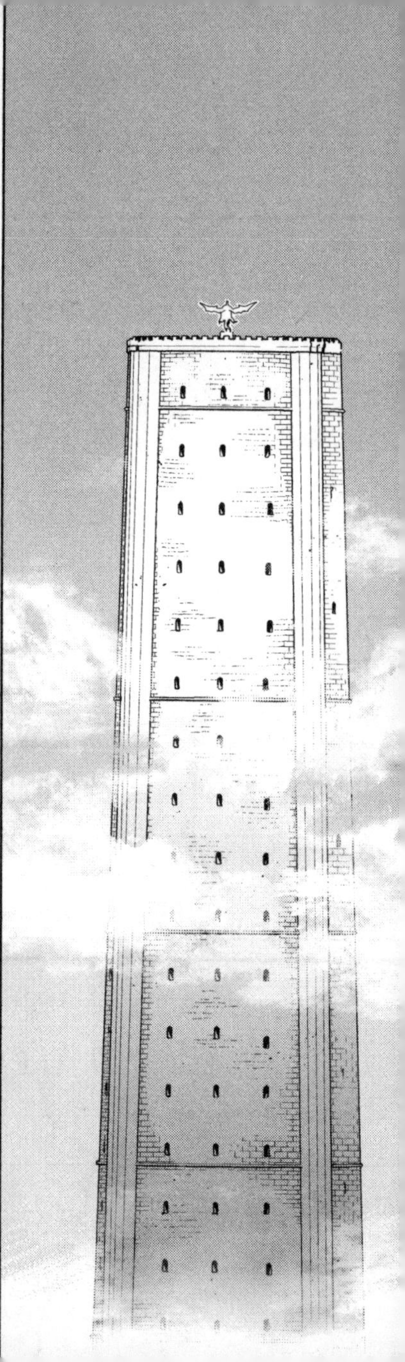
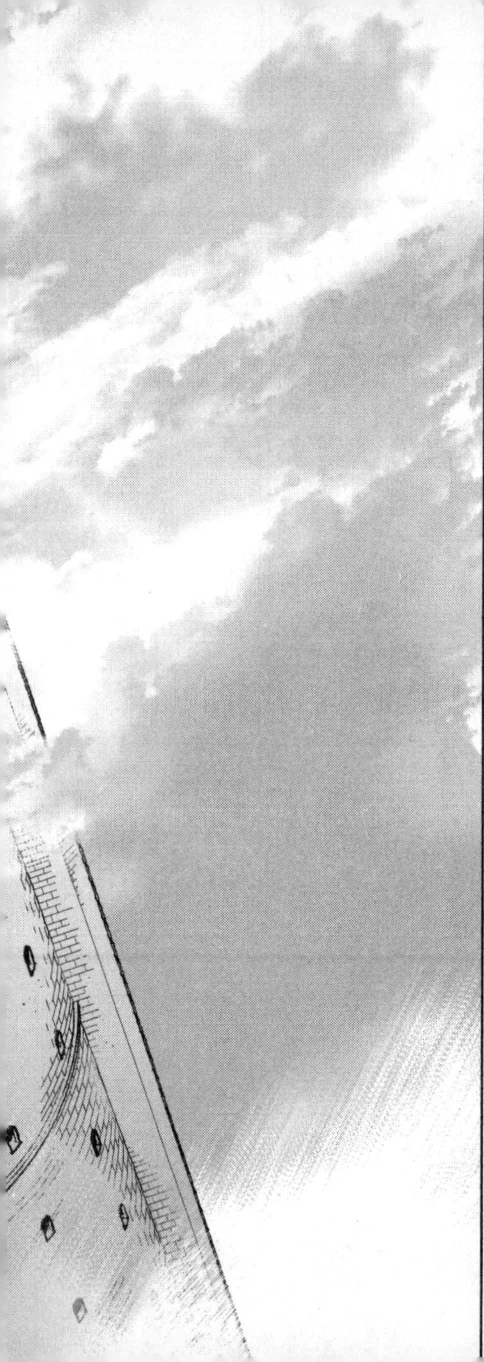

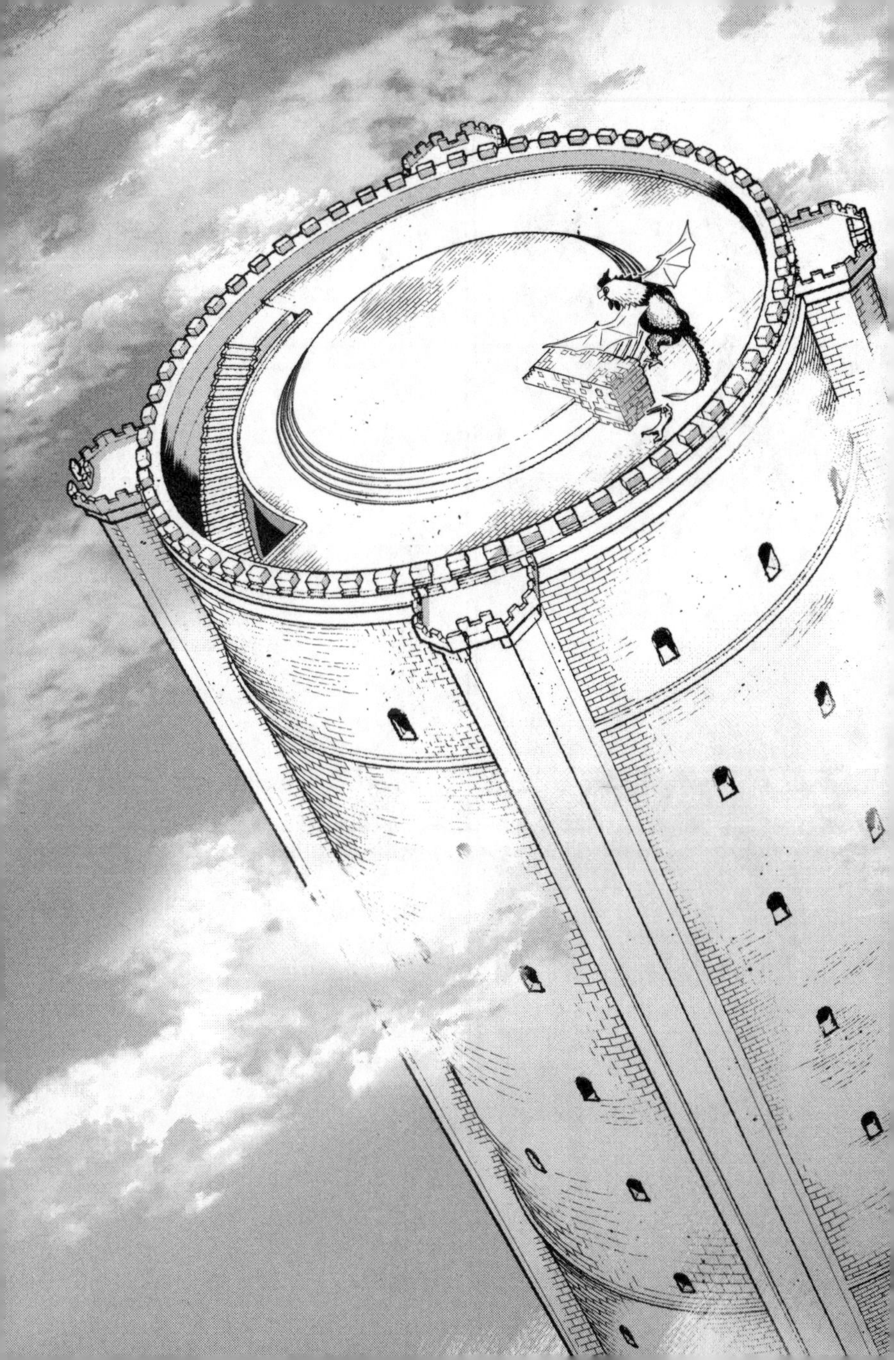

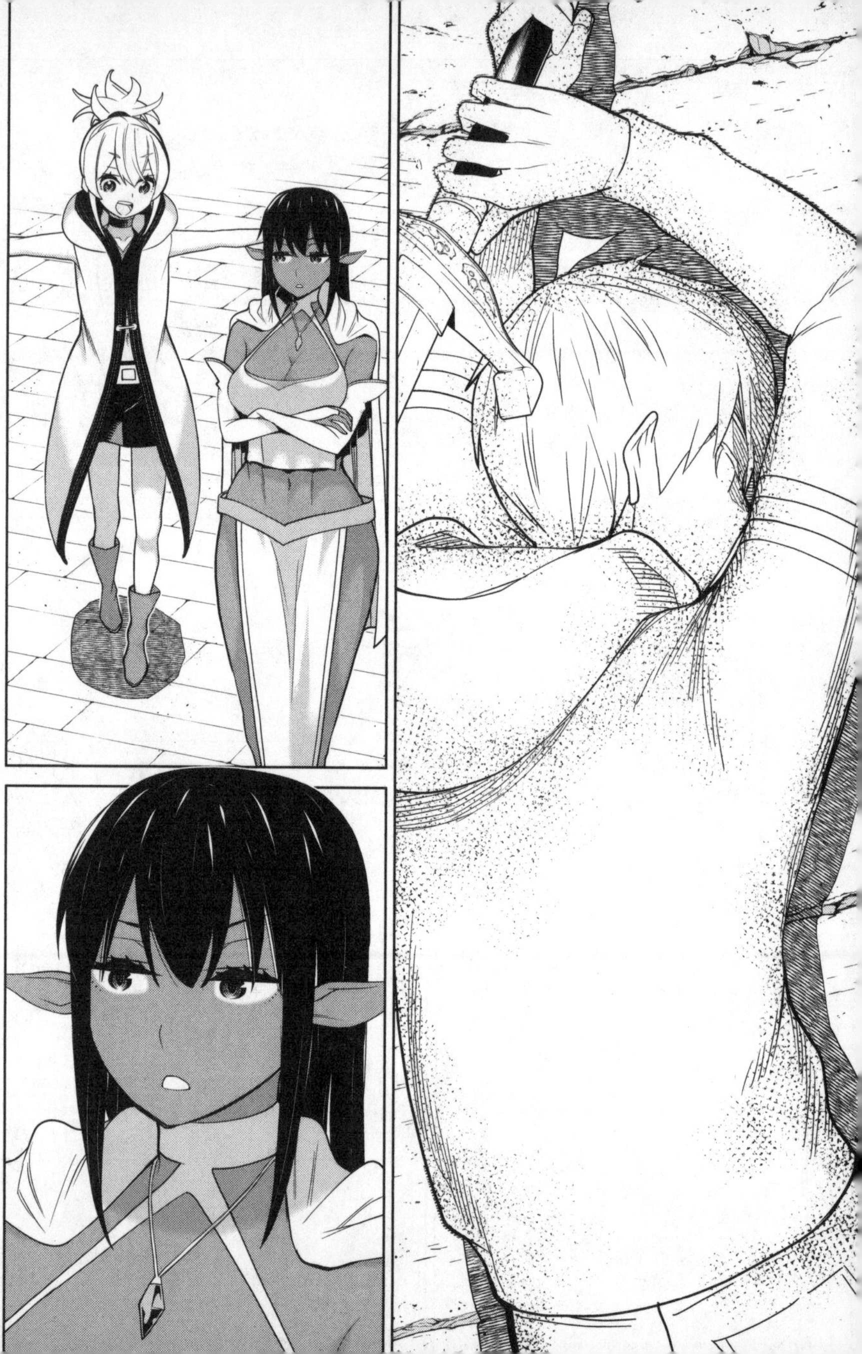

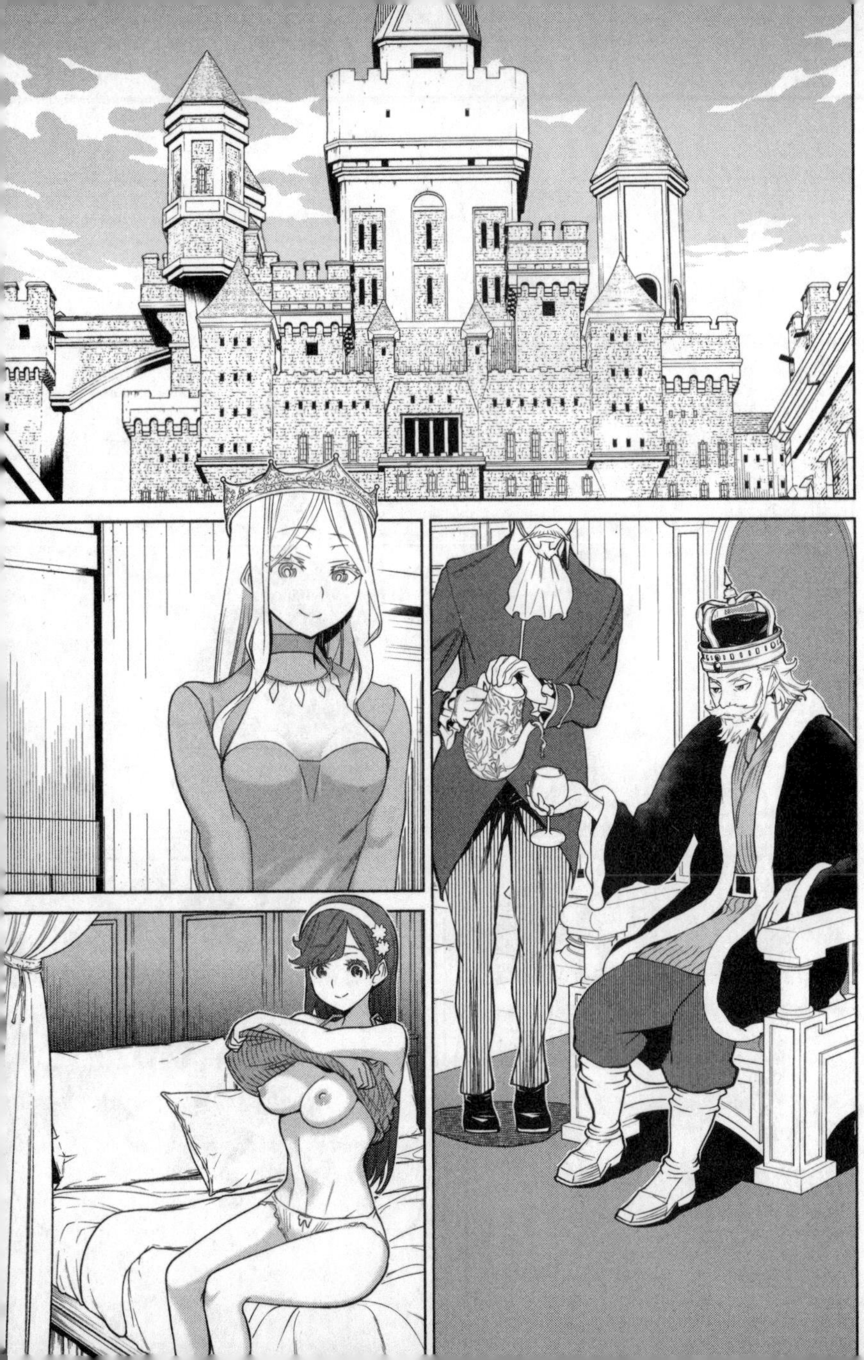

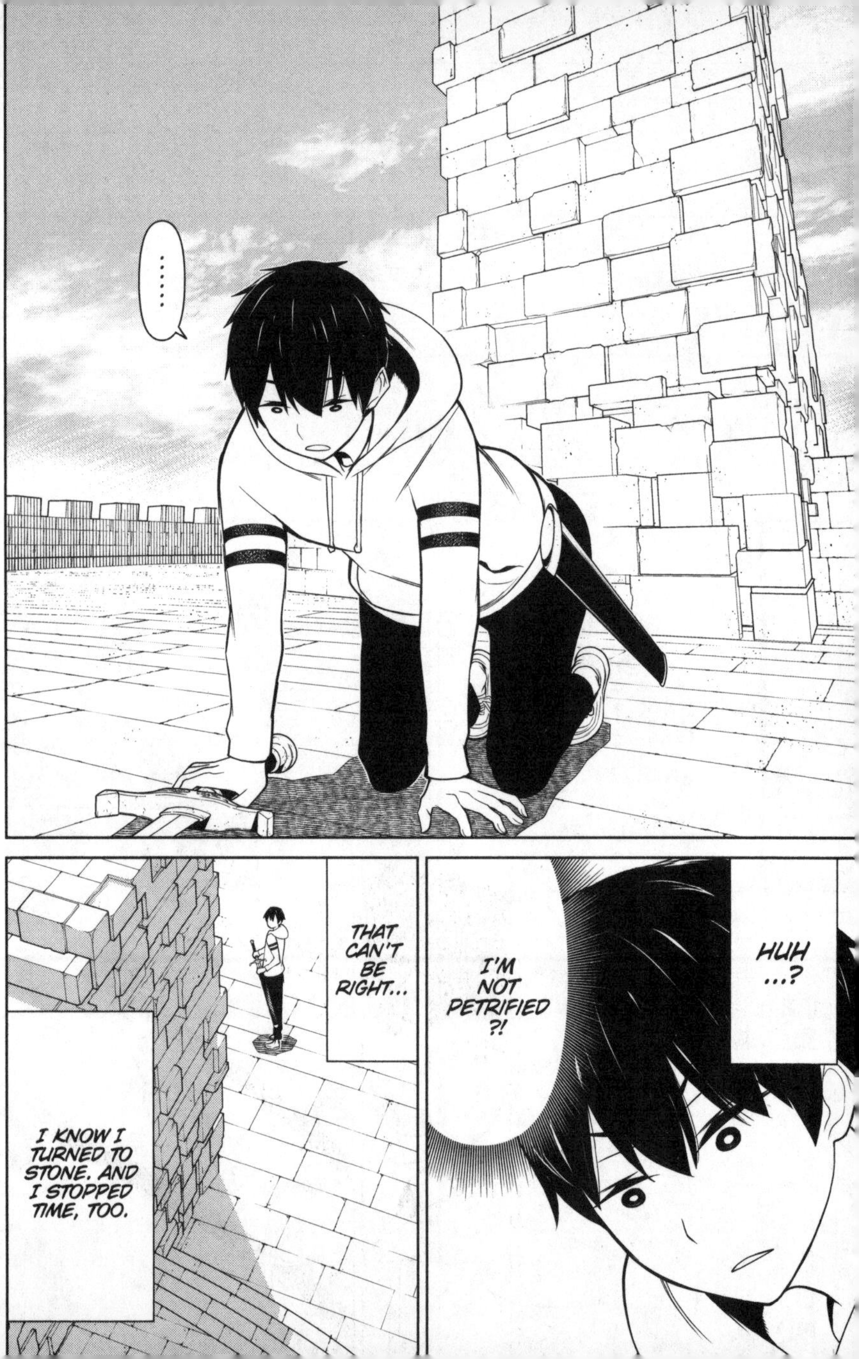
......
HUH ...?
I'M NOT PETRIFIED ?!
THAT CAN'T BE RIGHT...
I KNOW I TURNED TO STONE. AND I STOPPED TIME, TOO.

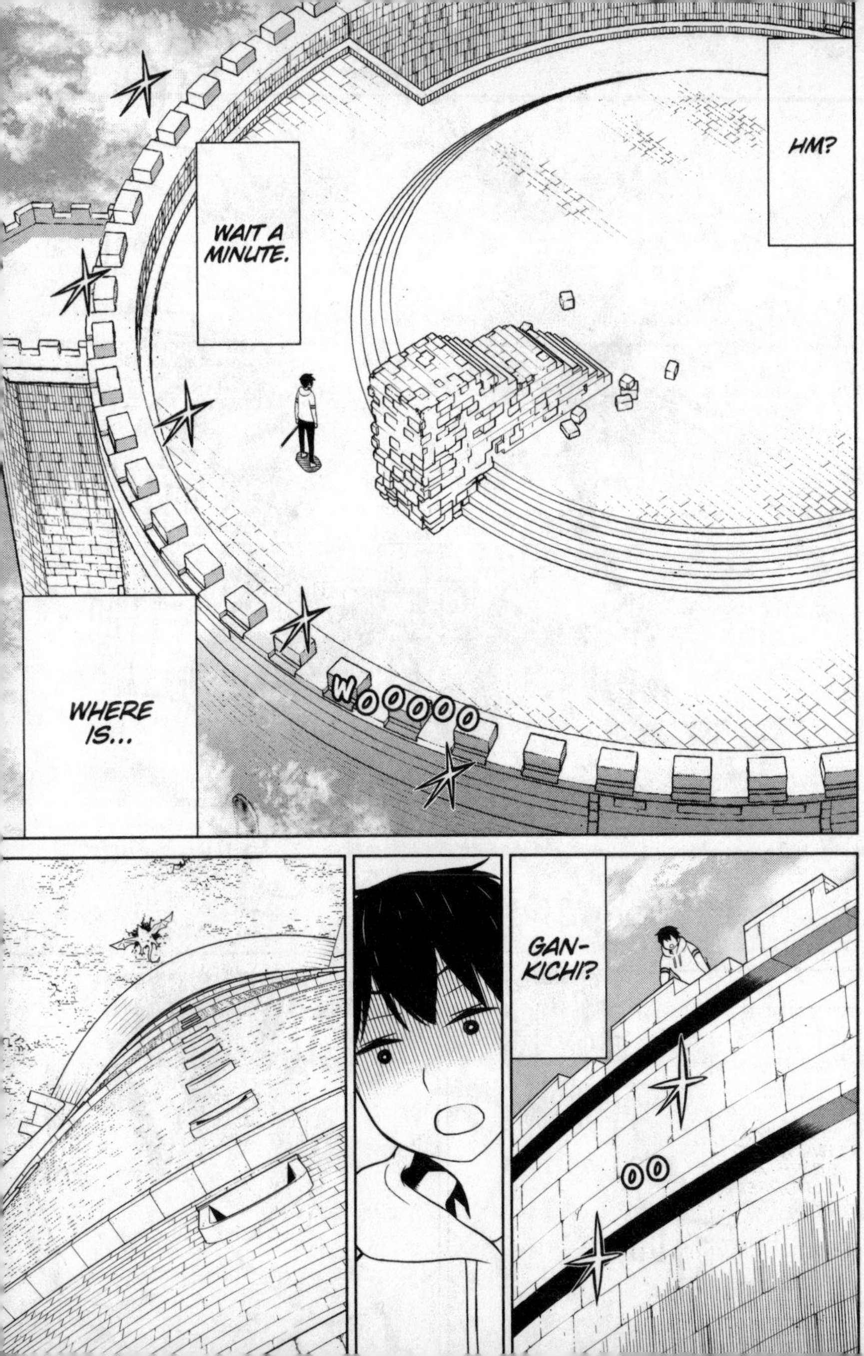
HM?
WAIT A MINUTE.
WHERE IS...
WOOOOOO
GAN-KICHI?
OO

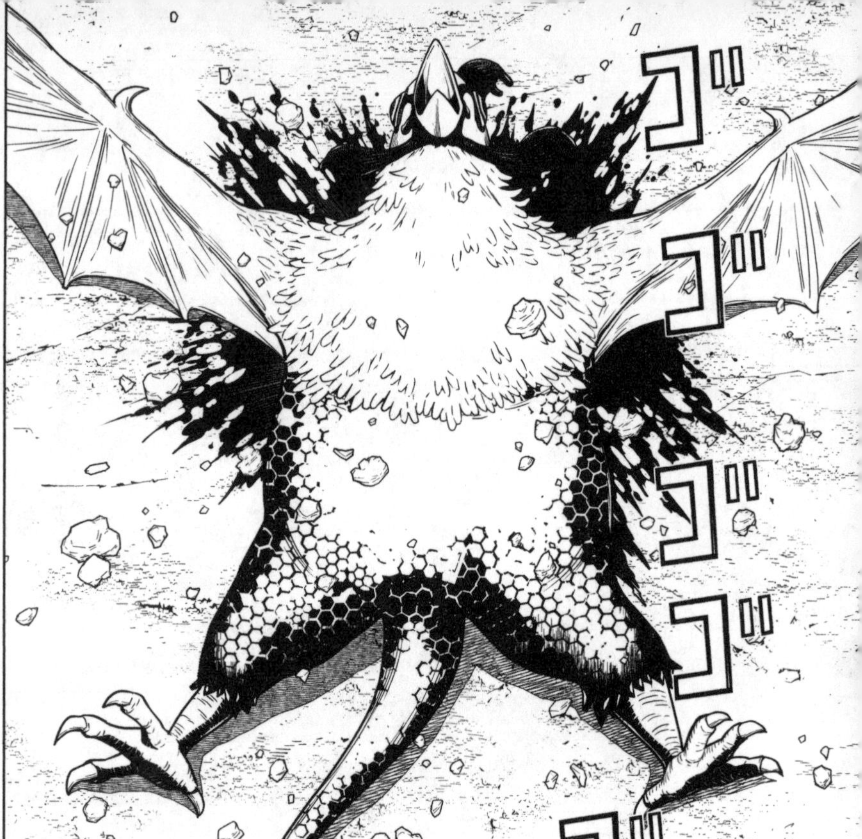
ゴ
ゴ
ゴ
ゴ
ゴ
GWOOOOOOOO
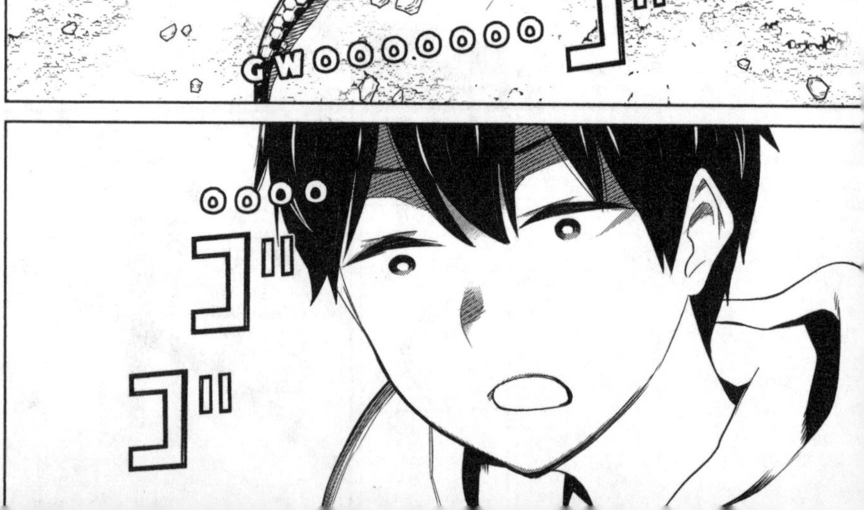
OOOO
ゴ
ゴ

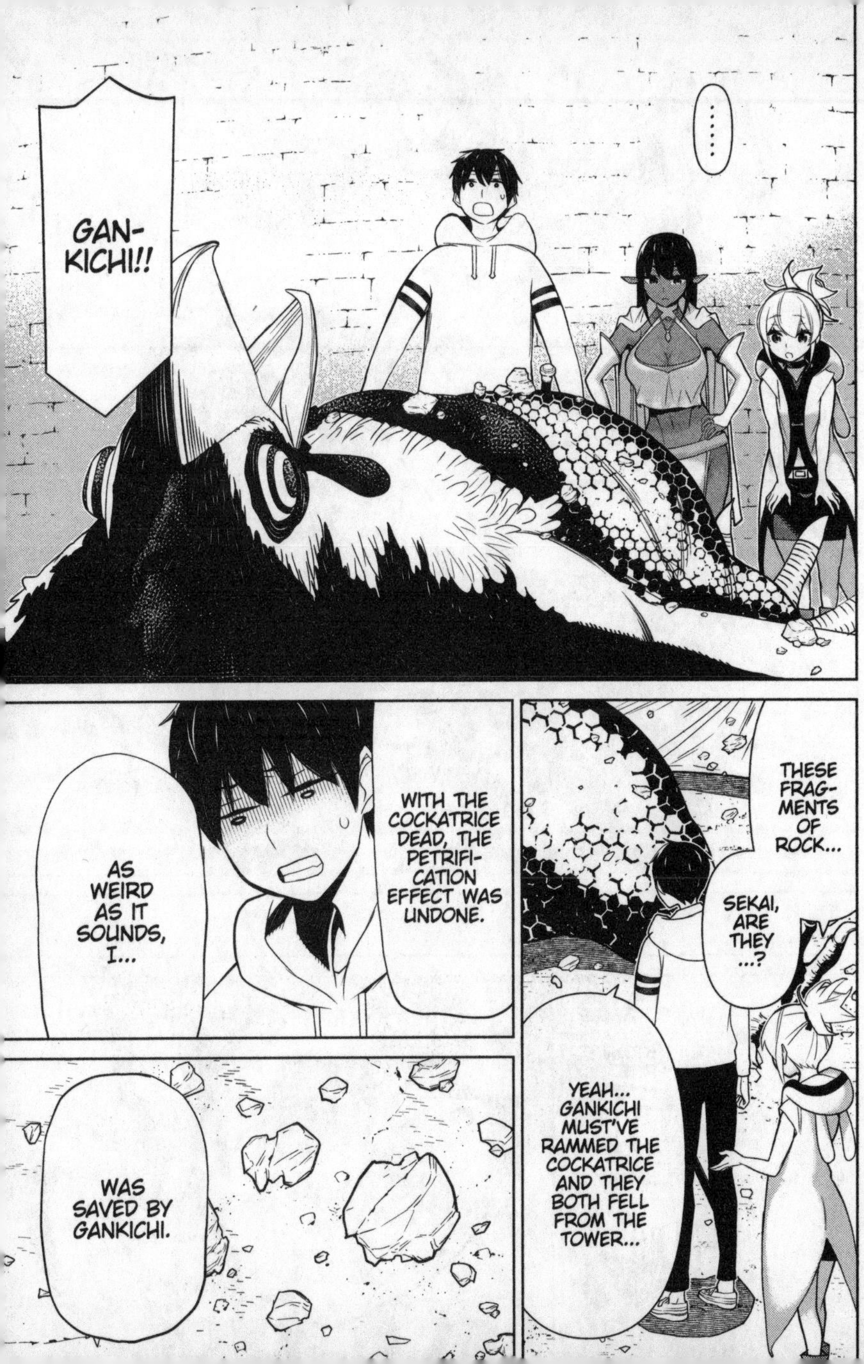
......
GAN-KICHI!!
THESE FRAG-MENTS OF ROCK...
SEKAI, ARE THEY ...?
YEAH... GANKICHI MUST'VE RAMMED THE COCKATRICE AND THEY BOTH FELL FROM THE TOWER...
WITH THE COCKATRICE DEAD, THE PETRIFI-CATION EFFECT WAS UNDONE.
AS WEIRD AS IT SOUNDS, I...
WAS SAVED BY GANKICHI.

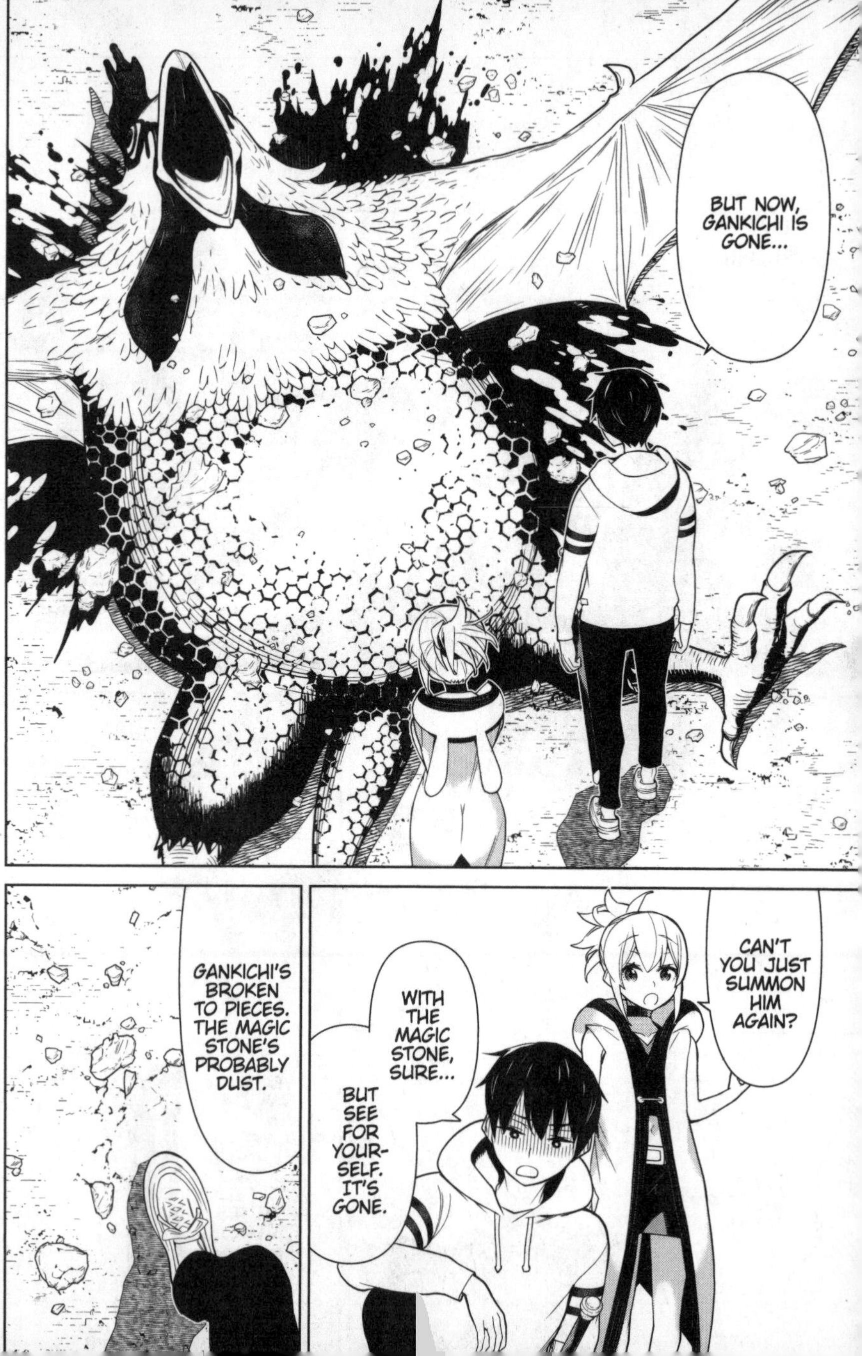
BUT NOW, GANKICHI IS GONE...
CAN'T YOU JUST SUMMON HIM AGAIN?
WITH THE MAGIC STONE, SURE...
BUT SEE FOR YOUR-SELF. IT'S GONE.
GANKICHI'S BROKEN TO PIECES. THE MAGIC STONE'S PROBABLY DUST.

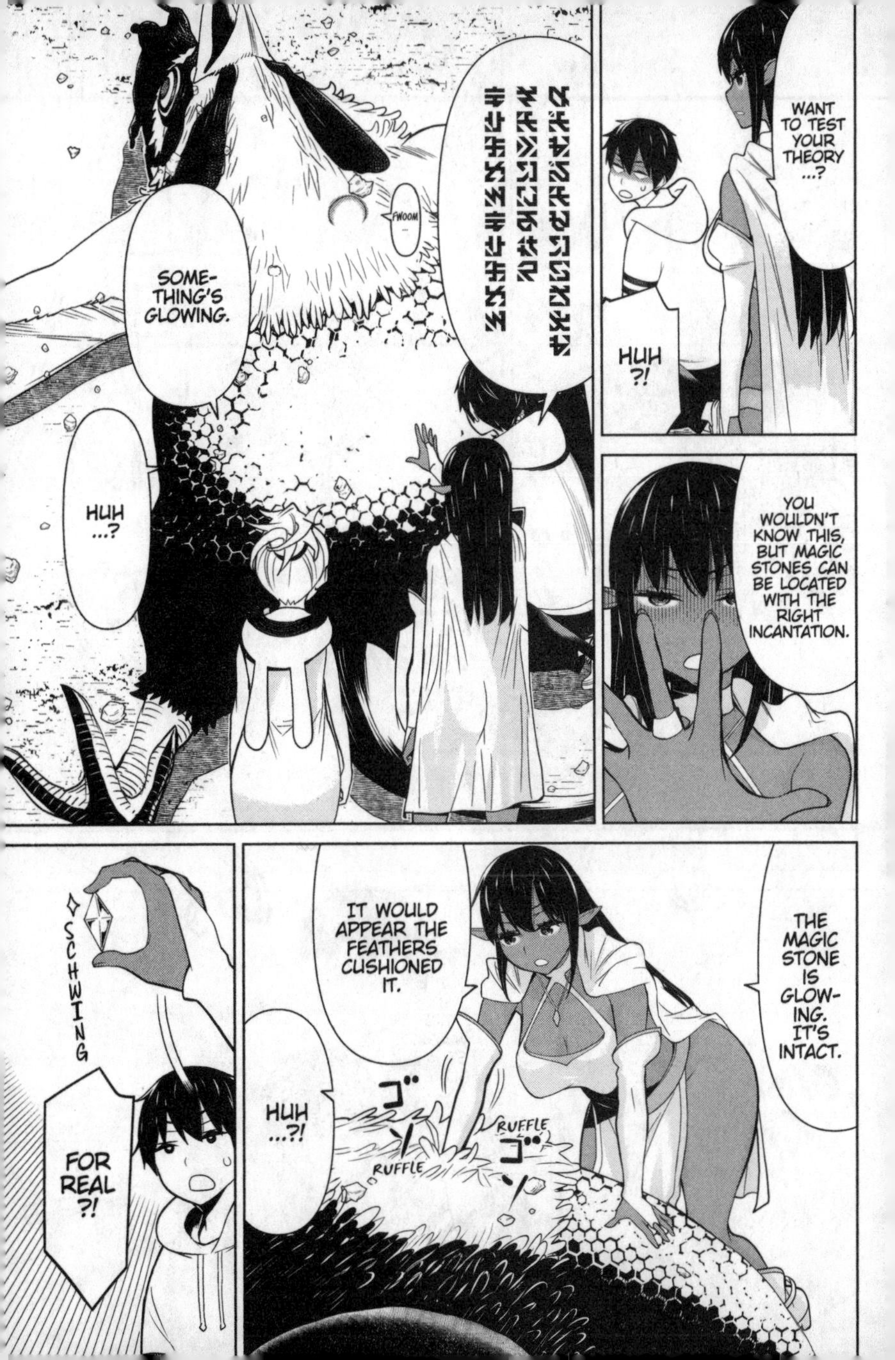
WANT TO TEST YOUR THEORY ...?
HUH ?!
YOU WOULDN'T KNOW THIS, BUT MAGIC STONES CAN BE LOCATED WITH THE RIGHT INCANTATION.
FWOOM ...
SOME-THING'S GLOWING.
HUH ...?
THE MAGIC STONE IS GLOW-ING. IT'S INTACT.
IT WOULD APPEAR THE FEATHERS CUSHIONED IT.
RUFFLE
RUFFLE
HUH ...?!
SCHWING
FOR REAL ?!

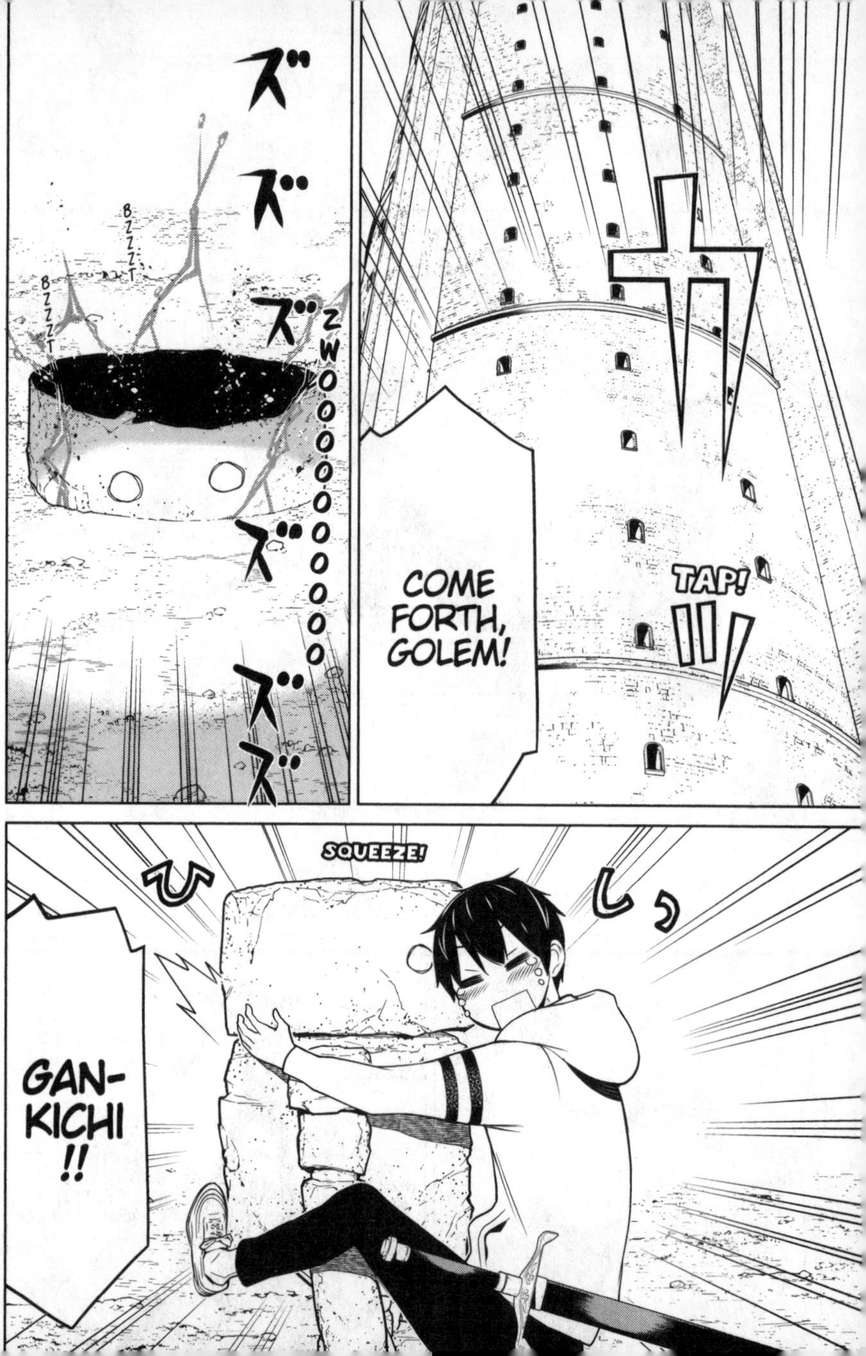
COME FORTH, GOLEM!
TAP!
ズ
ズ
BZZZZT
BZZZT
ズ
ZWOOOOOOOOOOOOOOO
ズ
ズ
ズ
SQUEEZE!
ひしっ
GAN-KICHI!!

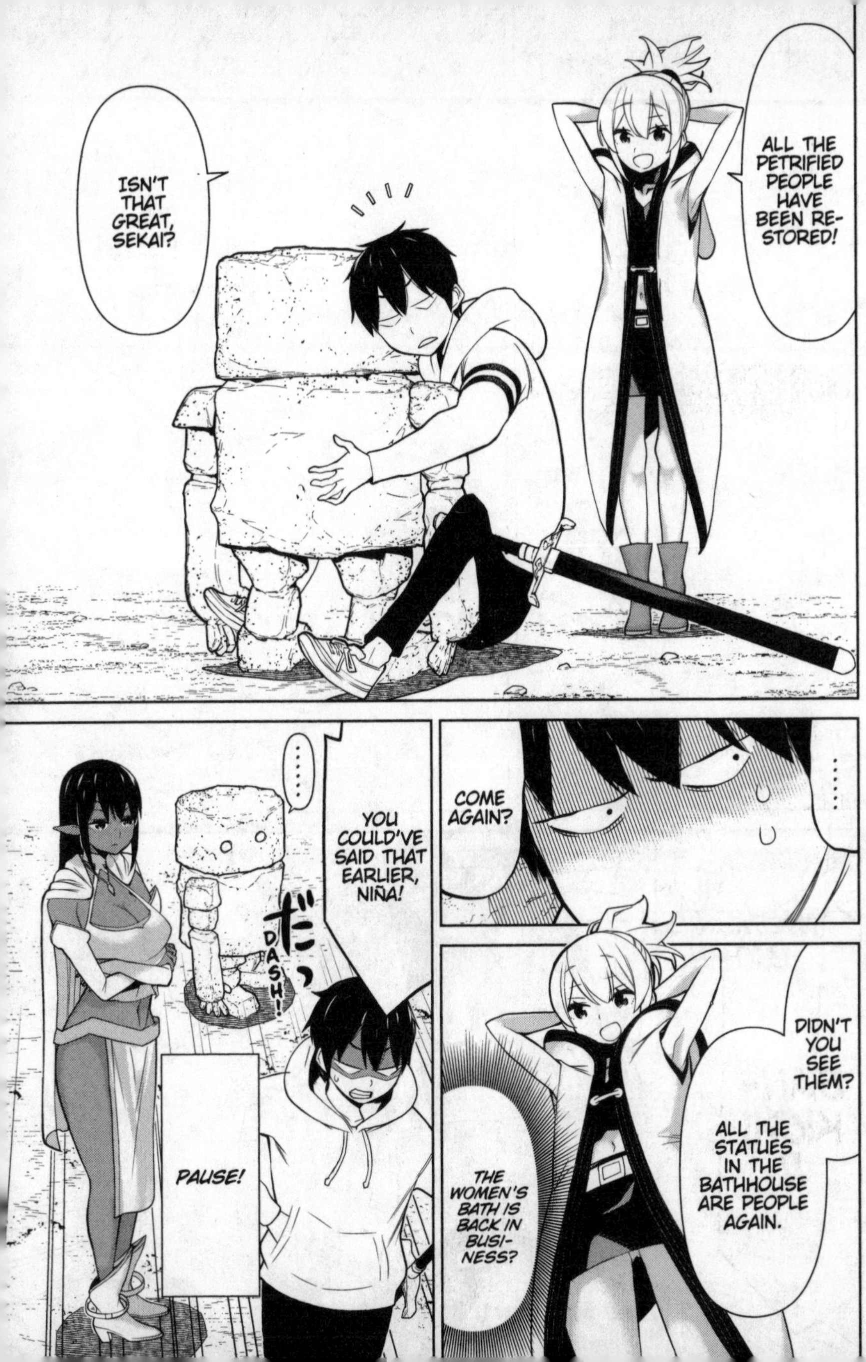
ALL THE PETRIFIED PEOPLE HAVE BEEN RE-STORED!
ISN'T THAT GREAT, SEKAI?
......
COME AGAIN?
DIDN'T YOU SEE THEM?
ALL THE STATUES IN THE BATHHOUSE ARE PEOPLE AGAIN.
THE WOMEN'S BATH IS BACK IN BUSI-NESS?
......
YOU COULD'VE SAID THAT EARLIER, NIÑA!
だっ
DASH!
PAUSE!

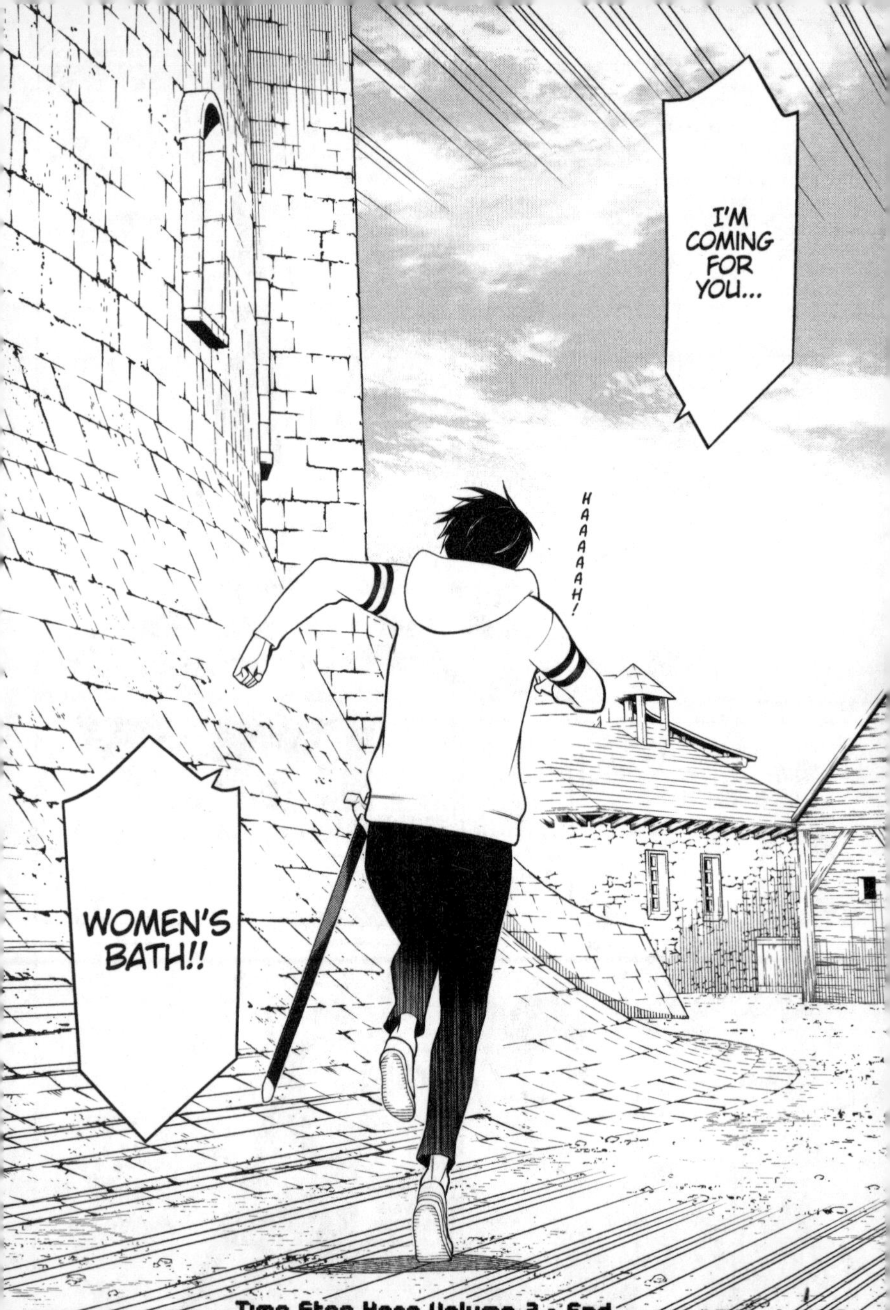
I'M COMING FOR YOU...
HAAAAAAH!
WOMEN'S BATH!!

Time Stop Hero Volume 2 - End